WHY WE BOAT
Running Rivers On Our Own

Vishnu Temple Press
Flagstaff, Arizona

Vishnu Temple Press

P. O. Box 30821

Flagstaff, Arizona 86003

(928) 556 0742

www.vishnutemplepress.com

Cover design by Sandra Kim Muleady.

WHY WE BOAT
Running Rivers On Our Own
edited by
Beverly Kurtz

This book is dedicated to

My Mentor
Buck Buchanan, who taught me that it is important to
give back to the rivers I love

My Muse
Katie Lee, who inspired me with her passion and wit

My Mother
Ann Titus, who has supported me in everything I've
ever tried. Her mantra of "No News is Good News"
gave me the freedom and courage to explore the twists
and turns of rivers and of life.

Table of Contents

IV - Adventures

V - Reflections

Introduction

The idea of this book had its genesis over a decade ago. The publishers of Vishnu Temple Press thought the bookshelves of River Rats were lacking a missal that reflected on the joys and trials of "do-it-yourself" or "private" river runners. Books abound by folks who are outdoor professionals—guides, outfitters, photographers, or scientists. But a significant population of people who spend time on rivers tend to be just ordinary folks who value their experiences enough to hoard and spend their limited vacation days and funds on adventuring down rivers. There didn't seem to be a lot of documentation on what that kind of boating is all about. We in the non-commercial sector know that private boaters have stories to tell too—of our adventures, of obstacles overcome, of what drives us and how boating rewards us.

And so the concept of *Why We Boat* was born. I didn't get involved until a couple of years ago when I retired from the corporate rat race and had some time to invest. Having never undertaken a project like this I approached it the same way I handled any challenge I faced as a professional project manager…I jumped in, got organized, and started talking to people. Social media proved to be an excellent tool for connecting with potential authors. The trick was to find people who boated (raft, canoe, kayak, SUP, whatever….) and were also interested in writing about that. The goal was not just to share an adventure story, but to write to capture the essence of why people spend money, time and energy doing private river trips. With that in mind I posted on multiple Facebook pages dedicated to boating. I also reached out to a few formal publications and colleges with a focus on the out of doors and writing. The result was overwhelming!

I received submissions from all over North America. The stories were diverse—tales about being young and inexperienced, and those about the challenges of continuing to boat when the body is less agile. Authors shared narratives of hope and loss, joy and fear, work and play. There were chronicles by rafters of course—but also many from people who built their own canoes or dories, experimented with stand up paddle boards or conquered kayaking. So many of the stories caused me to laugh out loud or to shed a tear that I knew that I was onto something. If I enjoyed reading these pieces so much, I was reassured that other boaters (or would-be boaters) would feel the same.

My biggest challenge with this endeavor was to decide which pieces to accept—I am so appreciative to everyone who sent in their work. I loved reading everything that was sent to me, but of course I had to make hard choices about which to include. Some submissions were so beautifully written that I had to include them just for that reason. Other pieces reflected so perfectly the feelings I have for boating that they seemed obvious choices. And some were so hilarious or heartfelt or insightful that they spoke to me on a visceral level, tugging at my heartstrings. The authors I selected have all been gracious with their time and energy in working with me on the final product. Most are not professional writers, which makes their efforts even more admirable. I feel that I've made 31 new friends and hope that someday I will have the opportunity to meet each of the contributors in person. Every author holds a special place in my heart.

Putting this book together was definitely a labor of love. I have done lots of technical editing in my life, but compiling an anthology was a new challenge. It was "learning on the job" as a professional editor. I am very grateful to Tom Martin and Hazel Clark who encouraged me every step of the way and always reminded me that I should be having fun, or I shouldn't be doing this! And I'm equally grateful to my long-suffering husband, Tim Guenthner, who thought I would have more time with him when I retired—instead I have spent innumerable hours in front of my computer and have dominated our conversations for months on end with editorial mumbo jumbo, analysis of book organization, and dilemmas over style. His support has been crucial to getting me through this undertaking. Now that this project is winding down, I look forward to sharing more adventures with him, playing in the mountains and on the rivers we love.

In the end, my goal was to put together an anthology of stories that other boaters can identify with, laugh with, and be moved by. I hope I've succeeded and that you enjoy reading these tales as much as I have.

Beverly Kurtz
Boulder, Colorado
May 2018

I
Memories

Why Whitewater
Walt Bammann

When trying to explain why my wife and I own two rafts, two catarafts, and two kayaks and have no room in the garage, I look back on thirty years of boating through some of the most beautiful and often remote corners of our great country and simply ask:

"Have you ever …………"

- felt the adrenaline rush from staring down the gut of Lava Rapid in the Grand Canyon before pushing on the oars to drop in?

- shared the laughter of your teenage sons while paddle rafting your own boat through Blossom Bar on the Rogue River?

- made love in a creek? a cave? a raft? a tent? a meadow? a collapsible chair? a tree? (who us?)

- sat on a porta-potty on the bank of the Colorado River watching the morning sun inflame the walls of the Grand Canyon?

- waved to over 30 passengers on a passing pontoon boat while on the same crapper?

- solar-showered under a tree only to discover nearby … a rattlesnake? … a "friend" with a camera?

- climbed in your tent to hold it down and it blew over anyway?

- sat naked with friends and a glass of wine in Sheepeater Hot Spring on the Middle Fork of the Salmon watching a full moon rise?

- gotten "the itch" in a hot springs?

- had the crowd cheer when your fresh cherry upside-down-cake came out of the Dutch oven intact?

- eaten shrimp fried rice—with tuna (oops)?

- packed poop in the crapper with a stick to make more room?

- chased a skunk? bear? rattlesnake? scorpion? outfitter? ... out of camp?

- eaten a sugar-free (bad recipe!) cranberry/pear cobbler? Mother pucker...

- been the first one up to sit alone in the morning mist with a hot cup of coffee listening to river sounds?

- drunk a River Margarita? Perhaps more than one?

- sat under a tarp two miles above the Class V Green Wall Rapid on the Illinois River listening to the rain and watching the river rise ominously?

- had a new Cataract oar break at high water while dropping into the infamous Green Wall Rapid?

- cringed in your sleeping bag at 2 a.m. as lightning illuminates your tent and you can only count to 1 before ... Kaboom!!?

- melted a hole in your formerly waterproof splash pants when they blew off a chair into a crackling bonfire?

- run left (oops) at Bedrock Rapid in the Grand Canyon?

- felt the elation of hitting your first "combat roll" in your hardshell kayak?

- stood at the top of the ramp at the Boundary Creek launch on the Middle Fork and thanked the Lord for the opportunity?

- helped your 2-year-old grandson climb into your garaged raft and scamper into the rowing seat? The anticipation ...

- walked weak-kneed and nauseous back to your raft after scouting a rapid?

- high-fived your buddies after successfully running that same rapid?

- portaged the Green Wall on the Illinois?

- needed to use the crapper three times in the morning on Lava Rapid day (three shits to the wind!)?

- felt foolish strapping your life jacket around your butt for protection, then bobbing down the tropical turquoise waters of the Little Colorado river on a 100-degree day? … and run back up, giggling, to do it again and again?

- had all the savory, slow-cooked Dutch oven prime rib you could eat on the last day of a Middle Fork trip?

- tricked your Arizona comrades into eating "Oregon" chili (add a dollop of peanut butter) 'cause that was all the food left on the last day of a marginally planned Grand Canyon trip? (They said it was good …)

- played football in the nude on a Grand Canyon beach? Tackle, flag, or two hands below the waist—no good choices …

- watched your wife and seven other women do a beach-umbrella strip tease to say, "thank you" after the nude football game?

- spent the afternoon of a 110-degree layover day lounging in a chair in a shady side-creek on the Salmon River?

- taken a picture of your group's feet to show off the sandal suntans?

- been afraid to go barefoot in camp for fear of getting your toenails painted should you doze off?

- listened to the wind and canyon noises quietly reverberating in Veil Falls Cavern on the Middle Fork?

- about crapped your pants when 200 yards above you Mother Nature suddenly looses a truck-sized boulder and it comes bounding down the canyon toward your raft?

- sat naked in a river sauna watching the soothing steam cloud envelope everyone when cold water hits the hot rocks?

- marveled as a hovering osprey suddenly folds its wings for a screaming, fish-catching dive just yards in front of your raft?

- had your truck not start at the takeout miles from anywhere?

- carried the ashes of a boating friend into his favorite river canyon and thinking perhaps someday our ashes and spirits will meet again?

- dallied at the takeout taking pictures and giving hugs to all your long-time river friends, as well as to many new ones, while promising to return next year?

If you can say "yes" to any similar memories,
then you've been as blessed as I …

Running the Big Red

Dave Mortenson

May 1961

The white jeep bounced and twisted as we made our way through the dense pinyon and juniper forest. The dirt roads were behind us, and we followed two faint tracks that weaved their way north across Great Thumb Mesa. I sat in the back holding on as the three pack frames and I flew into the air every time we hit a rock or fallen tree branch. P. T. "Pat" Reilly was driving and my father, V. R. "Brick" Mortenson, was riding in the passenger seat. At thirteen I was off on my first adventure down into the Grand Canyon. Although I hadn't yet hiked into the Grand Canyon, it had been part of my upbringing.

My father and Pat were river runners. Pat began his adventures in the late 1940s and my father began in 1955. I didn't understand much about running the Colorado River, but I had seen the movies, heard the stories, and had met some of the people whose stories were told. Historic names like Powell, Stanton, Flavell, Galloway, Loper, the Kolb brothers, and Nevills were discussed in my presence, much as past baseball players or presidents were discussed in a normal household of the early 1960s. River levels were a big topic, since both Pat and Brick ran in the floods of 1957 and 1958.

As we began our drive out Great Thumb Mesa, we stopped to look down a large canyon where we could see the Colorado River below and a rapid call Forster. Pat explained all he could see below with great enthusiasm. He spoke about the rock formations, the level of the river, how to run this rapid, and so much more that my young mind couldn't comprehend. When we reached the end of our 4x4 drive above 140 Mile Canyon, he once again explained what we saw. Again, it was too much for me, but as he spoke there were some names I recognized. He pointed out where Surprise Valley and Deer Creek Falls were located. I knew those areas from the movies and stories. He pointed out Powell

Plateau and told me about John Wesley Powell. Then he discussed Kanab Point and Kanab Canyon below, where Powell's second expedition had left the Canyon. He introduced me to more than history, geology, and vegetation. He, with my father, introduced me to a passion to explore and experience this place called the Grand Canyon.

We made the hike to Keyhole Bridge and back. At thirteen, this hike was really the first time in my young life when I did what adults did. I began to come of age on that hike. The knowledge that I was only the fourth person in recorded history to see something made me feel special. Yes, just Harvey Butchart, my father, Pat Reilly, and I had been to Keyhole Bridge. I wanted more of the Grand Canyon, and that opportunity came faster than I could have hoped.

Pat Reilly, Martin Litton, and my father began to discuss running the river again in 1961. Litton had rowed his first river trip with Reilly in 1956. They needed to do this before Glen Canyon Dam was complete and before the two dams being proposed in the Grand Canyon would end river running. My father approached me with the invitation of running the river with him and Pat. He explained that it would not be easy since they had to build boats, and I would be required to help. In 1962 it was not possible to rent gear as it is today. Pat had retired his two 1950s boats by sinking them near Pipe Creek in 1959. So, I became a boat builder's assistant and helped in ways I never could have imagined.

Since my father worked the swing shift for Lockheed, he and I would never really see each other except on weekends. He would come home long after I was asleep and I'd be off to school the next morning before he was awake. But each day after school I had different duties assigned to me that were related by my mother. Initially it was yard work, cleaning the garage, and other activities not related to the boat building. But each day I would see that our boat was beginning to take shape. On weekends I would assist my father and he would explain the boat building process. During one of these discussions he told me that the boat would be called the *Flavell II*. Brick had previously rowed Reilly's boat *Flavell*, which was named to honor George Flavell – the man who was the first to successfully run Lava Falls Rapid in 1896.

Out of sheets of marine plywood and oak boards, the *Flavell II* was born. She was 16 feet 8 inches long, 66 inches wide at the beam, and 20 inches deep at the chine. It was a low-profile craft, flat on the top along its horizontal axis, decks rounded to the sides. The bow had a depth of 15 inches while the stern had a depth of only 11 inches.

The boat was configured with a bench seat in a front cockpit that sat two people who faced forward. The boatman sat in the middle with another passenger seat in the rear. Four removable storage compartments were situated in the center of the boat. These compartments could be lifted out and carried to the campsite, which greatly simplified setting up nightly camps.

The front, back, and sides of the boat had watertight compartments that were filled with foam. The process of filling these spaces was not simple. The expensive ingredients were mixed, and the foam would chemically form. Sometimes! It was a very sensitive mix that was affected by temperature. It seemed the foam would either fail to work, or else work too well.

Another problem was its cost. So Brick came up with the idea of placing plastic bottles in the space and having the foam encapsulate them. In 1962, not many things came in plastic bottles. For example, soft drinks were either in cans or glass bottles. The source of cheap plastic bottles was found: bleach bottles. So, several nights each week, my mother would drive me all around where we lived in the San Fernando Valley in Los Angeles to rummage through all the local Laundromats' trash cans for empty bleach bottles. This was not a good way to build a shy thirteen-year-old's self-confidence. I would raid the trash containers as fast as possible hoping no one would notice. Waiting for laundry is boring, so strangers watched every move I made and surely wondered what I was up to.

Another task I was given was to make small metal fittings out of tubes of hardened aluminum. These fixtures would hold a lifeline for someone to grab in case they were in the water. I had to cut them on a band saw, drill, and file them. Each one took a long time to make, but every night I would produce a couple. We needed sixteen of them for the *Flavell II*. When Pat saw what I was producing, he wanted them for his boat, the *Susie Too*, as well. Thirty years later, I showed my daughter, Cece, Reilly's *Susie Too*. It had been renamed *Music Temple* and was on display in the visitor center at the Grand Canyon. I pointed out the fittings I had made, but she failed to understand my attachment to the little metal tubes around the boat.

The *Flavell II* was completed barely on time to make its first river trip in June of 1962.

Running Big Red

My first day on the river started at Lees Ferry. It was Sunday morning and all our party had arrived the evening before by car or plane. We spent the morning getting the boats and gear from Cliff Dwellers Lodge to the river. We drove down the paved, two-lane Hwy 89 until we came to a small, dirt road near the single span of Navajo Bridge. Pat was leading the way in his two-tone red and white pickup, pulling two boats in his trailer. As we drove along towards this deserted place, he excitedly told me about Lees Ferry and its history. I heard little of what he was saying since I was so overtaken by the beauty of the place. We crossed the Paria River, which had some water running in it, and some of the vehicles had trouble getting through the wash. With everyone pushing we solved that problem.

As we drove on, Pat startled me when he practically yelled, "Look at Big Red! Look at the flow!" The river was muddy red and was flowing at 50,000 cfs. It was much bigger and livelier then I had imagined. Its flow seemed so swift and was full of driftwood. The water was so silty that it appeared to be a red river. There was very little vegetation along the river shores, as high water was inundating what vegetation survived the annual flooding. Only people going downriver would come to this remote spot. Because Glen Canyon Dam was being constructed only 17 miles upriver, no river runners were allowed to run through Glen Canyon anymore, thus ending Lees Ferry as a take-out point. Our party of ten, plus a few family members who would shuttle our vehicles to the take-out on Lake Mead, were the only souls around for many miles.

We chose to launch the boats near a big, green tree that provided shade. The boats and gear were unloaded. Pat and Susie had planned and outfitted the trip, but compared to today's river trips we had few supplies to unload. We had no propane stove or tanks since we used firewood for cooking. We had no ice chests, although one of the crew brought some ice for drinks. We had no porta-potties, but we had a rule: men downriver and women upriver where possible (pants down, skirts up). As it was early summer, we had very little in terms of clothing and personal gear. No folding chairs, no tents, no frills. Suzanne Culley, the only woman on the crew, did bring a small guitar. There were no park rangers or anyone else overseeing our launch. Pat had notified the Park Service of our trip and told them how many would be on the river. But since little of our journey to Lake Mead would be in what was then Grand Canyon National Park, they paid scant attention to the few hardy souls who ran the river.

With everyone excitedly helping unload the boats, we soon had three new boats launched with appropriate champagne fanfare. Pat Reilly's *Susie Too* and Martin Litton's *Portola* were put in the water first. These two beautiful boats, made by modifying Mackenzie River hulls, became some of the first dories to run the Colorado River. When our *Flavell II* was launched, it became probably the last "Cataract" style boat ever built for running "Big Red." Although I didn't realize it at the time, I witnessed the end of one era and the beginning of another in Colorado River boats.

Martin's 16-year-old son, John, and I were given the task of watching the boats in the afternoon and to spend the night beside the river. When everyone went back to Cliff Dwellers, John and I spent the afternoon fishing for catfish. As afternoon turned into evening, I sat along the silt and rock shore looking downriver. I was excited but also a little intimidated by the whole situation. The movies and stories had made me well aware of dangers below. Pat had told me that I was probably the second youngest person to go down the river. I had just turned fourteen in May and was small for my age. I just wanted to do well and not fail the trust Pat and my father had put in me. I didn't sleep well that night until I remembered the story that someone had once taken a bear cub down this river. This funny thought relaxed me, and soon the sounds of the river put me to sleep.

Day 1 - Monday, June 25, 1962 - 52,200 cfs.

A little before noon, our party of ten people and three boats began our run down the Colorado. The river was flowing at 52,200 cfs. Suzanne Culley and I sat in the cockpit in the front of the *Flavell II*. My father handled the 9-foot oars as he sat in the bucketed seat that kept him in place. Behind him was Grant Culley. My father was pleased with the *Flavell II*. It was very smooth in the water, it had especially great lateral stability, and because of its low profile, it had great visibility. In rapids, the *Flavell II* would attack the water and dive right into the waves. To everyone's surprise, the boat's design seemed to keep the water out. There was a metal splashguard around the front cockpit that worked so well that we rarely need more than sponges to bail.

Running downriver we passed under Navajo Bridge where we saw my mother, sister, and Susie Reilly, who were going to drive the trailers to Lake Mead. The canyon was already very deep. Soon we came to Badger Rapid, which we ran without stopping to scout. The roar and the excitement of my first real rapid was unbelievable. As we slid down the tongue, I reviewed my mental checklist of what I was going to do when we flipped. We didn't flip, and I hardly got wet. It was fun, and my silver-colored pith helmet made a great shield against the waves.

Next we came to Soap Rapid and my father wanted to run solo. Grant, Suzanne, and I walked down along the rapid and watched as the three boats made successful runs. Brick took the *Flavell II* right down the middle of Soap to see how the new boat would do. When we re-boarded at the foot of the rapid, he was clearly overjoyed at how well she handled. Down we ran through Sheer Wall, and past Boulder Narrows with lots of fresh driftwood deposited in the 1957 flood. We camped on river left at Mile 19.1.

As camp was being set up, Grant Culley mixed a drink using his ice and 151-proof rum. The mixing of a unique drink became a nightly ritual. The group named the place "Lemon Hart Cove" in honor of the rum. I was assigned the task of gathering firewood, which was easy since it was everywhere. After helping Pat make a fire ring with rocks in the sand to hold a large grill, we cooked steaks over the open fire.

21

Pat helped me place several sticks upright in the sand at the edge of the river to measure the water level. He explained that he wanted me to do this at each camp, so we would be able to tell if the water was going up or down.

Day 2 - Tuesday, June 26, 1962 - 53,300 cfs

First thing in the morning I got up to check the river level. Pat was already there, and he explained the river was up a little. Now these sticks made sense to me. After breakfast we were off around 8:00 a.m. We pulled over to look at North Canyon Rapid and Mile 21 Rapid before running them. We ran everything else "wide open" as the boatmen say, until we reached 24.5 Mile Rapid. It was the roughest Pat had ever seen it and he decided the boats should be lined. It was his first time lining boats in Marble Canyon. I asked my father why we were not running the rapid, and he explained about safety and being on our own. He was right about being alone. We would not see another person until we reached Bright Angel Creek and Phantom Ranch. Then Don Harris and Jack Brennan passed us in two powerboats on July 5th at Royal Arch Creek. Georgie White's large party of 46 passed us on July 8 below Tapeats. The next and last person we would meet was Carl Peterson on July 13th who would tow us across Lake Mead to Temple Bar.

We spent the whole day lining the boats through the rapid, unloading them, and then portaging everything to the head of an eddy below the rapid. Camp was made on a large, sandy beach. After dinner, Pat and I climbed up something he called Stanton's Marble Pier. We found an old survey stick from the 1889 expedition led by Robert Brewster Stanton, the chief engineer of a railroad company. Pat told me the stories of the drowning of two of the crew on that trip, Henry Richards and Peter Hansbrough, who didn't wear life jackets, and of the aborted attempt to build a railroad down the Grand Canyon. As we climbed back down, I was less embarrassed about the large, green life jacket I wore, adorned with two bleach bottles added for more flotation. As I was not a good swimmer, my father required the bottles in addition to the life jacket. That night the last of the ice was used for a drink they called "Stanton's Sidewinders."

Day 4 - Thursday, June 28, 1962 - 52,200 cfs

It was another amazing day for me. We passed the beautiful formation of Royal Arch and then visited graves at President Harding Rapid: those of Peter Hansbrough who died in 1889 on Stanton's trip, and of David Quigley, a Boy Scout who drowned in 1951. The Quigley grave affected me the most since I was a Boy Scout and he had died only eleven years earlier. Thunder and lightning darkened our mid-day, but we reached our camp at Nankoweap early in the afternoon. Several of us hiked up to the prehistoric granaries high above the silt and driftwood-covered flatlands by the river. From the granaries I remember looking downriver at the straight, warm, powerful river cutting down-canyon, with so little vegetation along its silty shore. Years later I would be shocked at how this view of the river had changed from this lofty location. A cold, blue, meandering river, whose shores were overgrown by vegetation, had replaced the wild Colorado River.

That night at camp I learned about another side of river running. There were large driftwood piles that covered acres of land. Nailed to a mesquite tree was a sign that read, "Georgie White Royal River Rats 1944 to 1960." Pat became very irritated by this self-promotion by Georgie, and loudly explained to all of us that she completed her first trip through the Grand Canyon with Elgin Pierce in 1952. Since Martin had ridden with her that year from Toroweap to Whitmore, he had much to add about Georgie. As was requested by the Park Service in those days, we set fire to the driftwood. As Pat and Martin drank "Nankoweap Depth Bombs," they celebrated the burning of the sign. Again, I was witnessing things that only time would reveal to me as significant. First, after completion of Glen Canyon Dam, the river and its shores would greatly change. And second, I was seeing some of the early skirmishes between private and commercial river runners.

Day 10 - Wednesday, July 4, 1962 - 49,900 cfs

We camped above Hermit Rapid and I suffered greatly at night from blowing sand. There was silt and sand everywhere. Signs of wild burros were all around the mouth of Hermit Creek. We were on the river by 7 a.m. and ran Hermit Rapid with a dry run. About a mile below, we saw bighorn sheep, which I found to be very exciting. I felt we were intruding on their domain.

We ran everything that day wide open. Boucher, Crystal, Tuna, Serpentine, and Bass were all big-water rapids that I now found very exciting to run in the *Flavell II*. We floated under the Bass Cable and the remains of the cable car were still there to see. We passed the *Ross Wheeler*, Charles Russell's abandoned boat, as we made our way down through Waltenburg Rapid. We landed at Royal Arch Creek about 11:15 a.m. where we camped.

It was here, at Elves Chasm, that I became aware that people treated the unbelievably beautiful canyon very differently from what I was taught. At this jewel, we found a very messy camp from some previous party. There was paper, clothing, food, and all kinds of junk left at the campsite. Cigarette butts and paper wrappers floated in the pools, polluting one of the most beautiful spots I had seen along the river. We cleaned up the mess and I remember thinking of how careful we had been in our camps.

There was a register book there and we signed in. Pat and Martin got all excited as they saw that Georgie White was using it to advertise her rate of $300 for a trip through the Grand Canyon. Once again, different personalities and styles of river runners were surfacing.

That afternoon everyone did his or her own thing. Most went up above Elves Chasm exploring. My father wanted to take a bath in the creek by the river and I went fishing. He asked Suzanne to stay upstream until he was done, so he felt he was alone in the wilderness. No sooner had he gotten his face all suds up, standing there in two inches of water, then the Don Harris boats motored around the bend and pulled in right in front of him. I tried yelling to him, but the river noise was too loud for him to hear me. I watched as the two-boat party unloaded and stared at this naked man. Finally, my father rinsed his face and discovered he had three women in front of him. What did he do? He said, "Hi!"

Day 14 - Sunday, July 8, 1962 - 43,200 cfs

We left our camp at Tapeats early just so we could land on the left side of the river at Mile 135 to watch Georgie White's baloney boats go through this narrow part of the river. "Baloney boats" was a term Reilly and Litton used to refer to the three ten-man life rafts Georgie tied together to make one large boat. Sometime in big rapids these rafts would flip on top of each other with people sticking out like pieces of baloney. We had shared camp with her party at Tapeats. Pat seemed disappointed as their baloney boats easily negotiated this tricky part of the river. Yet he gave the boatmen praise for their abilities. Pat had spent yesterday afternoon visiting with Bonnie, Chet, and LaMar Bundy who he seemed to greatly respect. He learned from Chet how crowded Glen Canyon was becoming and that 400 people had recently landed at Kane Creek in just one day. All were there wanting to see what was soon going to be flooded by Lake Powell. None of us could imagine that this was going to be the same story for the Grand Canyon in just a few short years.

We made our way downriver and made a quick stop at a salt cave to view the "Christmas Tree," and then continued to Deer Creek Falls. We all climbed up the gorge to Surprise Valley and had lunch at the mouth of the valley. It was very hot, so we spent some time in the shade by the beautiful pools of Deer Creek. After lunch my father and I went up into the valley to climb up to Vaughn Spring. Near there I found several prehistoric granaries. It was exciting for me to make these "discoveries." Pat had told me that he knew of no prehistoric sites in the Deer Creek area, but in later years I spent much time in this valley and found many more sites.

It is very revealing to me today, as I reflect on my first visit to Surprise Valley, how people have mistakenly accepted things that are wrong. The name Surprise Valley has been moved from the valley where Deer Creek flows to the barren area between Tapeats and Deer Creek. The early maps by C. E. Dutton clearly label the Deer Creek area as Surprise Valley. Vaughn Spring has been moved, again incorrectly, to a location way up Deer Creek Canyon. Then there is the issue of the spit handprints in the gorge area above Deer Creek Falls. These were not there in 1962, nor in the early 1970s. Clearly, they are modern day "enhancements" that are being sold as prehistoric. The collective knowledge of the Grand Canyon has increased greatly in my lifetime, but in this case the record has gotten it wrong.

Day 18 - Thursday, July 12, 1962 - 32,800 cfs

We left our camp at Spring Canyon early in the morning. Soon we were above Mile 205 where my father decided to give an oral account on his reel-to-reel, battery-powered tape recorder of what it is like to run a rapid. He began recording his explanation as we approached the tongue of the rapid. Down we went into the waves and then I got a little concerned. He was so busy talking into his microphone that it seemed we were not running this rapid very well. Soon we approached a wall and it became clear to me that we were going to hit. I prepared for the flip. With a loud bang, the *Flavell II* struck the wall and the boat totally filled with water. Somehow we managed to stay upright through the rest of the rapid. Later that night at camp we all had a good laugh at Brick's recording of "How to run a rapid," accompanied by great background sounds of much panicked breathing.

At Mile 211, my father had me row the boat through this minor rapid. The boat handled very well but not because of my ability to row. Other than lining up correctly I was totally out of control, but we made it. I developed a great deal of respect for the *Flavell II* and the river. Hiking in the Canyon was something I felt very comfortable doing. Being a boatman was a whole different story for me.

We landed for lunch at Diamond Creek. There was no road or takeout in 1962. We found just the remains of the old hotel and a small stream. It was here that Pat, Martin, and Brick initiated the six of us who had never run the river before into their exclusive club. They blindfolded me, had me sit in the stream, and told me to bail. Pat drilled me about my knowledge of the river. "Name three rapids above Bright Angel. What is the biggest rapid? Who first went down the river? Why are Georgie's boats called baloney boats?" As Pat drilled me with questions, the others splashed me with water, yelling for me to bail. When it was done, they welcomed me into their world of river runners. I'm still proud to have been accepted into this special group of men and women.

Just before dinner Carl Peterson came walking into our camp from downriver. He had been able to come upriver to Diamond but no further. Pat offered him dinner and the drink of the night – "Lemon Hart Failures." As I listened to the discussion after dinner I was aware that this trip would soon be over. I was excited about making it through the Grand Canyon, yet it all seemed to happen too fast.

Day 20 - Saturday, July 14, 1962 - 28,500 cfs

We camped on river right at Mile 262.5 the last night on the river. Carl had intercepted us the day before and had my mother and Susie Reilly with him. I sat in the powerboat with Carl that day as we headed for Temple Bar. Between the Bat Cave and Emery Falls, I completed my transit of the Canyon since I had been up this far on a powerboat with Pat and my father in 1957. I was too excited driving the motor boat to even notice.

Carl took control and guided our three riverboats in tow into the bay below Emery Falls, which was falling directly into the lake. We continued across the lake until we exited the Canyon. Below Pearce Ferry a large powerboat greeted us. It was Bill and Fran Belknap who took two of the boats in tow. We were able to travel faster then and soon pulled into God's Pocket to look for the gas that Don Hatch had left for us. Searching through all the driftwood we were unable to find the gas—but we did find great driftwood. We lunched below at Iceberg Canyon. By 6:30 in the evening we reached Temple Bar.

The resident ranger, Mac Miller, and his wife, Fran, greeted us. He informed Pat that 238 people had come through the Canyon that year. My father told me that that was nearly the number of people who had run the river in all its history when he ran in 1955.

A lifetime later

The Grand Canyon has been in my life for 50 years. As a small boy I met people and heard stories from those who are legends today. When I was a teenager I hiked in what is today called the backcountry. Most significantly, I ran the river before Glen Canyon Dam changed it. As a hiker in the late 1960s and '70s, I witnessed how unregulated use of the Canyon by river runners almost destroyed the place. Hiking in the 1980s and '90s I saw the results of the development of rules and regulations to protect the Canyon, while user groups fought over a limited resource.

Then, in 2001, just weeks after my father's death, I ran the river once again. To honor him I wore his silver pith helmet down the river. I ran Lava Falls wearing that hat. He always lined Lava. When we pulled in for lunch below Lava, I walked upriver to be alone with memories. When he and Pat Reilly brought me to this special place called the Grand Canyon, they changed my life. In 1962, we had no guidebooks or references explaining history, wildlife, or plant life. I learned by experience and through the words passed to me by my elders. I experienced the power of nature and was engaged by the mystery of prehistoric and historic sites. The stories of past explorers were shared with me, along with the personal experiences of Pat Reilly and Brick Mortenson. All this was on my mind as I looked upriver at Lava Falls … and I thanked them.

In 2002, I ran the river once more and this time my daughter, Cecelia, became the third generation in my family to be a river runner. On that trip I passed to her the stories and memories given to me. Then in 2011, I was the permit holder of a trip where we replicated and ran the boats Reilly parties had run in the mid-to-late 1950s. My son Leif and his nine-year-old daughter Natalie were on that trip. Nat became the fourth generation of my family to be a Grand Canyon river runner. When they all completed their transit from Lees Ferry to Grand Wash, I'm sure that Pat Reilly, my father, and all others who came before welcomed them, as they had me.

Mad River Escapades
Marty Wolf

"July 12 [1969] Saturday: What a mess! Al & Mart went canoeing, and got lost. They ended up taking a 2-day canoe trip, in 10 hours. Meanwhile, Dad, Mom, and I were frantic, searching all over the stupid river trying to find them. We had the police, park rangers, and sheriffs all looking for them too. Finally we found them." [Journal entry, Mim, age 13]

Can you get lost on a river? I don't think so. Can you get delayed or waylaid? Or sped up past your designated (and never-before-seen, sometimes hidden) landing? Absolutely, especially in those ancient days before cellular phones, wireless networks, and GPS satellites (or in areas inaccessible to them). Can you not know specifically where you are, even though this river winds and rushes around and through a countryside you're very familiar with from the vantage points of its roads and walkways? For sure—everything looks, feels, smells, and sounds so different from the flowing river, whose ripples, waves, riffles and rapids, banks and riparian greenway can completely mask or distort the known cultural landmarks seen from roads or depicted on a map. Can you become disoriented, plunged into an altered state you wish would never end, while focused on the immediacy of avoiding submerged or emergent rocks, gravelly shallows, and downed trees caught against the bank in the middle of a sharp bend? Can you lose track of your location in the larger world when concentrating fully on aiming for, and staying within, the safest inverted-V funnel through obstacles in sudden rapids, mad with delirium as you shoot out the bottom into a calmer stretch? Ah, yes indeed you can. Overtaken, found, delivered. Definitely not lost.

Our madness started in the summer of 1968 when I was a quiet 16-year-old and my younger brother was a scrappy 14-year-old—and when, for some reason, our parents allowed us to use our pooled allowance and summer job savings to purchase a canoe kit that we worked on over several weeks in the unfinished basement of our house in Springfield, Ohio. Up on Dad's two old worn sawhorses, the boat slowly took shape: wooden centerline, stems, gunwales, thwarts, decks, ribs, seats. Then a canvas skin was stretched tight and secured with longitudinal wooden strips at gunwales and centerline. Finally, it was coated outside with two layers of fiberglass resin—first a yucky yellow layer followed by a second, more aquatic turquoise finish.

That resin may have contributed to our madness; its chemical solvent fumes permeating and lingering throughout that basement long after each layer had dried. Of course, few worried about respiratory protection back then. For months the family got to relive and consume that odor in meals made from foods retrieved from the huge chest freezer at the bottom of the basement stairs. There was no question of throwing the food out—that would have been too wasteful for a family of seven living on the salary of a religion professor at a small college. Besides, despite Rachael Carson, this was before there was much real concern about the potential or actual dangers to humans of an ever-growing number of chemicals in our modern world. That was still a year before the Cuyahoga River in the northeastern part of our state notoriously made nationwide news by catching on fire in '69. It was before the Clean Water Act, the Clean Air Act, or the EPA—but just a few months before the National Wild and Scenic Rivers Act was signed. Anyway, after the canoe skin was cured, we only needed to mess with a couple more chemicals to produce a mass of foam flotation for each end. We installed those under the bow and stern decks, and then put together and installed the wooden, mesh floor. We were ready for the water!

We hoisted the canoe on top of the family station wagon and did a few small lake trips to get used to what we immediately realized was a very tippy canoe (that foam flotation was going to come in handy several times in the coming years), and to coordinate, practice, and solidify our positions and strokes. We had paddled canoes at a summer camp or two, and rented canoes a few times during family camping trips (classic Americana: '60s station wagon with a luggage carrier on top, pulling a pop-up camper, crammed with five kids spanning six years—parents seeming unfazed in my memory—out seeing America's National and State Parks and Monuments … priceless). But we were pretty much beginners—though we felt very empowered as we had saved our money and built this canoe ourselves. Here we were, freely paddling about on local reservoirs! It was mesmerizing to watch the twisting vortices of air spinning down in the water off the end of my paddle with each stroke. I was starting to learn the subtleties of ruddering from my stern seat (especially when Al wasn't paddling) and twisting my paddle into a J-stroke to move us straight ahead, or to correct a bearing without switching sides.

We were also both beginning/intermediate birders, and I even got confident (or cocky) enough to wear my binoculars around my neck after the first trip. It was exciting to paddle along shores and see a fishing osprey gliding low overhead with bent wings, a kingfisher's dipping flight along the lakeshore, or an utterly exotic wood duck preening in an inlet. It was a delight to hear a pileated woodpecker calling, or an indigo bunting singing in nearby woods. And sheer pleasure to then paddle silently into a marshy area and freeze a patiently fishing bittern in the reeds, or spot a swamp sparrow with a beak full of bugs before it dived into a low shrub.

Soon enough, though, we were eager to get onto our local Mad River. There are at least a couple river-running outfits along the Mad today, not counting below its confluence with the Miami River in Dayton—but in those days such things were nonexistent in Ohio. This may have partly been because a river in those days (and not just in Ohio) was a convenient and much abused open sewer or pipeline for unwanted wastes and storm runoff. We would never see another canoer, rafter, or floater on our trips on the Mad River—and why the hell would we see a kayak, anyway? This wasn't Alaska! Good thing our first training runs were in the fall—it wasn't until the next spring we were to discover firsthand why the river got its name.

We did one or two trips on the Mad from the north, paddling about six or seven miles south to a spot upriver from the Ohio Edison power plant (where there was a dam—both are gone now) on the west edge of Springfield. Dad dropped us off somewhere near the Champaign County line, or maybe Tremont City Road, and planned to meet us two to three hours later at a takeout a little south of Upper Valley Mall. That trip was fairly tame and straightforward but a real joy. We let the river take us along, drifting and paddling. We came upon turtles sunning on logs along the banks and on herons wading, ignoring us, intent on their prey, then suddenly flushing as we came too close. A muskrat swam across the surface carrying plant matter in its mouth, its snout and eyes just above the water, then diving under as we were about to overtake it. We were seeing a new perspective from the river, viewing territory we had never before seen, although we had ridden in cars on the two-lane US Highway 68 that roughly paralleled the river through farmland half a mile east. Who'd have imagined what was just over there, hidden in the long strip of trees?

Our next adventure was to put in below where Buck Creek joined the Mad—just below the dam at Ohio Edison—and to travel some ten or so winding river miles southwesterly to a take-out spot (near Snider Road, or Spangler Road) where Dad would meet us in three to four hours. We were to discover that this stretch was very different from the straighter, northern run. We had a beautiful, fun paddle for about five and a half miles, winding toward the southeast for a bit, then bending southwest, skirting an island as the river wound west-northwest for a longer stretch, then bending in a northerly direction. We floated mostly through wooded and agricultural areas, passed under a highway bridge, then a railroad bridge. We passed under another smaller road bridge and maneuvered a broad, left-hand turn as the river took us more steadily southwest. We were loving the journey—seeing and hearing the local bird life, watching the spiraling slipstream of our paddles, discovering this new flowing course through the trees and the land. We relished the physical and sensual experience of paddling, passively floating when we could, guiding through bends without too much push so we wouldn't get torqued around by the faster moving current on the outer side, and avoiding trees clogged along steep outer banks that the current pushed us toward. We were learning how close we could skirt the inner bank without scraping bottom, developing a sense of the river's changing currents and speed as its course curved or narrowed, learning to feel and read the river … experiential learning in the flow-zone, on the go! Nothing like it.

Shortly after passing what we decided must have been the Enon Road bridge (unlabeled of course), we floated through a gentle, left-hand bend, down a south-southwesterly straightaway, and into a right-hand bend. The river turned more sharply and just kept turning, becoming two connected but opposite oxbows forming a backward "S" over a fairly short distance. Midway through the second hairpin we suddenly tipped slightly, momentarily too far, started taking in water, and couldn't regain balance as we quickly swamped and were pushed under. Sudden cold! Yikes! —Find your feet! —Grab the paddles! — while also trying to grab the suddenly very heavy canoe full of water that was being carried along just below the surface. Whew! Adrenaline rush! We managed to guide, push, and pull our canoe toward the inside sandbar where it and we were more secure, then rolled it onto its side and lifted it enough to drain the water. No damage done—oops … I realized my binoculars were still around my neck. Of course they had been submerged with me when we dumped. Raising them to my eyes, I could see one ocular lens had a film of moisture on its inside face, blurring the view. Damn. But what a rush! We were both soaked and grinning from ear to ear. Taught a little lesson in hubris by the river. OK, we caught our breath and rested a bit in the sun, then climbed back in and continued on our way.

We paddled on without incident for another half-mile, tackling a nice stretch of mild rapids that fed us into a sharper oxbow turn that we rode through with experienced handling at both ends! Alright—feeling good. By the time we met up with Dad we were still exhilarated by the trip, our spill and recovery, and all the many experiences of the journey.

The following spring, we picked a Saturday to again canoe the winding lower stretch of the Mad—same put-in and take-out as before. When we arrived at the put-in just below the Ohio Edison plant we could see the river was flowing higher and faster than we'd last seen it. We soon discovered what a difference the increased volume of water made, with its greater mass and momentum. There were fewer opportunities to rest and just float along, or to watch birds and explore. It took more vigilance, and we found many more downed trees and other debris snagged along the banks, with branches appearing below the surface as we flowed along. This faster spring river was fuller, deeper, and wider in places; in many bends it was scouring deeper into the outside bank. This was a different river!

In the stern I got pretty good at switching sides quickly, swinging my paddle behind my back to the other side to avoid spraying water onto Al. I was also seeing how a subtle difference in my stroke through a curve could either be amplified—sending us into a rotation with the risk of a broach and sudden swamping—or effectively be balanced with the forces of the bending river torrent—allowing safe passage, though with plenty of shivers and goose bumps! In this swollen spring river there was less response time for error. We had a couple spills accompanied by that sudden "Oh no!" intake of rushing water as we tilted and capsized, that instant cold of immersion, that thrash-and-grab reactive alertness, so fully aware while trying to hold on and float to safety, trying to avoid further obstacles as the flow took us onward.

After each swamping we managed to find footing downstream to get the canoe hoisted and emptied. It could be tricky getting us both back in if there wasn't a shallow enough sandbar or decent handhold along the bank to steady that tippy canoe! Our next mishap came in that same sharp, double-hairpin, "backward S" curve that got us on our trip the previous fall. It happened when we were uncontrollably forced by the twisting current against a broken branch stub on a snagged tree on the outside bank of the left curve—puncturing the hull just below waterline. Oh man! As water gushed in through the two to three-inch opening we continued forward around the curve, gradually filling, slowing, and sinking. By the time we reached a submerged sandbar, our seats were just below the waterline. After climbing out (standing in knee-deep water) we rolled the canoe over, lifted it up to drain, and were able to set it down on the adjacent bank. After we took a short break sitting in the sun, catching our breath, and contemplating the situation, Al took his shirt off and stuffed it into the hole to temporarily plug it, and we launched into that Mad River yet again.

That puncture would be our first of two that season. Back in the basement after that trip we were able to splice a broken rib, apply a canvas patch, and coat that over with fiberglass resin—as good as new. The second, larger puncture (on our next trip) rendered us unable to reach our planned take-out, and thus meet-up spot with Dad, so we all got a first taste of the disorienting panic that can ensue in such a situation (again, long before cell phones). We got to the nearest downstream dirt road access and walked up it until it met the paved road that parallels the river through that stretch. There we ran across Dad driving on from the previous access point; he'd been on a systematic search, driving down every river access road he could find after we failed to show at the planned time.

Come summer of '69, we were off to Wisconsin for a few months. I was working as a (soon-to-be high-school senior) student intern at the Wisconsin Audubon Camp for adults east of Sarona in the northwest part of the state. Mom and Dad, with Al and our younger sister Mim, were in Madison where Dad was doing some post-doc studies (and/or teaching) at the university. They brought the canoe along to the house where they were staying in Madison, and did some occasional paddling on Lake Mendota.

During my free time at the Audubon camp I would take one of their aluminum canoes out on the little Twin Lakes, and sometimes would follow the connecting passage over into Big Devil Lake. I would paddle around, watching common loons and listening to their wild haunting calls, hearing the constant singing of red-eyed vireos and an occasional wood thrush in the surrounding woods. On moonlit evenings I would hear the steady, high-pitched drone of thousands of mosquitoes in those woods, and the sudden, loud smacking of a beaver's tail on the water when I approached too closely. I became expert at silently paddling a two-seater canoe by myself on flat water using the J-stroke. I spent timeless spells wrapped in the deep experience of being a part of nature out on those lakes. To me those explorations and observations from a canoe were truly about living, being—not just "making a living," as my mentor of many years, H. D. Thoreau, had written.

One Saturday about a week or so before the historic Apollo 11 Mission, my family members in Madison, who were out seeing some of the sights upstate, drove up to fetch me. We decided to go east to the Flambeau River so Al and I could paddle a section of it in our trusty (tippy), homemade canoe. Our likely put-in, as best I can figure now, was on the South Fork at the Lugerville/County Road F access, with plans to meet our family and the car at the County Road W bridge landing, about 10 miles downriver. We estimated the trip would take four to five hours. This stretch wound through wild, mostly undeveloped forest and was supposed to have a number of mild rapids.

It was an amazing and beautiful trip. Though it was a weekend, I don't recall seeing any other people, but we ran across many birds: saw a bald eagle perched in a snag over the river, great blue herons, a red-shouldered hawk, yellowthroats, an indigo bunting. We heard red-eyed vireos, wood-pewees, ovenbirds, least flycatchers, and several warblers. The brown, tannin-stained waters moved us along, carrying us through riffles, calm water, and three or four rapids in the first hour—including a couple of sets coming fairly close together. We were very jazzed! We came upon several elongated islands which we liked to circumnavigate, comparing the waterway and banks on opposite sides and looking and listening for birds or other wildlife. We got out to explore one of them briefly, making sure to avoid poison ivy, which I was horribly sensitive to. Later, after some flat water, a few minor rapids, and a big bend, we ate our lunch on a large island, enjoying the sunshine and gentle breeze—but with just enough mosquitoes to make us want to get back in motion on the river as soon as we could manage. Paddling on downstream we came to another nice series of rapids, the middle one followed by a cluster of interesting parallel islands angling into the current.

We really got into river mode after that, drifting along with the flow, enjoying the physical movements of paddling, switching sides periodically to give one arm more of a rest, watching the trees on the banks stream by. It became an altered state, one with the moving river, centered in the present while scanning downstream now and then for any upcoming rapids or bends calling for maneuvers in the near-future. We barely noticed a bridge crossing overhead or a house through the trees past it—if anything, we took them as an insult and slipped quietly by with the water, back to the wilds of our river entrancement. We figured we still had an hour or more to enjoy! (I *was* wearing a watch, but …)

After a stretch of quiet, winding water we reached a series of fun rapids within a half-mile of each other, and then several islands scattered through a couple miles or so of more gentle running water again, and then ran another good rapid. We were now starting to wonder if our take-out hadn't been hiding back there at that bridge. Oh well—nothing to do now but keep on!

We came to a wild span of rapids that wouldn't let up much, yet wasn't too difficult for us—no mishaps, but so invigorating! Then the river split around a nice, long, tree-covered island, and quickly fed us right into more rapids, followed by some snaking bends, and then yet more good rapids. Yee-haw! Charge! —and before we knew it we went right into a new series of more intense rapids that tested our alertness and skill more than any others we'd hit that day. But we made it all the way through! Yes! Our hair and clothes were pretty wet, we had some water sloshing in the bottom of the canoe, our eyes were wide, grins plastered on our faces, adrenaline flooding our bodies—and just ahead we saw another bridge across the river. We knew we had to pull over here, and see if we could figure out where we were; we were sure now that we had missed our meet-up with the folks and Mim. But wow, what an incredible trip! The Flambeau! Our wildest and maddest trip yet, in our homemade canoe—but no punctures or broaches! But it wasn't quite over yet …

We found a landing near the bridge. It turned out we were at the County Road M crossing, some seven or eight miles and four hours beyond the planned take-out and meet-up point. Oops. We emptied the canoe and carried it to where there was car access, and then walked up the dirt drive through the trees to wait by the road for Mom and Dad to hopefully drive up—or else to flag someone down for help getting to a phone and finding the number for the state forest office (had we really thought that far ahead—at 17 and 15? I doubt it). As it turned out, they did show up within about 45 minutes, relieved to see us safe and sound after a long and frantic four hours of searching and, yes, enlisting help from all available authorities! We were so sorry, Mission Control (and Mim), but we couldn't help it, and had had such a great time … at one with the river's space and flow.

Eight days later, watching the televised moon landing with others at the camp as Neil Armstrong and Buzz Aldrin walked and leaped around on that moon, I understood the significance, the awe, and accomplishment of that mission. But, and it may seem silly, I felt like that paled in a way to what Al and I had done in our canoe on

37

that river. We were here, on this planet, fully experiencing its waters, its forests and life, in a homemade craft powered by teen muscle and by moving waters responding to gravity's pull, to topography—and the waters also responding to our human muscles, brains, boat, and senses—all forces of nature interacting and interwoven.

Ah, for those days of yore—mad youth, free spirits, and mad river adventures! Did I mention we had no life preservers? In those less litigious days, I don't know that there were laws requiring their use, and I don't recall it ever coming up as a safety concern either in the family or at any place we canoed. We knew how to swim, right? It was definitely way before the age of brain buckets. I forget what ever happened to that canoe. Today, at 65 and living in Colorado since my young twenties, my wife, Chris, and I have 10-foot kayaks (with life-jackets, as well as GPS-equipped smart-phones—or, at least, my wife does—Ha!), and some good friends with whom we kayak on nearby reservoirs and the South Platte River in Colorado's Front Range mountains. Time in our kayaks has really brought back memories (when it's not on a weekend with the crowds of other river recreationists). We hope to get onto other rivers in the state, including the Colorado—but that will be on relatively tame stretches now (alas). The era and our age make mad river escapades much less likely, for good or for bad. But I'm so glad that Al and I had those grounding, character-building, nature-submersed, wild and reckless canoeing trips back in our younger days! And that we had the chance to lose our moorings just enough to find ourselves, truly, out on a river. As Thoreau wrote, "Not till we are lost, in other words, not till we have lost the world, do we begin to find ourselves, and realize where we are and the infinite extent of our relations."

A Backpacker Takes a Ride
Jeff Ingram

I did once take a commercial (rowing) trip down the Colorado River through the Grand Canyon, about 40 years ago. It was by invitation, free, and a mistake. In many senses. The only redeeming factor was that I had a chance, in the middle of the fierce controversies over the river in the 1970s, to take a look at the condition of the river shore.

My other two trips were privately organized and led. I was one of 1,100 travelers to go down the Grand Canyon in 1966. In September of that year, Martin Litton got together his dories, a few friends and their boats, and some people interested in keeping dams out of the Canyon. We spent three weeks exploring. Trip of a lifetime.

In January 2001, I participated in a month-long adventure led by two more of the Canyon's premier advocates who are publishers at Vishnu Temple Press. This was surely as close to a true wilderness trip as the Canyon's Colorado can offer. The environmental awareness of this group was several grades higher than what I experienced 35 years earlier.

These are not particularly extensive credentials to allow pontification about the virtues and perils of authentic—individually organized and led, fully participatory and cooperative, wilderness, human-powered river trips. Nor am I any use in consulting about packaged tours (the true name for commercial boating). I find them deadly restrictive; they make me even grumpier than I normally am. I tend to bounce against the walls, even when there are none. And when there are, I prefer to consider scrambling up them. But then, you see, I am a backpacker, a landlubber.

Why didn't I become as fascinated by boating? If I had, I was in the Southwest early enough to have floated Glen Canyon. Yet what that country said to me was, "Come walking." I cannot tell you why, though I have often wondered. In some measure, the practicalities

39

of river running always loomed larger, though that is almost always a phony excuse. Ignorance of opportunity seems like a cop-out too. Whatever, while backpacking, hiking, and poking around in odd places irresistibly seduced me again and again, river running remained a rare joy.

Certainly I enjoyed the few real river trips I have been on. The revelations smoothly floating by. The excitement and rituals of running rapids. The opportunities to face into the canyons, walking or climbing about in the spaces rock makes as it is being eroded and carried off. Bringing me right back on land again—

> The comfort of the rock:
> Surrounded home, walls the blanket,
> The roof dangerously blue.
> Across a slot the view, felt, needs to be underfoot,
> Under feet firmly placed,
> Steps shaped to contour,
> Drawn on, up, around, over
> Grain, grit, gripped.
> Those waves and slants walked out,
> So defined, setting me free—
> As my ache for the rock is,
> Here written out, defined and eased.
> Isn't it?

Yes, there are times when sharing talk and food, games and conversation transform people into more than fellow travelers. Yet groupiness is not the point of wilderness travel for me. People are OK, but there are billions of us, and plenty of opportunities to spend time with some of you. A wilderness trip may require a group for the sake of logistics and safety, and some companionship. My peak Grand Canyon experience was a three-week, trail-less backpack in the western Canyon with one other, also surly, person. While he tended a camera on the river shore, for me there was day after day of glorious exploration. And a certain loading of fear.

I can only make sense out of such adventures if they excite issues about what it is all about, what am I doing there. Sharing may help. Too often it deflates enthusiasm without restoring the experience; wilderness is too interior a matter. And it requires keeping up, matching paces—or sitting together in a boat. I cannot escape falling behind, to think, to remember. Journals help, an excuse to concentrate, to find out if there is anything going on, or if that feeling of being struck is only vaporing. And I have been tricked, now and then, into trying to create some match—

> Across and Back Again
> Low, flat; wild.
> Wind, wind, wind.
> The Canyon open,
> We spill out, across,
> And down.
> Gone behind: The walls,
> A catapult, the world flung back.
> This plane the floor—cracked.
> We hang, suspended between steps,
> Among steeps, wandering:
> Space's float;
> Motes expanded in apprehension.
> We drop;
> The bottom's found.
> Long, slow.
> Snap up.
> Fading.
> Each step imagined,
> Created,
> Made to happen;
> Determination's precision:
> No grace, exhaustion's choreography resounding to ascent's perfect pitch.
> Hushed, done.
> Ecstatic, collapsed.

As I said, I'm a landsman. The Canyon is a grand, the grandest, space. "A universe," I once enthused, "embedded in the earth," with, basic to it all, the River, scouring and deepening. And providing a medium for travel. With travel comes the opportunity for learning, appreciating, understanding its canyon. Uniquely, the medium for having your understanding cohere. Walking takes too long; package tours are way too short. On a river trip there is a balanced pacing, tuned to our minds, going at the river's speed to imprint the longitudinal development. Stopping often enough to imprint the variety of cross-sections and habitats. Conversation can be heard whether you are on a quietly directed boat or on shore. Talk materially helps here, especially if supported by labels, explanations, or even speculations. You are able to relish your evolving understanding of the plurality of this singular place. You absorb the full force of that very American idea of a National Park. You are being given a book and are provided with the time to read it. On a package tour, a gaudy summary is dished up. Walking, you get to study a chapter. During a wilderness river trip, you can read, pause, reflect, discuss, and absorb the entirety as you go.

If this is education, such a trip can provide anyone with an advanced degree. Or a bit of doggerel—

Pleistocene Canyonscene

The ice sheet paused.
An age deterred,
Astounded at Earth's gaping,
Glacier-deep already:
Time's layerings a haven,
Accepting even lava's falls.

Wilderness, a National Park Wilderness, is a vital, powerful, contested idea. On a river-paced trip, however, it just seems obvious. What seems cuckoo are the schemes: dams, railroads, mines, motorized tour barges, tramways. Yet just as the leavings of the would-be profiteers show up here and there, so the Canyon's human history is littered with political argument. A truly privately conceived wilderness river trip provides a metaphor for the potency of the wilderness idea. Indeed, that is how Parks and Wilderness have come about; individual citizens, moved by an idea, working together, cooperating to bring the concept to reality. Leadership is important, of course, to add strength to the effort to promote and advocate for Parks and Wilderness, which can only grow successfully out of citizen initiatives, eschewing the desire to profiteer. To be whizzed through a Park or over a Wilderness is to be denied the chance to learn, as well as the chance to understand that you are needed. On a trip run by cooperation, every person is of value. Likewise, every person is needed to support the effort to protect the wilderness you are passing through.

The Packing Party
Lloyd Knapp

My first trip on the Colorado was a few decades ago. Nine months earlier, with a precious invite in hand and truly Grand expectations, I had purchased my first raft. There was one thing of which I was certain: I wanted to row the river myself. Even back then, getting access to the Colorado River was becoming a big issue and I knew I might never get another chance.

My new boat was a carefully chosen Maravia Williwaw 1. Over the late fall and winter, I worked diligently equipping the boat: four oars, custom aluminum frame, Rubbermaid 105-quart ice chest, ropes, straps, and an almost staggering miscellany of other gear. Everything I bought was with the Colorado in mind and was the best quality I could afford. By spring, the boat was as ready as I could possibly make it.

There were several other beginners in our group. We were known as the "Duckies" to the more experienced boaters. Almost every weekend we were out running all the local rivers to be found near southern Oregon. With the typical high-level flows of spring, we encountered some big water like we expected on the Colorado. Our put-in date for the Grand was June 20th.

On these trips I realized I had done a pretty good job designing the raft frame for my tall body. With my feet against the footbrace, I could straighten out my legs and firmly wedge my butt into the seat. This placed my body in a solid, stable position from which I could really pull on the oars when necessary. Wedging my butt tightly into the seat was the key element. There was no chance of sliding sideways off a smooth-topped ice chest or drybox in choppy whitewater. My concept worked well. The little 14-footer turned on a dime and maneuvered beautifully. It was not like a big, heavy gear boat. To me it was like being in a little sports car. I came to love that boat. Clearly, I had left my days in little inflatable kayaks behind.

I was also beginning to learn those subtle lessons that define the very nature of our sport. 1) There is something innate within the human spirit that thrives on the anticipation of and preparation for a big adventure. For us, these feelings are critical. If the preparation aspect of the trip isn't fun, then take up another activity. 2) Multi-day river trips through remote river canyons are expeditions, not fly-away, carefree vacations. A degree of independence and work are required.

The preparation and journey really help define the entire experience. In my case, river touring is what I really go for. Unlike many aspects of travel, the final destination becomes unimportant because that's the takeout—meaning the trip is over. To avoid post-trip letdown, I then start thinking and planning my next adventure.

It also really all comes back to the tribal thing—a small group of interdependent people moving respectfully and gracefully through the wilderness. It's the way humanity was meant to be. It is the time when human nature can be at its best—or at its very worst. I've seen it go both directions, everything from beautiful to weird, with an amazing variety in between. The tribal thing sounds pretty good, but it can definitely go either way.

In May of that year our group celebrated another solemn ritual well known to those people who disappear down into remote river canyons for days or weeks at a time—the packing party. It took most of a Saturday. There were at least 12 of us there who had been invited on the trip. The mission was to prepare and pack all our non-perishable food. It had to be organized and coordinated perfectly. We planned to be in the Grand Canyon for at least 21 days to cover a distance of 278 miles, from Lee's Ferry all the way down into Lake Mead. There were 16 of us. At three meals a day, that's a lot of food—a total of over 60 meals to be prepared.

Our Trip Leader (TL) was awesome. Leading up to this momentous ritual at the packing party, she had led several gathering trips to local grocery stores and markets. Woman-the-Gatherer: I wonder how many times in prehistory Woman-the-Gatherer fed the family when Man-the-Hunter came home empty handed. The gatherers had spent at least $600. The TL had menus made up and laminated, one for every one of those 60 meals.

Her husband and a few others had collected 60 or more used, white, plastic paint buckets, five to seven gallons each, complete with the original lids. These buckets were the ideal container for conveying our food down the Grand. Other needed supplies had also been assembled; Sharpie pens and, of course, the inevitable duct tape.

We went to work cleaning and washing out the buckets, carefully checking the lids and rubber seals. All the food that had been purchased was brought in from various vehicles and stacked and organized on tables set up in the living room. Clean buckets were placed out on the deck with associated lids. Team leaders were issued menus. The job was to pick out necessary food items for a given meal and put them all in the same bucket. For example: Lunch Days 5 & 6 in one bucket, Dinner Day 19 in another, Breakfast Days 9 & 10 in a third, etc. Another person would accompany them to double check. Both the bucket and the lid were then labeled accordingly.

This was to be our sustenance. It had to be done right. We knew there would be a lot of full buckets going downstream with us. Once we were on the river, a few slip-ups, with key items in the wrong bucket, might render an entire recipe unusable. Just the thought of looking for a missing ingredient brought visions of a dire situation. The entire team might end up on a wild goose chase looking through other buckets. It would be a nightmare. And then all those hastily opened buckets would have to be packed again and re-sealed. Clearly there wasn't any room for errors.

Notably impressed by all this, I worked at my tasks diligently. The stacked-up piles of food slowly diminished as buckets began to fill. Copies of the recipes went into the bucket along with the food. Our leader had a master copy. However, nothing was to be permanently sealed—not yet anyway. Even after all this, our Trip Leader was going to go through every bucket one more time, to make sure it was right. Only then would the buckets be pounded shut, and taped. When the last stragglers left that day, she was still there with all those open buckets.

The packing party was a momentous occasion, and a memory I cherish to this day. Despite all the adventures with my new raft, the packing party was a real eye-opener, revealing that this Colorado River trip was going to be a pretty big deal. But there were more preparations to come.

Another big factor in the logistics department was the heat of the Grand Canyon. In mid-June it would be hot. Damn hot. I had lived in Arizona, so I understood. (One day, during our trip, I remember rowing and sweating through the many miles of flat-water—it was 118 degrees in the shade. Other days reached up closer to 125 degrees.)

But finally it was time to go to the river. As a "Duckie," I readily admit to a bit of apprehension. It was quiet in our van as we rolled down the road leading from the North Rim of the Grand Canyon, winding down the hill past the Vermilion Cliffs toward the put-in at Lee's Ferry. The thought of the Colorado River, and all that big water ahead of us, had me a bit nervous. Perhaps the others felt the same way. Maybe that's why it was quiet in the van that day.

But there was still a lot to do when we got to the put-in. It kept us busy. All our empty ice chests were assembled, loaded into two vehicles, and our leader and her chosen team were off for another gathering spree. This time the gatherers were off to Page, Arizona—for ice and the food that would be refrigerated. I knew it was a long drive. It wasn't far as the raven flies, but a long way around in canyon country.

While they were gone, the boats were inflated and made ready. All our gear went into the boats. There were also the thirty-five buckets to deal with. They were collected from the vans and set out on the bank—the weak and flimsy appearing buckets containing our provisions. The boat crews somehow crammed them in.

Hours later the gatherers returned. The ice chests were packed full, and kept as cold as they could be. These were also lifted into the boats. The next morning, the day of the put-in, one more trip was made locally for more bags of ice to top-off what we had. We knew the ice would not last indefinitely in the heat, but it was the best we could do.

Another team took a clean bucket and mixed four to five gallons of tabbouleh right there at the put-in. This became a staple for lunches and proved to be very popular.

Then it was off to the darkened, little building for the spiel from the park ranger. He was known to us only as "Blue." "Pee in the river," he said, "Send that stuff down to Lake Mead where it belongs." After a number of other rules and regulations were explained, the meeting ended. That short talk was our final preparation, then it was back to the boat ramp and we were off. Our little tribe passed under Navajo Bridge, the last really big symbol of Western civilization we would see. We would be on our own for the next three weeks.

Once on the river we were able to be pretty carefree about our food. In the end, the bucket brigade, and the pre-trip attention to detail paid off. As buckets were emptied, they were filled with trash or smashed-aluminum cans, the lids were pounded down, and they again found their way back into the boats.

Although numerous precautions had been taken, the ice in my cooler only lasted until Day 6. It had been sealed and taped with duct tape at the put-in. I had also covered it with a reflective space blanket to radiate heat away from the contents below. The meals it carried were for Day 4 and part of Day 6, so that worked out pretty well. The bigger ice chests, 128-quarts, and a 156-quart lasted longer, but by Day 10 just about all the ice was gone. The 156-quart ice chest was nursed along with a few cold items, worth their weight in gold, until we made Phantom Ranch where more ice was purchased. For me, an empty ice chest wasn't all bad. It just meant I had valuable space for extra gear storage.

The tabbouleh lasted for about a week. Most of it had been happily consumed. We knew it was time for the bucket to become a trash container when people would take one hopeful look inside, then politely decline. Another popular item on our trip was a salad made primarily of cabbage. This is one vegetable that survives pretty well in the heat with minimal or no refrigeration.

Our buckets served us admirably. Not only were they packed with precision, they survived several flips. Dubendorff Rapid claimed a 15' SOTAR. The boater was really experienced and I'm still not sure what happened. Even after all these years the story of that flip is still a little unclear. Around camp there were proposals to give the hapless boater the river-name of "Dubie." It didn't take hold. For that matter, none of his other given river-names ever took hold either.

Granite Rapid turned a 14' Hypalon boat upside down. The rower held onto an oar for a little bit too long. In rafting there comes a time to simply let go of everything, grab onto your seat with both hands and hang on. He should have let go of the oar. The power in the long wave train at Granite, transmitted through the handle of the oar, ejected him right out of the boat. His girlfriend in the front of the raft was still talking to him and giving advice. He was in the water, hanging onto the boat for all he was worth. She didn't think to turn around and see that he was gone. As the raft finally careened out of control and then flipped, he heard her last desperate command, "Row hard left." In the discussions that followed later in camp, it was decided that a factor in his favor was that he was hanging onto the left side of the boat.

The fabled fifth wave in Hermit did the Maytag thing with another raft, flipping it a couple of times. And my own raft flipped in Lava Falls. Lava cost me a pair of sunglasses. However, not one of our used, cheap, hand-me-down buckets failed. In fact, if I had had a few more loaded buckets in my raft, I might not have flipped. My passenger had gotten out on the bank and was video-taping the whole thing as I flipped a few feet in front of her. In other words, I could have used a bit more weight up front, to "high-side" and power through those big waves. I can come up with many other valid, reasonable excuses that would explain and justify why I flipped—or not. In any case, after all these years I'm not the least bit worried about it. I really don't care. Besides, I'm saving all those excuses for an entire book about my flip, and I'm not surrendering up all that valuable evidence just for this narrative.

Anyway, I got surfed sideways, and—wham! That boat went over so fast it wasn't funny. I came up under the boat, bumping my helmet into something. I did have the presence of mind to reach up and push the boat downstream with both hands, at the same time propelling me upstream. One more shove like that and I came up behind my upside-down sports car speeding down through the runout waves at Lava.

I grabbed for the raft. Missed. On my second grab I caught the boat. I don't know quite how I did it, but by the time I hit the bottom of the rapid I was already climbing onto the bottom of my upside-down raft. My rescue was swift and sure. We had the boat turned over in no time. At least my buckets were dry inside.

For weeks afterward, I had nightmares about that flip. Over and over in my dreams my mind replayed the incident in great detail. Again and again, I saw that left tube coming up out of the water and felt myself being thrown out of the boat on the right side. The dreaded feeling that I was about to swim …

Weeks later, when the video came along, the boat had obviously flipped in the opposite direction from how I remembered it. It was clearly the right side of the boat that came up and over. Oh well, so much for the reliability of dreams. I now know why eyewitness testimony is notoriously unreliable.

It was our meticulous preparation that made our trip successful as well as memorable. We had no supply or food issues. Way down the river, Day 18 or 19, I don't remember, a couple of guides taking an empty J-rig down to Lake Mead pulled over and gave us a bunch of ice, fresh food, bread, cheese, and some lunch meat. They had offloaded their passengers, and the big side tubes from their J-rig upstream at Diamond Creek. At this point the remaining supplies on the big boat were a liability for the guides who were facing a short turnaround time before beginning another trip. To us they were gifts from out of the blue canyon sky. Our ice had been gone for days.

We stopped at Travertine Canyon. There was another group there, a commercially guided trip. Although there were just a few of them, the place seemed badly overcrowded. I smelled something there I hadn't smelled in weeks. Burning tobacco. I couldn't help blurting out, "Oh my God, a cigarette!" It just seemed so out of place. No one in our tribe partook of those things. In just three weeks, that small tribal thing had distanced us from one aspect of humanity.

Later I stopped and lingered a few minutes by myself at Separation Canyon. There was no whitewater ahead of us. I just wanted a little mental process time alone in one of the most spectacular places on earth. Although at times my rowing had been less than spectacular, I had come out OK.

When I caught up to the others it was early afternoon. They had pulled all the boats together into one large, air-inflated flotilla, made up of all our boats in a roughly circular pattern. I pulled in alongside, grabbed a couple of carabiners and attached my boat to the others. We floated that way for hours, quietly talking and sharing our experiences. The unruffled river carried us along.

I turned around, undid my chair, and sat it up on top of my ice chest. I tucked one arm inside my shirt and tried to look like the famous Major John Wesley Powell, the first explorer of the Colorado River and its canyons. Powell had lost one arm in the Civil War at the Battle of Shiloh. He had directed the first expedition down the Colorado from a chair mounted to the deck of his boat, the *Emma Dean*. That was in 1869. Finally someone noticed my mimicry of the great explorer, and quickly pointed out that Powell had lost his other arm. Who was I to argue? Hell, at that time I didn't even know which way my boat had flipped in Lava Falls.

This last day and night of our trip is one of the top ten most memorable experiences of my life. We were headed all the way down to Pearce Ferry in the upper reaches of Lake Mead. The water was averaging about 18,000 to 22,000 cfs that year so the final row into Pearce Ferry would only be through a few miles (we hoped) of flat water. Where we were, the current in the upper reaches of the reservoir was moving us nicely along at about two to three knots.

In late afternoon, someone set up a small stove on a drybox to heat water. We passed around some of the bread, cheese, and a few remaining sodas. Occasionally Larry and I would have to row to remain in the current. He was directly opposite from me on our little flotilla. He had access to his right oar, and I had access to my left oar. For just us two to move the entire group of eight boats was interesting but it worked. There were no eddies here, only a minimum of rowing was required.

To make the final row out to Pearce Ferry easier, we had decided that we would continue on the river for as long into the night as possible.

From down in the canyon we couldn't see the sunset, but it must have been a good one. The canyon walls above us were painted in soft hues of pastel yellow, orange, red, and then purple as the sun went down. Eventually it was all in monotone shadows. Then the shadows steadily darkened until there was a complete absence of light. As evening slowly became night, people took out pads and sleeping bags and laid down on dryboxes and other flat areas. The unruffled river carried us along.

Just about the time it was really dark, a full moon came up from behind the low cliffs on river right. The light and the scene became spectacular, almost surreal. Our eyes adjusted, but I noticed that my depth perception was limited. At one point we came close to a vertical cliff that came down to the water's edge. I saw it, but couldn't tell if it was ten yards away or one hundred. Somehow, we avoided the towering face with just a few strokes on the oars. We slid by with the massive base of the darkened cliff just a few feet away.

The sounds and signs of wildlife came on in amazing abundance. Beaver, a lot of them, were constantly slapping their tails on the water as our flotilla was carried downstream towards them. Dozens of bats flew overhead, their silhouettes crossing the disk of the moon. There were several varieties, from small to large. Owls and other animals, some recognizable and others unknown, called in the warm, night air. A band of coyotes talked to each other.

Briefly, I shined my flashlight onto the bank, and held it still as the current moved us. Occasionally the beam would sweep across a small pair of reflective eyes shining out of the darkness. I knew the desert came alive at night, but "Wow." My words fail to adequately describe this scene. Many of our people appeared to have gone to sleep. But I knew most of them were simply quiet—as if spellbound by the magic of this incredible night. The unruffled river carried us along.

In the end, well after midnight, it was only Larry and I sitting up at the oars. We communicated with brief hand signals. I finally gave up, motioning that we should pull over. We rowed for shore. Someone on the raft behind me reached up out of their sleeping bag and tied our flotilla onto a tree sticking out of the bank. Wearily, I pulled out my pad and sleeping bag, putting it across the drybox. I was gone in minutes and slept the sleep of the just—the just plain tired.

When I awoke it was dawn. I looked up and the trees and cliffs were moving. Dazed for a moment, I realized the flotilla was again underway. Someone had untied us, and two other rowers were quietly guiding us. They had done it without making a sound. Another small stove was set up and hot water was available for coffee, tea, and instant cereal. At this point any food was fair game. The tabbouleh and the cabbage were long gone. Except for a few treats, we had been on canned, dried, and packaged foods for days. We were down to the last of our supplies. At least there would be no need to pack a lot of unused food up the bank at the take-out. The unruffled river carried us along.

We floated by the Grand Wash Cliffs, striking in the splendor of the early morning sun. We continued downstream until the banks became less steep, the river became wide, and the current diminished to nothing. At last it looked and smelled like the reservoir that it was, Lake Mead. We unhooked our boats from the flotilla and began to row. Pearce Ferry was less than 30-40 minutes away. By the time we arrived it was already hot. We were experiencing the heat of mid-July. Damn hot.

Our little tribe had done it! Later that afternoon, I knew it was really over when we crossed Hoover Dam, and then rolled down the hill into Las Vegas. The city seemed like a howling, desolate wilderness compared to where we had been.

It had been an incredible three weeks. The whole trip, including transportation, had cost me less than $350. That was due to the organizational skills of our Trip Leader, a firm commitment to the concept of self-support, and carpooling in several vans to and from our homes in Southern Oregon. For me, it all really began with the packing party. It ended up making for one damn good trip.

Desolation, Demoiselles and Falling Feathers

Herm Hoops

At age 68 my body is paying the price for a lifetime of abuse. Lifting heavy boats, ice chests, and river gear has taken its toll on the lumbar area of my spine, and arthritis, where nerve bundles pass through the vertebrae, complicates the effects of my fused neck. Severe bursitis in both hips makes standing more than ten minutes, or walking any distance, an exercise in severe pain. As the time approached for my annual spring trip, Val urged me to get the injections that would ease my pain. Almost any doctor can inject steroids into a person's hip joints. Performing epidural steroid injections, where the needle must be inserted between the vertebrae, is a bit more complicated and painful, and it cannot be performed by just any doctor. Because my orthopedic doctor had left the area, it took some doing to find a qualified professional to administer the injection, but a week before the trip I had been treated and my pain eased somewhat. For the patient it is an experience akin to medieval torture on the rack while being lanced with a red-hot iron. It takes about an hour of patience to complete the process, knowing the results are worth the agony.

This trip was to be a very special one for me because I had promised Val that it was likely my last solo early-spring trip on the 130 miles from Ouray to Green River, Utah, ending a 30-year tradition. But it was also special because my good friend Bob Decker from Vermont was coming along.

Over those thirty years I had rarely taken others along on this spring journey. In fact, I had only taken three others on what is normally my solo "follow the ice out" or "donut" trip. In 1988 Andy Robertson and I became trapped in river ice at Sumner's Amphitheater and, in a trip of notoriety, we walked fifty snow-packed miles across the remote desert to Myton. The following year, Cindy Doktorski, a co-worker with a wonderful, near-Franciscan personality, went on the trip. And, in 2012, Dan Warthin, who has been rafting with me since his early teens, came along. Dan loves the river canyons, but I suspect one of his motivations was to keep a watchful eye on me as I had recently been diagnosed with pneumonia, and then inhaled toxic smoke from a car fire while trying to save my house. I tired easily as I had not yet recovered and Dan, one of the best boaters I know, rowed most of that trip.

Bob would be the fourth to share this trip, although the plans were for him to leave me at Flat Canyon and continue his journey with others. What a common name—Bob, for such an uncommon person. His name is really Robert K. Decker, and he is one of the most talented people I know. I had been very close friends with Bob and his wife Beverly for many years, even as I moved around the country. But when we divorced, my ex-wife moved back to their area of northeast Vermont. I no longer stayed in touch with them because in a divorce, friends are like the furniture and other assets: you get the couch and I get the table. It wasn't until a few years ago that I re-established contact with them in a tear-filled reunion at their home.

Over the years, most of our time together has been at their beautiful house in the woods above Lake Willoughby. The times we spent there together were a jovial, introspective sharing of our lives and interests. They were the sort of times that a person might choose to experience in perpetuity if that sort of decision had to be made. But Beverly and Bob never chose to experience my wonders and secret places along the rivers of the Colorado Plateau. Perhaps Beverly was being protective of Bob and his family history of heart problems, or maybe they didn't feel comfortable experiencing my way of life.

So, they had never been on a real river trip. Oh, Bob went with me on day trips on Maine's Androscoggin River in the 1960s when I was in the formative stages of my river rafting experience. And one time they met me to do a day trip through Split Mountain Canyon in Dinosaur National Monument. But they had not experienced multi-day river trips, of at least four days, to explore secluded paradises that have an irresistible, mystical grasp on most people. A few years ago, Val and I were eagerly looking forward to sharing that special experience with them when they planned to fly to Utah and spend six days with us on the idyllic lower San Juan River. Just before the trip, late one night, we received a call from Beverly. Bob had tripped coming off a boat dock and fell into an Adirondack chair, breaking his orbital socket in eight places. It was disappointing and disheartening, but for obvious reasons the trip was off. So it was with great anticipation that I was looking forward to spending time with Bob on this trip. To share my world with him, as he had done with his world for me.

When I first launched at Ouray in the 1970s it was a small cluster of run-down, Ute houses with a small, decrepit store selling five-year-old Ring Dings, cigarettes, cola, and other life essentials. Its porch seemed to be held up by a couple of permanent regulars who sat there like silent statues. Today the store is gone and the houses mere piles of wood and memories. It has been surrounded by oil tanks, and the constant loud groan of oil trucks speeding by and across the Green River to the oil patch in the Book Cliffs: the Uinta Basin's Cibola.

We launched in the grey dawning of the day and drifted under the Green River Bridge and, for the next ten miles, were assaulted by the perpetual ugly growl of oilfield traffic. Monsters of the oilfield. Semi after semi, pickup truck after pickup truck, one man per vehicle. A parade of waste, whose audience began with the county commissioners and their families who profited handsomely from this crime against humanity.

A large log and then a beaver accompanied our journey for a time on this moderate current of silty water flowing from Wyoming and Colorado. Some would ask why I begin my trips at Ouray and endure the obscene intrusions, rather than launch 35 miles downriver at Sand Wash like others do. Maybe the oilfield intrusions remind me that I, too, rely on petroleum for my boat, and my lifestyle. Perhaps the noise heightens and contrasts the value of silence and natural sounds on the rest of the trip. But this section, for almost a third of a century, has been my transect of trends above the deep canyon.

Soon the growl of truck traffic was replaced by the deep whine of a drill rig perched on the shore near Pariette Wash. The rig, poised Washington statue-like, was topped by an American flag. A fitting tribute for mega companies who take public resources at a song and sell them to foreign countries at an obscene profit. At Willow Creek the sound of the drill rig was supplanted by that of a gravel crusher and loud pump generator, drowning out the ever-present goose calls and morning birdsong. A light breeze began blowing upriver as the intrusions disappeared and we sank deeper into the canyon. At King's Canyon, high above the river on the skyline, another drill rig sat silently, a reminder of the incessant, overwhelming threats creeping ever further into this spectacular place.

The wind rose in occasional light, upriver puffs, then grew into stiff breezes and matured into a major wind storm. I searched for a camp, protected from the wind but not under cottonwood trees, whose falling, hundred-pound branches could be a serious hazard. After several miles I spotted a nice place on the inside of a river bend. It was sandy and protected by willows and a small grove of developing young cottonwoods that were maybe ten feet tall. The wind was howling, and it took the better part of an hour of hard rowing to cover the 300 yards to the beach.

Our camp was in relative quiet while the wind roared through the old-growth cottonwood grove across the river. High above, maybe a thousand feet, blasts of wind hit scalloped formations of rock—sounding like bombs going off, blowing dirt and rocks into the air. It was as if the earth was inhaling until it could no longer hold its breath, and was then filling its cheeks and blowing at something. Sometime in the night the wind subsided, and first-night jitters evolved. Sounds in the night—an unknown, alien world out there in the dark is waiting to attack. No attack came, and after a cup of coffee I fell back to sleep.

We were on the river before dawn as scattered clouds began to pick up the sun's glow. Soon the layered cliffs also turned light, then pink and then red. The trees' new leaves became a brilliant fire green in the light; they looked as if they were freshly waxed.

In a few short miles we pulled into the boat ramp at Sand Wash. A large group was preparing to launch, and another one-boat trip was packing their gear. A plane had just landed on the butte a thousand feet above the ranger station, and it would take the passengers almost an hour to walk down the steep trail to the boat ramp.

Step by step, I slowly made my way up to the ranger residence where Jim, Mick, and I spent several hours chatting about job issues and river threats. Before he left, Jim drove me back down to the boat ramp. The large party had gone, and I began talking with the couple who remained there packing. In the conversation I mentioned that I had almost died of hypothermia down at Cedar Ridge Canyon in a blizzard about this time the previous year. The man, a hippie carpenter from Colorado, had launched this time last year as well—a couple of days after I had passed Sand Wash. In an odd coincidence he had seen my marks in the snow: "Mick. Help. Herm." with an arrow pointing downstream. He saw where I had drug a fence rail through the snow. He had wondered what it meant and what he should do. I told him the story—how I had dragged the fence rail as I was stockpiling as much wood as I could because I knew it was going to be a long night. How I had burned that 12-foot log, foot by foot, musing on its origin as I realized it was burning so hot that it had to be maple, ash or beech—and so it likely had journeyed down the Green or the Yampa river to arrive at my camp. And how before I left camp the next day, I used what was left of that log like a giant pencil to make my note in the snow. As I recounted the events of last year's blizzard, he commented that I had solved a great mystery for him. Later in the day we met on the river and floated together and talked for a few miles.

I rowed 20 miles that day, much of it against a stiff wind. The sun had dropped below the western wall of the canyon. To the right, about a mile downriver across from Stampede Flat, was a well-used camp. But as we rounded the corner, a white sandy beach about fifty yards long and ten yards wide presented itself on the left. It was deposited by last year's high water and the winds of winter; likely no one had ever camped there before. The pristine sand beach so attracted me that I rowed over to it for the evening's camp. I set up my stove in the boat, ate a simple supper, and filled my thermoses. Then I clambered ashore and set up camp. The boat rocked back and forth in the eddy waves as they splashed and eroded the shore. I had tied my boat off to a questionable branch of a box elder tree and, because my sand anchor also seemed tenuous in the deep, soft sand, I clipped the bow line onto the Paco Pad I was sleeping on. That way if the boat took off in the night I would receive notice!

Camp was in deep and cool shadow; below, the river turned sharply west. I happened to look toward the cliff at the bend in the river as it, and several demoiselles in a scallop between two ridges, were being painted in brilliant light by the setting sun. Geologically, demoiselles or hoodoos, are tall, thin spires of relatively soft, sedimentary rock topped by harder, less easily eroded cap stone that protects the columns from the elements. I counted over a dozen, ranging in height from five to thirty-five feet. I sipped coffee and watched the contrast increase and the color turn from goldenrod yellow to clotting-blood red. The view was mesmerizing, stunning. As the canyon and sky darkened I pulled my sleeping bag up and lay back to watch the nightly gathering of stars above. Upriver a small rapid whispered, and the river continued lapping endlessly at the shore of our sand bar home. I drifted into deep sleep.

Suddenly in the night, I had no idea what time, I sat bolt upright; something had changed. I immediately clicked on my flashlight. Assured that my boat was still tied securely, I drank in the scene before me. What had awakened me was how the world had suddenly quieted. There was no longer an upriver rapid whispering from the distance, and no nearby river lapping at my sand bar. That happens sometimes at night. Maybe it's a change in the direction of the night breeze, or maybe it is just one of the tricks of the moon, which now began to creep its reflection from the sun on the massive walls across the river. My thoughts were briefly interrupted by several shooting stars streaking across the sky. Moonrise on the cliffs is no less dramatic than sunrise. Ever so slowly, as your eyes adjust to the soft light, contrast and details of the rock become highlighted. Bob hadn't said much, but this is what I brought him along with me to experience. Oh, this folly of sitting in the sand in the moonlight!

Yet deep in my mind something was troubling me. Bob and I both knew that I would not be able to walk up Flat Canyon for him to see the gardens of yellow marsh marigolds, blue forget-me-nots, Indian paintbrush, scarlet gilia and watercress in the small pools there, let alone walk the easy two miles to Cathedral Door Arch and the small waterfall. Despite my injection I just would not be able to walk that far. We would just have to figure out what to do the next day.

I laid back to sleep again and slept unusually late. Once underway, I drifted the boat down to a small beach beneath the scalloped cliff of the demoiselles as the overcast light of daybreak slowly washed down the far canyon wall. I had discussed the location with Bob and we agreed that he could easily be located here and continue his journey as planned. We climbed the loose talus slowly, every step up taking a half step back. For me, it was a little like the high climbers on Mount Everest: step, pause, breathe, step, pause—it continued for about an hour before we reached the base of one of the demoiselles. To our right, a small trickle of water ran over the silky-smooth rock and fell in dribbles to accumulate and continue its journey under the influence of gravity. It nourished a small corridor of greenery along its course.

We were unable to climb to the actual base of the demoiselle, which was maybe fifteen feet high. But off to its side were several ledgey outcrops of Wasatch sandstone, each about ten feet high in setback layers. The Wasatch was deposited as a shoreline in a giant, shallow Lake Uintah some 55 million years ago during the Eocene epoch. The name *Eocene,* from the Greek *eos* (dawn) and *kainos* (new) refers to the "dawn" of modern fauna that appeared during that epoch. The face of the exposed rocks here looked like Swiss cheese. In the tawny colored rock were small pockets that had been eroded by the wind and dissolved by water. Near one small pocket a purple milkvetch had just begun blooming. A claret cup cactus boasted multi-flowers of red while sparsely scattered, rangy, orange globe mallows added their color and provided contrast with the tawny, rocky talus.

In the cold desert, it's this brief period of spring when plants must make their gain and assure continuation of the species. Like the food pyramid, but easier to overlook, the entire ecosystem depends upon the soil that grows the plants, the plants that provide stability and food for the insects, birds, and grazers. Each has its place in a healthy and stable ecosystem on which all survival depends—including humans.

I shared my last Pabst Blue Ribbon and a drag off my last Pall Mall with Bob. We sat silently for a few moments, gazing at the massive, layered rock wall across the way. The sky had turned blue and the river whispered below. A light wind began stirring. It was time for me to go.

I left Bob there where he would easily see all others descending the river, and then I worked my way down the talus to my boat. I waved, drifting downriver until he faded out of sight. I was now alone. I thought of demoiselles and how they were formed. I remembered *Les Demoiselles d'Avignon*, a Picasso painting—The Young Ladies of Avignon—and wondered how the name was translated to these slender formations. The free-standing rock columns were almost feminine in nature. To a lonely explorer or geologist in this remote land, were they perhaps reminders of lovers left behind? Another connection was rolling in my mind, but right now it had only just begun to ferment.

One of the things that made Bob Decker special was his concern for people, for his friends. Last year, after nearly succumbing to hypothermia in Desolation Canyon, I announced that I might continue my solo tradition. It brought a lot of weird looks and finger wagging comments from people. I also received a phone call from Bob, who rarely phoned me. Bob began with his homily of my responsibilities to other people and of my duties to life in general. He expressed his concern for my well-being, and my future. Bob was an excellent businessman in the finest sense of the word. He had a knack for melding an interest and an idea and transforming it into an income. He had called me up to try to make me understand that I was older, less able to run rivers, but that I could make an income from my knowledge and experience. I could sell my photos, my writings, my presentations to groups, organizations, and advertising agencies. He talked to me from the heart, he was concerned about me, my safety, and my health. Bob wanted me to consider different alternatives for earning money, while safely staying connected to the river.

It is hard to explain this river attraction (addiction) to other people. Once you feel it in your heart and recognize that it is the rivers, not blood, coursing in your veins, other options are, well, just not options. In my case, many people helped me along the way, and they did it for no fee or compensation … or even with any expectations. The river canyons are magnets that hold those sorts of folks to their fate, and somehow, I had become one of them. Life becomes so wrapped around the doing of the thing that it becomes like the peel wrapping around an apple. When you remove the peel, the apple yellows and deteriorates.

There are few others on the river this time of year. As I neared Steer Ridge Rapid an old fear arose in me. I had rowed this rapid a hundred times, but always, always, it began a wild, almost uncontrollable fear in me. I worried that familiarity might breed contempt, and that some unknown, unexpected event could change my life—as it did for Renny Russell in 1966 when his brother Terry drowned at this rapid. Or as it affected the families of the several others who failed to return from this spot. That fear is with me all the time on the river. Frankly, Steer Ridge Rapid, Joe Hutch Canyon, or Coal Creek Rapids are not difficult. They certainly do not rank in the top ten list of Big Drops of the Colorado River system. Still, to screw up here, especially alone and at this water temperature could be … well, fatal. And sometimes shit just happens. So, I glanced around the boat to make sure everything was secured and that my PFD was snug. Then I reviewed my response to potential outcomes in my head. The boat entered that glassy "V" of smoothly moving water, glided over a lilt or two, and quickly entered what, to some, would be an undecipherable maelstrom. Seconds later I was through it, and ready—indeed couldn't wait—to go through the process again. For me that intensity and focus never changes.

Few know of my fear; indeed, I firmly believe that is why river runners wear reflective sun glasses. They don't want others to see into their brain to see that swirl of emotions and fear. And to look into their eyes is a gateway into what is running through their head, and that is a contemplation that cannot, should not, be shared with anyone else. I don't wear sunglasses. I've learned that polarized ones make reading the river currents impossible, and I've learned that no one can peer through the steel shutters behind my retinas.

Besides, in this game, even though there is a "game plan," it is not like a high school basketball game. There are no cheerleaders in uniforms jumping and splitting on the floor during time-outs—because there are no time-outs. Even if there is an audience ashore, they are irrelevant and there is little they can do other than yell and whoop it up from shore. And if you have a poor run, at least among old-timers, no one would dare bring that up, because the person rowing the boat knows what went wrong and why. The last thing that they or anyone else need is a coach publicly chastising them. And so, I ran before the non-existent crowds and cheerleaders to win my game, my game against the march of time. Rapid after rapid, fear after fear, struggling against the wind and the dragons of my mind.

Bob will travel far from where I left him at the demoiselle. In a long journey he will follow gravity and the Green and Colorado rivers to the ocean, and Bob will work his way up the food chain, stabilizing the ecosystem on which I … and you, depend on for life.

Bob passed away on Saint Valentine's Day, 2014. His wife Beverly had sent me a vial of Bob's ashes to share on this last river trip. Beverly had a vision that I would receive a message from Bob in the form of a falling feather. I jokingly replied that each morning I was covered with goose down from the multitude of holes in my sleeping bag, but that I wouldn't count that as a missive from Bob. I doubted her vision, and I don't want to try and read something into what occurred on our trip. There was no falling feather. But there were demoiselles—the geological formation and the title of a Picasso painting. But hours after I had left Bob, my fermented thought emerged much as a dragonfly emerges from its cocoon. *Calopterygidae* are a family of damselflies in the order Odonata. They are often metallic colored and found along streams or rivers, and they are commonly known as broad-winged damselflies or demoiselles! Beverly had a tattoo of a dragonfly on her wrist.

ROBERT K. DECKER
February 14, 2014

Robert K. Decker, 72, of Westmore, beloved husband of Beverly Decker, passed peacefully surrounded by love and light on Valentine's Day. Their love was a star-matched forever love that transcends time and space. Together, they experienced two centuries of living in four decades of their "storybook marriage."

II
Growth

Take a Chance on Me
Amanda Gibbon

Reading the *USA Today* magazine this weekend, I turned to an article called "The 5 Massage Tips Everyone Should Know." In a publication that is otherwise only suitable for a cat's litter box, I thought this might be something useful. The first tip described how to screen your Yellow Pages for a suitable professional. Tip two was something about how to read a Spa Massage menu. There was a tip about appropriate massage gratuity. I laughed, thinking how silly I had been to have thought I might learn something about the art of massage itself. The names of major back muscles perhaps, or some new thumb maneuver. No, no, no. Here I could learn to whom to make out my check. Let this stand as a metaphor for our times.

The night before I hiked into Phantom Ranch, I couldn't sleep. I had the same nightmare that had repeated itself, intermittently, for months. I am in the boat, I am rowing through Crystal Rapid, I flip, and I am pinned under the boat while the river washes me over the rock garden at the bottom of the rapid. I wake up just as my head is hitting the first rock. As nightmares go, it is a rather plausible one. The rock garden exists, Crystal is a big rapid with plenty of opportunities for screwing up, and I was a completely inexperienced oarswoman.

Prior to the trip where I was to row, I had been to the Canyon three times. Twice my family had gone on commercial dory trips. They were fantastic experiences—fantastic enough to prompt my big sister to become a river guide, and for me to drool at the opportunity of returning to the Canyon's expanse. The trips also introduced us to Tom and Hazel, two people who would become close friends and would invite my sister and me to experience the river again, this time on a private trip. When this opportunity arose, I jumped at it immediately and, with confidence, wrote to Tom that I wanted to row. My sister had done it, hadn't she? I'd seen other people row who had little experience, so why not me?

Soon after I wrote that e-mail, the nightmares began.

In addition to the recurring nightmare, I had voices of experience telling me that I was right to be terrified. The night before I left for the Rim, I slept at my sister's in Flagstaff. Her neighbor, friend, and fellow guide, popped in while my sister was out. He bounced around her house, speaking quickly, making slightly off-color, sometimes funny jokes, grilling me on our gear—it was January and the river would be COLD. Then, he proceeded to complete the circuit of my terror. When he found out that I would be hiking in at Phantom, in January, and rowing—he asked if I was crazy. When I said, 'Yeah, I'm a little nervous, but I've rowed a little bit before and I think I'll be okay," he went on to detail all of the big water right below Phantom (as if I hadn't recited the rapids' names and ratings for the last few months), how little time there would be for me to get my bearings at the oars, and, once again, how COLD the water and air would be. He, who had guided in the canyon for twenty-five years, laughed at the reckless misadventure that I was about to undertake and then, with stern concern (this I believe, on behalf of my sister who he was a bit in love with and who, in his mind, was about to lose me, her little sister) asked if I was really sure that I wanted to do this. Let's just say, I didn't sleep a whole lot better that night.

Anyway, with concrete advice from my sister (specific rapids, things to watch for, general guiding advice), a heavy pack, and my boyfriend Greg, I started down the Kaibab Trail to Phantom Ranch. We met up with the trip. I took over a boat, gladly enlisting the help of my friend Jason to row and ride with me on the first afternoon, and set off on another marvelous journey on the Colorado River.

After two days at the oars, getting a feel for the boat, I laughed in disbelief when Tom said he was planning a two-night layover at Crystal Rapid. Two whole nights to listen to the rushing water of Crystal? This must be a cruel joke. We hiked the canyon and I fell asleep listening to the rapid. I walked to the water's edge and stared at it, trying to figure out the lines, watching water slam into the left wall, looking at the narrow entrance on the right. And then, in my less productive observation time, I stared at the rocks sticking up at the bottom of the rapid.

I would like to say that after scouting the rapid for two days, listening to the advice of experienced boatmen on my trip, and trying to visualize me and the craft making its way downriver safely, that I had an alert, relaxed and clean run. I didn't. But I didn't flip either. I ran left and ran into the wall pretty hard. I slammed the nose of the boat into the same wall that frequently flips boats. The wall that makes the right run the more prudent, yet more technical run—a run that on that day was even more difficult because of the low water level. So we went left. I hit the wall and then, well, some combination of the river gods and physics graced me and let me through. The tightness in my chest finally disappeared as the rock garden sailed by on the right and I found myself on top of my boat, not pinned beneath it. I smiled weakly and thanked any deity who wanted to take credit for my safe passage. This was my inauguration.

This is a part of what running the river by yourself is about. Although some may say that this is a story of foolishness ripe with liability lawsuits, I would say that they missed the point. In rowing a river, there is real knowledge involved. There is a skill to master and a river to learn. In the rest of my days on the Colorado, I learned about eddies and water currents, about what it means to miss a pull-in and get stuck on rocks. I was responsible. I had agency. I could row well, or I could screw up. There was no cushion between me and myself. There was no interlocutor to guarantee that my ride would be safe. Instead, there was a connection to the river, to the walls and falling rocks of the canyon, to my fellow travelers as we made decisions and built camps together. And in a beautiful, jarring, and sometimes terrifying way, there was a connection to life itself with its precious, fragile, and ancient stories.

In many ways, this story may serve to show how ridiculous it is that novices navigate the Colorado. However, this is not the conclusion that I draw from my own experience. Our places of wilderness give us the opportunities, as humans, to challenge ourselves, to be our own judges. To take risks that we think are appropriate and to face our place in the natural world—including the possibility of a river giving you just enough, shall I say, water to drown yourself.

It seems that as a society we are willing to give up so much of our agency and freedom if someone else will take responsibility. We are willing to cede our health to doctors; we give up our common sense, trusting that someone else has thought more of our safety than we have—and if they haven't, we find it grounds to sue. We doubt our judgment in the face of trained professionals. We go to a massage therapist for our back rub instead of to our partners. There is a part of this that seems right and good. Probably a massage therapist DOES know more than your husband about the art of massage; but in that choice, we also give something up. In addition to giving up the pleasure of sharing a massage, we also give up the belief in our ability to do it ourselves. We let so much of life become a mystery—from the appearance of artichokes on our table to the magical processes that make the engines work in our cars—that we have a tendency to stop thinking of ourselves as an active part of the mystery. We become passive and disengage from some of the most exciting parts of life. And with that, we lose.

On the Colorado, I am so glad that I've felt the power of the water against the oars. I am glad I've looked at a topo map and had to figure out how to get down, now that I've gotten myself up. I am proud to have rowed a boat through a good portion of the canyon. I am proud to have done it myself.

Don't Fuck Up
Hilary Esry

"Follow Steve. Don't fuck up." Good advice. Just over the horizon line, Cramer Rapid announces its presence with a persistent, undulating roar. A periodic burst of spray leaps into sight above the horizon. It sounds BIG. The others have assured me it is the biggest water I have yet kayaked, and it is the final rapid between us and the take-out on the River of No Return, the Salmon River in Idaho. This final Class IV rapid culminates a week on the Middle Fork of the Salmon with water so pristine and clear that I spent the first day dodging rocks that were two or more feet below the surface of the water. We soaked in riverside hot springs and hiked high above the river to see it wending its path through the mountains of the Frank Church Wilderness. We watched as two black bear cubs tumbled and scampered on the river bank under the observant eye of their mama. One cub climbed to the top of a too-small tree, the lithe tree bending halfway to the ground as it swayed. With the exception of a few inholdings, we escaped man-made life and immersed ourselves in the heart of the wilderness. Steve peels out of the eddy. I smile. "I can do that," I reply, laughing, as I enter the current and fall in behind Steve.

Whether kayaking or rafting, there is nothing better in this world than running rivers. The camaraderie, the disconnection from civilization, the sense of both community and self-reliance, the physicality and mentality of the sport, the feeling of freedom, the power and grace of the water, and the stunning natural beauty of river corridors leave little else to desire.

I was introduced to the idea of river running as a child, when my father announced that a distant relative had lost his mind. It seems he was securing himself in a boat and careening down whitewater rivers with no regard for his life. What would happen if he flipped upside-down? He was confined in the boat! He wouldn't be able to escape. It was nuts! He would surely drown any day now. How could anyone be so reckless, so irresponsible, so crazy? It was beyond my father's comprehension. I nodded in agreement, but secretly I thought it sounded fun.

In my early twenties, I dated a man who had recently returned from a Grand Canyon rafting trip. In a blatant ploy to lure me back to his house, he offered to show me photos from his trip. It was there that I first witnessed the towering height and delicate beauty of Deer Creek Falls, the dazzling, pale-blue waters of Havasu Creek, the lush oasis of Elves Chasm, and the magnificence of the canyon in general. I fell in love—not with him—but with the river and the canyon and the idea that someday I, too, might be privileged to experience it.

Two years later, I floated the Colorado River. No, not through the Grand, not yet. I was canoeing Horsethief and Ruby canyons. A recent flood had washed debris into the now-muddied water. Among the detritus, we paddled past the bloated carcass of a calf floating in an eddy. That night, we slept out under a blanket of stars at Black Rocks, a section of river known for the large, water-smoothed clusters of dark grey, metamorphic schist that populate both river and beach. Here, sandstone, in hues of red-orange and cream, dotted with green desert scrub, rises in cliffs and spires above the darker rocks below. We lay on the soft sand beach, the summer day's warmth radiating from the dark rocks surrounding us. It was a long, hot wait for sleep. As I lay there, a Perseid meteor slowly traversed the sky, shedding a transient ribbon of glitter in its wake. Nature is as beautiful as she is indifferent.

After two decades as a hiker and backpacker, I returned to the river for my first multi-day raft trip: a whitewater excursion through Ruby/Horsethief and Westwater canyons on the Colorado, followed by four days on the lower San Juan. At Black Rocks, we sat in full-size camp chairs with our feet in the cool river, inhaling the enticing scent of coconut milk and Thai red curry spices as the cliffs before us melded into the sky in the soft, orange glow of sunset. With one riverside gourmet meal, I converted from backpacker to river runner. And, of course, we slept out under the stars.

A few days later, I sat in a borrowed RPM kayak, about to launch on the San Juan. I had a strong desire, but little idea of how to kayak. My friend checked to be sure I was properly fitted in the boat and knew how to wet-exit. Sensing my nervousness, he laughed and said, "I give you five minutes until you flip." With that, he returned to his raft. No sooner had we launched than the wind kicked up. I struggled relentlessly to keep the kayak's bow pointed into the chop. The waves grabbed at the low-volume tail, nearly capsizing me repeatedly. Each time, I somehow managed to flatten my hips to the surface of the water and stay upright. I was white-knuckled, stiff, and scared. I lasted two hours on adrenaline and luck, then hauled the boat up onto my friend's raft. My nerves were shot, but I was even more enthusiastic about learning to kayak. In hindsight, I was much better at bracing before I learned to roll.

One of the allures of whitewater is that every now and then, you hit the exact right line at the exact right moment so that the timing of the waves and the timing of your blades allow you to glide smoothly, elegantly through what had, moments before, appeared as churning chaos. It is pure joy! And you desire to linger and revel in the sensation.

Of course, those moments are fleeting and rare. Much more common is the adrenaline rush that comes from actually feeling the force of the water as it crashes into your boat and your body. Just below your consciousness, mental subroutines conspire with muscle memory and adrenaline to make constant course corrections as pushy turbulence deflects you off your intended line. Viscerally, you calculate Plan B and Plan C until you reach the next eddy or the end of the rapid. It's a kind of active meditation. There is an addictive satisfaction in meeting the challenges of the river.

With some of the biggest whitewater in the US, the Colorado River through the Grand Canyon presents a much sought-after challenge. And, after a quarter of a century of dreaming, I finally had the chance to raft it. "That was a riffle?" I exclaimed, as we passed the confluence with the Paria. It felt like a Class II rapid to me. A few days later, we stood, perched precariously on well-rounded rocks lining river left, gazing into the maw of tumult that lay before us, scouting our route. The noise of the rapid, like low-pitched static, drowned our words and alighted on each nerve ending in our bodies, filling us with electric courage, albeit tinged with trepidation.

This was my first big-water river, and each rapid seemed larger than the last. I was the only passenger on an oar rig that my friend was rowing. In some previous rapids, he'd given me the job of locating a particular guide rock or feature and informing him as we approached or passed it. In this rapid, I had only one job: hang on and don't fall backwards into the cockpit as we punched through or careened over the waves. In other words, stay in the boat and out of the way. A kayaker I'd met only a few days before stood nearby, planning his route and screwing up his nerve. This was his first Grand trip, too. When everyone was as comfortable as they were going to be with their lines, we started the anxious walk back upriver to where we'd tied our boats. Some chatted nervously, others were absorbed in silence, gaining their composure for the task ahead.

A calm confidence is required in whitewater. Doubts get amplified. If you think you will mess up, you will. Feeling intimidated by the immensity of the waves, I caught up to the kayaker and gave him a huge hug—well, as huge a hug as you can give through two PFDs. I didn't know or care if he minded. I needed the reassurance of a hug, and he looked like he might need it too. He and the other kayakers ran the rapid first to set safety for the rafts that would follow. I untied our raft and watched as he disappeared into the churning froth below. He emerged a few seconds later, upright. I smiled and relaxed just enough to begin to feel the excitement welling from my chest to my face.

"Ready?" the oarsman asked. "Ready," I said. I coiled the rope, tucked it under the bow line, shoved the raft from shore, and hopped into the bow. I looked around, doing a final check to ensure that everything was tied down and tucked in and that no straps or ropes were in a position to cause foot or hand entrapment should we flip, stilling my nerves in the process. I perched on a stack of Paco pads between the two straps that attached them to the raft frame. As we entered the current, I slid one hand under each strap, leaned forward and took a long, slow breath.

The first wave hit us hard, slowing our momentum and dousing me with frigid, silty water. Then, suddenly, we were with the river: perfectly aligned to the waves, traveling over them more than through them, enjoying a smooth, exhilarating roller-coaster ride. As we crested each wave, I gazed approximately ten feet down into the trough ahead, eagerly anticipating the thrilling drop and subsequent climb. I shouted "Whee!" and "Woo-hoo!" with each descent. When we eddied out below the rapid, the oarsman looked at me skeptically and shook his head. "Don't ever go 'Whee!'" he said. I smiled. He'd had a perfect line. And I had a new dream: to return and run the river in my kayak.

My friend continued to have good lines. But, a little more than fifty miles downstream, we watched helplessly as a potential disaster unfolded. Another oarsman in our group performed a stern squirt in a fully loaded 18' raft! The guy had hit the hole at the aptly named Upset Rapid. At the scout, we'd all agreed on a right line. But, perhaps at the urging of his spirited ten-year-old son, he'd taken the meat line—a "down the middle through-the-hole" line that according to the Martin-Whitis River Map is "not recommended." Bow pointed to sky, the raft hesitated. It stood there for an eternal moment, then slowly began to fall. It crashed into the water right-side-up with everyone still aboard. The adult passenger's eyes were as wide as the kid's grin. That was close! I exhaled in relief and shook my head at our good fortune as we stuffed the ends of our throw ropes back in their bags.

At camp that night, the sky was free of light pollution and the canyon walls created an impressive frame for the stars. The dim outline of the canyon rim against the night sky formed the image of a reclining woman; I matched her pose and enjoyed the solitude until the moonlight on the walls overwhelmed the image. More than an hour had passed since the last remaining night-owls drifted off to their tents. In the moonlight, the canyon walls looked ethereal—like a thin veil that could blow away or simply disappear in a breath. I sat up slowly, breathing in the scene one last time before begrudgingly making my way toward my tent. A toad scooted by, just outside the beam of my headlamp. He froze when I looked at him, paralyzed by this sudden intrusion of unnatural light. I apologized and turned my head, watching him peripherally as he sneaked away into the shadows. I walked to my tent, unzipped it, and quietly removed my Paco pad and bag liner. This was no night for shelter.

At some point in every multi-day trip, you give yourself over to nature. You drift to her schedule for waking and sleeping. You travel downstream when she allows, hunkering down from wind and blowing sand when she demands. If you dare continue downstream against the wind, she'll blow your raft into an eddy and back up to the top of a rapid to let you run it again, and again, until one of you relents. Wind is a four-letter word. You might even begin to believe that nature isn't so indifferent after all. Eventually, you give up your illusions of control and begin to literally and figuratively go with the flow. There is a calm contentment that settles in when you are moving and working in syncopation with the river and its environment.

Of course, not everyone experiences rivers this way. I've seen plenty of kayakers and oarsmen who seem to be in constant battle with the river, cursing the whole way down, imagining they can dominate an indomitable force. I enjoy watching my friend, Brian, taunting him with admonishments to love the river: "Oh look, Bri, she wants to give you some tongue!"

When we shift into river time, however, and live in cooperation with our surroundings, we are often rewarded. A ringtail cat scampers down a tree only a few feet away, keeping one eye on us as he disappears into the vegetation. A desert fox scrambles over a boulder and across our path at dusk. Two young deer exuberantly frolic on an island just downstream from our camp in the soft pink glow of sunrise. These are the moments I live for.

There is also freedom in wilderness. The immensity of the imposing canyon walls, the rushing power of the river, and the vastness of time itself clarify your stature. On this scale, you are miniscule, irrelevant. The river doesn't criticize or care who you are, how you look, or how you smell ten days into a three-week trip. Canyon walls don't care if you live or die or even that you exist. Wilderness is a place to be free from external judgment—and from internal judgment if you can manage it. In wilderness lies freedom in its purest form, life in its most honest form. You are free to indulge in all the beauty and child-like joy the world has to offer. Some of us require alcohol or other inebriants to reach such an uninhibited state of mind. Some of us just need the river. That's part of the allure—the beautiful, vulnerable, raw reality of being.

Vulnerability. Yes, there is danger in wilderness, too, as there should be! Wilderness is not for the tame. Little reinforces a sense of vulnerability more effectively than a desert thunderstorm. You can often portage an intimidating rapid, but there's no escaping the weather.

I recall a particularly strong summer storm in the Grand Canyon. We set up a tarp in the rain, finished dinner clean-up, and retired to our tents. It wasn't long before the storm intensified, and thunder wasn't the only thing crashing. That was the sound of aluminum banging on aluminum, kitchen tables clanging into dryboxes. My friend and I hurriedly unzipped our tent and darted toward the carnage. "No, you stay here and make sure the tent doesn't blow away!" he bellowed through the wind and rain. He spoke from experience. I'd heard the story. I dove back into the tent, chuckling at the fact that I was most useful as deadweight. Since I was already wet, I left the tent unzipped enough that I could peer out into the storm. When the lightning flashed, I could make out an impromptu waterfall pouring over the canyon rim a thousand feet above, intermingling with the wind and rain, and dissipating before it reached the river.

Thunder grumbled and growled. Trapped by the high canyon walls, it reverberated down the canyon, amplified as it advanced, and crescendoed to a frenetic furry. The sound was felt as well as heard. Fear is pointless in the presence of such overwhelming force. Protected from the tempest by only the thin tent fabric, and comforted by my insignificance, I watched and listened in delighted awe. A sudden downdraft twisted and collapsed the ceiling of the tent, repeatedly bashing it into my forehead. Thwump! Thwump! Thwump! The sound of my laughter joined the thunder, echoing off the canyon walls.

Toward morning, thunder of a different kind rolled through the canyon—a rockfall! As daylight dawned, we could see a bright, white scar on the rockface downstream and across the river, in the approximate location of the next camp. We made quick work of packing up and headed downstream to check on the group camped there. There is a strong sense of community among boaters. There are no strangers on the river—oddballs perhaps—but not strangers. River runners all have stories of helping and being helped in turn. Fortunately, no assistance was needed that morning. They were fine.

The cliff face had sheared off just upstream of their tents. They had one more story of vulnerability and the awesome power of nature—and damn good luck to be alive to tell it around countless future campfires on countless future rivers.

But today I am kayaking the Salmon. Ahead of me, Steve disappears over the horizon, dropping into Cramer Rapid. I am just far enough behind. An enormous hole extends from the left bank to the center of the river. The right side roils with turbulence. A narrow tongue of green threads the churning froth. The line is obvious and easily read, but I'm happy to follow Steve nonetheless. At the bottom of the tongue, a white-capped wave looms in front of my bow. My body is relaxed. My hips are loose. My mind is calm. The conscious part of my brain is a spectator now, and registers a slight surprise that this wave is so large that I'm paddling up it. As I reach the peak of the wave, time slows. I am momentarily suspended above the river, peering deep down into the hole to my left. Briefly, this singular moment is all that exists. And, it is enough. I feel content. It is almost as if the universe has offered me a fleeting glimpse of some unspeakable truth. Time resumes its normal pace and soon I am sliding down the wave and through the whitewater of the wave-train below—kayak, body, and water moving as one. I eddy out and my conscious brain reengages. I am elated. And I didn't fuck up.

Going It Alone
Jane Dally

In the summer of 2013, I was (still) recovering from a relationship break-up that had landed me squarely on my ass. To manage the pain of my heartache, I did the only thing I knew how to do: I ran away from it. I ran to the place that has always, since I was a little girl, been my place of solace—the natural world. In particular, that summer I determined to do as many multi-day river trips as I could. I would string together as simple a life as possible, focused only on the present moment, meeting basic needs and the tasks at hand, and far away from the worries and ruminations of my "other life" back at home.

By mid-July, I had done pretty well for myself, having already done four multi-day river trips with friends in the Four Corners region where I live. But when I pulled an Upper San Juan River permit from Sand Island to Mexican Hat, everyone I asked to accompany me was either too busy with other life activities, or wanted to head up to the mountains to catch the wild flowers, or said that it was too hot to do a desert river in July, or complained that the water was too low to make it worth their while. Who, after all, would want to go on a mid-July, low water San Juan River trip? I did! So rather than stay at home, mope around, and feel the feelings I was so desperately trying to avoid, I decided to go by myself.

It would be my first solo river trip. I had done other solo trips; on patrol as a backcountry ranger in Denali National Park and in my free time as an Outward Bound Instructor in the Boundary Waters of Minnesota—both summer and winter trips. But I had never done a solo river trip before. I had heard about other locals who had done solo river trips in the area, but I had never considered it a possibility for myself.

Some of my friends that July were guiding commercial trips in the Grand Canyon, Westwater Canyon, and Cataract Canyon. So I felt a little bit embarrassed that I wasn't doing something more "bad ass" than the Upper San Juan. But I also reasoned that it would be a perfect trip for my first venture into solo boating. For one, I knew that section of river well, having floated it perhaps ten times in the previous two years. Also, the rapids are rated a reasonable Class II at the water level I would be paddling it (less than 1,000 cfs). The logistics of the shuttle, as well, were easy—grab a ride from the store keeper at Valle's in Mexican Hat and Voila! River trip on!

I sought guidance from my friends, Rick and Kate, who almost exclusively do river trips in their duckies (inflatable kayaks) because they are lightweight and easy to handle. I followed their lead and decided to take my own tandem ducky (an Aire Tom Cat), rather than my 14' raft, for the same reasons they love to travel in duckies on multi-day trips. Rick and Kate gave me the "inside scoop" on gear required to fulfill the permit regulations: turkey roasting pan as fire pan, jumbo Ranch dressing jug as groover. I also needed to carry first aid and repair kits and I pared down my raft kits to fit into my tandem ducky. I thought five gallons of water for four days should be plenty, even in the heat of the summer. A lightweight sleeping bag and a few clothes made up the bulk of my main dry bag. I wouldn't be bringing a stove or fuel to spare myself that weight and hassle; I just brought a small drybag of simple "cold food" that would last the four days. A pump and an extra paddle finished out my rig.

I called my friend, Michael, and told him where I was going and asked him to call the BLM River Office in Monticello, Utah, if he did not hear from me by Sunday evening. He said, "Sounds like you're going on a vision quest of sorts." Little did I know, in that moment, that his words set in motion an intention that I had not consciously created, but that would, in fact, come to fruition through the course of my travels.

I left my home early in the morning that July Thursday before first light. I knew that it would be hot that day—in the high 90s—so wanted to launch as early as possible. As I drove through a portion of the "Rez" (the Navajo Nation) between Cortez, Colorado, and Montezuma Creek, Utah, I noticed some sheep crossing the road accompanied by their lambs. My attention was diverted to the lambs momentarily, cooing out loud at their cuteness. When I looked back to the road it was veering in a sharp curve to the left. I overcompensated my steering, and sent my Honda Civic spinning in a 180-degree circle. For several seconds I felt my little silver bullet speeding backwards, first on the pavement and then thrashing through sagebrush and rabbit brush, dirt flying past the car windows and over the windshield. The car came to a stop, the engine stalled. The sheep were gazing at me blank-faced (as blank as I am sure mine looked to them). I got out of the car, walked around it, and, seeing no major damage, got back in and started it up. It rolled easily back onto the pavement. I turned myself back toward Utah and my destination. "So begins the Heroine's Journey," I said out loud to myself, hands still shaking.

When I got to the put-in at Sand Island, there was only one other party there—a large group of students from Northern Arizona University's Outdoor Adventures program with their instructors. I took my ducky out of the car, inflated it, and began to rig it for the trip. At one point in my rigging I heard a man's voice giving instructions to the group; this voice was very familiar. I looked up and saw David Lovejoy, a long-time Prescott College professor. I had taught Adventure Education and other courses at Prescott College myself for eight years, but I had not had much contact with any of the faculty since I moved away in 2011.

I approached Dave, glad to see him. "David!" He turned toward me, not five feet away, and said, "Who is it?" "Jane. Jane Dally." "Oh, Jane. Nice to see you!" At first, I was surprised that he had not recognized me, but then I remembered that I had heard through the grapevine that Dave had been gradually losing his eyesight due to some irreparable, congenital condition. Even though I had been quite close to him, he hadn't recognized my face. I shook his hand, and we talked about what each of us was doing there: me—a solo trip, and he— instructing a kayak course for NAU Outdoor Adventures students. "God," I thought, "he can barely see and he's leading this course?" Then, in an instant I thought, "Well, if anyone can run the San Juan with his eyes closed, Dave Lovejoy can!"

After my boat was rigged and my shuttle complete, I said goodbye to David and his crew and we both said, "Maybe see you downstream!"

I shoved off and floated for some time without paddling, settling in to the flow of the river and the beauty of the landscape. I immediately felt relaxed and grateful to be there, and so glad to be soloing this trip. I began noticing details of the land and scenery that I would most likely have missed if I was with a group because I would be talking to others or worrying about the million details one does when traveling in a posse. The sense of quiet and aloneness was incredibly comforting for me. I wondered why I hadn't done this a long time ago!

One of my goals on this trip was to stop at as many places as I could where in the past, traveling with groups, I had floated by saying, "Someday I'd like to stop there and check that out," or "That would be a great hike to do someday." I was committed to stop at as many of those places as possible. The first of such places was at Mile 2.2 on the Navajo side of the river. There was an interesting looking canyon there that I had always wanted to explore. I pulled my ducky up on the gravel shore, unclipped my water bottle, and started walking up the drainage.

I had barely left the water's edge and entered the narrowing canyon when I got a feeling that something was watching me. I turned around, back toward the river and looked up. There, in the sandstone cliff was a small cave, and two barn owls gazing silently at me. We stared back at each other for several minutes. Then the owls crept back into the shadowy recesses of the cave and out of sight.

I continued my hike, feeling grateful for having experienced such an unusual sighting. In hindsight, I should have remembered the words of my Cherokee-Choctaw teacher who had told me that in many Native traditions owls are an omen, a sign of something bad to come. But I didn't. I continued, exploring the small canyon for perhaps twenty minutes before returning to the river and my boat. As I approached my ducky, I noticed that my paddle, which I had neatly tucked in the forward compartment, had fallen off the kayak's tube. And in an instant, I knew with a gasp what had happened. One of the inner air bladders of the ducky had blown! I had forgotten to let some of the air out of the tubes when I pulled it up on shore, and the heat of the day had expanded the bladder to the point of bursting. I had heard friends talk about this happening, but never in a million years did I expect it to happen to me—especially within the first several miles of my first solo river trip!

I struggled to get a hold of a rising sense of panic. "Don't panic," I said to myself. "You can deal with this." I remembered that I had brought along the repair supplies that, according to the guy at the local boating shop, were needed for the ducky. I had never actually repaired the inner bladder of an inflatable kayak, but I assured myself that I could figure it out. The first thing I knew I needed to do was to find the actual leak. I had begun to unpack the repair supplies I needed and to unzip the outer tube when I heard an unusual "chug-chug-chug" sound on the river. From around the bend floated a raft with a motor on it and three people: two men and a woman. I waved them down, trying not to look overly frantic.

They landed on the shore where I was and I said to them, "I just blew one of the tubes in my ducky. Can you guys help me find the leak?" Having been an outdoor educator for nearly thirty years, I felt ashamed to be asking for help, and even more ashamed that I had allowed such a boneheaded thing to happen. Why didn't I think to let some air out of the tubes?! I silently chided myself.

I found out that the three of them were fish biologists studying the native species in the river; "Fish Heads" in the local vernacular. The two young men were so nice and helpful. They easily found the leak within five minutes, and pointed it out to me: a small tear in the end seam of the tube. They asked if I had the repair supplies I needed, and I said, "Yes, I think I've got it from here." I thanked them profusely, and watched them chug their way around the next bend.

I set to work repairing the leak, telling myself the process would be easy and quick. I used the repair tape suggested by the manufacturer. I then pumped both tubes up, and pushed off into the water thinking I was on my way. But no sooner had I congratulated myself for a job well done and tragedy narrowly averted then I heard a "psss" sound coming from the repaired tube. "Damn!" The tape must not have held. I paddled a short distance farther downriver looking for a good place to land. As I paddled, I realized that the outer tube, although becoming flatter as the bladder deflated, was actually helping to keep me afloat.

I relaxed some knowing that the double layer tube system was doing what it was designed to do: provide flotation even in the event of the inner bladder leaking.

I soon developed a plan to pump, paddle, pump until I caught up to the Fish Heads again, at which time I would either ask them if they had any repair supplies I could use or join their little posse. I became so comfortable with the pump, paddle, pump system that I began to relax and look around and enjoy the trip for what it was. I even could laugh at what a boneheaded, newbie mistake I had made. I stopped at a toehold route (steps chiseled into a sandstone wall by the ancient people of the area) that I had always floated past and was really drawn to investigate.

Once out of my boat—tubes deflated to avoid another blow out—and onto the sandy bench just below the toehold route, I discovered a slightly worn path leading to the left. I followed it, and lo and behold, discovered an entire abandoned pueblo site complete with rafter holes hollowed into the sand stone wall, an extensive petroglyph panel, and potsherds everywhere on the surface of the ruin site. This was exactly the type of experience I was hoping for on this solo trip! I felt very fortunate to have stumbled upon this site as I had never had the chance to stop and explore it, and because it looked as if not many people had visited the site in recent years.

I explored the site for at least an hour and then got back into my boat and continued down the river: pump, paddle, pump. I soon floated into David's group, told them what had happened and informed them that if I couldn't manage to repair my ducky I may need to hop onto one of their rafts for the remainder of the trip. "No problem," said Dave. "Would love to have you. Keep us posted." I also caught up to the Fish Heads close to where I planned to camp that night. They gave me some black, sticky patches they said were meant for raft repair, but may work for my ducky. Before parting I asked where they were planning to camp. They said, "Big Stick," which was just downstream from where I planned to camp for the night. I told them that if I couldn't fix my ducky I may need to jump on to their raft and complete the trip with them. They seemed open to that idea, and added, "We get on the water early. Seven or so. So you better catch us before then."

"No problem" I said, thanked them again for the patches, and paddled toward Chinle Wash.

Once in camp, I set to work repairing the inner bladder of the ducky. This time I used all manner of glue, tape, and patches that I had in combination with each other. I even folded over the end of the inner bladder where the tear was and duct taped the folds firmly together. I didn't want to take a chance with this repair not taking! I went to sleep hoping that the bladder would hold air in the morning.

I slept well that night and awoke at first light. I decided to go for an early morning hike up one of the "Mules' Ears" which are diatreme formations on river left near Chinle Wash. I crossed the wash, and steadily made my way up the scree slope below the diatreme. At the top I could see for miles both up and down the San Juan. The air was just beginning to warm and in that pure air I felt a freedom, peace, and joy that I have relished on all my journeys into the wilderness, but that I had not yet felt on this trip. I wondered what it would be like to actually live in this land, so harsh and also so beautiful. Allowing myself several minutes to relish the experience at the top, I decided that I better make my way back to camp and check to see if my repair job would hold under the pressure of inflated tubes.

Once in camp, I pumped up the tubes, slid the ducky in the water, and loaded it. I said a little prayer, climbed aboard, and began paddling. With great relief and satisfaction, I noted that there was no "pssss" sound to be heard from the tubes, and they seemed to be holding their pressure without any sign of deflating. It was one of the most memorable experiences I have had in all my many wilderness expeditions! I felt so relieved that I could now turn my full attention back to the trip without worrying about my boat. I was also proud of my perseverance and self-reliance in solving my own problem—with a little help from the sticky, black patches from the Fish Heads!

I began to completely enjoy every aspect of the trip: the movement of the river, the beauty of the land, the warmth of the sun, and the wildlife I encountered. Miles down the river, as I emerged from a narrow portion of the canyon, I noticed several desert bighorn sheep on the shore ahead of me. I stopped paddling and floated silently toward them. To my surprise and delight they did not spook but, in fact, moved closer to the shore near where I floated. The ducky came to rest in the mud at the edge of the water and I watched fifteen rams, ewes, and lambs, within five to ten feet of me, as they grazed and drank from the river. It was one of the closest sightings I had ever had of large mammals in the wild. I recalled the words of the ranger checking me in at the put-in saying that it doesn't really matter how many people there are in your party, you will see the same amount of wildlife. "Ha!" I had never, ever, seen this many sheep on the San Juan, especially this close. I felt fortunate and grateful for the encounter and slowly and silently floated downriver, leaving the sheep to continue to graze. I camped soon after that and slept very well with a deeply rested mind and body.

The next morning I awoke knowing that I would have to run Eight Foot Rapid that day. As I approached it mid-day, I cautiously landed my boat on river right to scout it. Being solo, I thought it a good idea to take every precaution I could to travel as conservatively as possible. The margin of error was small as I was the only boat in my party.

Not many people scout Eight Foot from the right. Rick had shown me the scout route high on the cliff overlooking the rapid. One can see most of the rapid from that one elevated vantage point. It looked very doable and I planned to "sneak" it on the left, again playing things conservatively. As I walked the cliff edge back to my boat after scouting, I almost stepped on a dead bat lying in the dirt. "Dang! Not another omen!" I gasped, and vowed to pay careful attention to every detail of the run. It came off without a hitch, and I peacefully floated on downstream feeling confident and relieved to have only Ledge Rapid yet to worry about.

I boat scouted Ledge, standing up in the ducky and scanning the preferred route and obstructions to avoid. I had become accustomed to boat scouting on northern river expeditions, where we would run loaded boats for weeks at a time through rapids of varying difficulty. Getting out to scout each rapid would have been too time consuming when we had to make 10, 20, or 30 miles a day. So, standing in a small boat became second nature to me and transferred easily to paddling a ducky.

I decided to make the beach just below Ledge my last night's camp. There was a bit of shade I could hide under and soft sand to lay my sleeping bag on. I made a little fire in my turkey roasting pan that night, even though it was still quite warm, just to celebrate my maiden solo voyage. I turned in early, anticipating a smooth float out the next day.

In the middle of the night, I abruptly sat bolt upright, pulling myself out of a deep sleep. It was pitch black, but in my chest, I felt a tightness I have only felt when I have been in the company of mountain lions. I groped for my headlamp and frantically turned it on. I saw nothing and heard nothing, but the tightness in my chest was all the more apparent. I yelled and clapped my hands together hard several times: both things that I have done when trying to scare away mountain lion or bear. Still there was nothing in the small orb of my headlamp light, which I scanned all around me.

After several minutes, I reluctantly lay back down, my heart still pounding, not sure whether to believe that something had been there or not. It took me several hours, mainly spent straining my ears to pick up on any slight noise, before I fell into a fitful sleep. When dawn came I got up and walked around my sleeping area and, indeed, found the tracks of a mountain lion not ten feet from where my head had lain.

Feeling very grateful for the sunlight and the ability to see my surroundings, I ate a simple breakfast and packed my gear, occasionally standing to look over my shoulder. I loaded my boat for my last day on the water and paddled silently past the Fish Heads' camp just downstream of mine. No sign of them stirring yet, so I knew it must be early. As I approached Mile 20.5, I decided I wanted to do a hike that the local guides call "The Stairmaster," because it involves a steep climb up an anticline slope.

I climbed gradually in the still-cool morning air and, reaching the top, I could see Monument Valley stretching out to the south with its graceful monoliths, spires, and plateaus merging into the distant horizon. A deep sense of peace came over me, and I felt as if I was the only person on earth. It was a strangely comforting feeling, and I felt very connected to the land and sky and river stretching before me. I also felt so very grateful for the opportunity to be experiencing this moment: silent, serene, sublime, solitary. I slowly made my way down the slope and silently slid my boat into the water to glide the last few miles to the take-out.

Since it was a Sunday morning the take-out was quiet. The only person stirring on the shore was a Caucasian man, a tourist in clean city shoes and slacks, standing at the water's edge looking upstream and down. I imagine he was wondering what it would be like to float the river that flowed so placidly past him. I landed and pulled my boat onto the sand. The man was silent for a few minutes watching me deflate my tubes. He then walked over to me and asked with disbelief, "Is it just you?"

His question reminded me of a month-long canoe expedition I had done with three other women in the fall of 1989 on the Hayes River from Lake Winnipeg to Hudson Bay. On one of our last days on the river we had floated into a party of moose hunters and their Cree guides. One of the guides looked at our group, and then asked, "Where's your men, girls?" We looked at each other and answered, "We don't have any." The men glanced at each other silently. Then another of the guides asked, "Where's your gun, girls?" We smiled at each other and calmly responded, "We don't have any." Eyebrows raised, they looked again at each other and then back at us, heads cocked to the side like dogs trying to comprehend something that was foreign to them. We waved and nodded our heads to the men and floated on downriver to finish the last few miles of our 500-mile journey.

I pulled myself out of my momentary reminiscing, realizing that I had not answered the man yet. I stood up, smiled at him, and said, "Yup. Just me."

Is it Fish We are Really After?
Audra Ford

I've always been a late bloomer. My confidence, charisma, and even my looks all came to me later in life. I grew up as a quiet and, what I considered, a rather awkward girl, not quite sure of the world and what I was seeking. Despite my reticence, I never shied away from thrills or an adrenaline rush. In my youth, I remember begging my parents to let me ride the fastest, highest roller coaster at the theme park, vehemently exclaiming to my father that I wanted to ski the black diamond runs on the ski hill, and even adding "swimming with great white sharks" to my bucket list. When I got my first taste of whitewater, it was no surprise it hooked me like a trout to a fly. It reeled me in hard and fast, and after gaining a few river miles, I quickly learned that whitewater rafting is so much more than an adrenaline rush. It encompasses an auspicious lifestyle surrounded by jovial crowds, picturesque scenery, and most importantly, an unprecedented sense of freedom and self-worth that can only be discovered on the river.

My rafting pilgrimage started as a passenger on round boats. When the weekends rolled around in late spring and summer, I was always eager to hear if any of my river friends were chasing the whitewater on Idaho's famous class III or IV rivers. I would graciously accept invites when they came, and always made sure to let whomever was captaining the boat know that I was a strong paddler so I could sit up front and get the best view of the rapids. After several of these day trips I began to form lasting bonds with my newfound river tribe and made valiant efforts to make sure they knew how appreciative I was to be invited on these trips, for my addiction to the river was flourishing.

The spring and early summer of 2012 proved to be extremely fortuitous as I was given the opportunity to paddle on several different rivers and various stretches of the mighty Payette. Perhaps my favorite memory of that spring was a warm Saturday in April paddling down the South Fork of the Boise River. Normally, this river averages at about 2,000 cfs. This particular Saturday the river had spiked at a record-setting 6,000 cfs, an almost unheard-of level for this stretch of river. My river crew ecstatically jumped at the opportunity to run the river while it was running high and I was fortunate enough to receive an invite to tag along on a paddle boat. After losing our captain to a monstrous wave and witnessing an upside-down raft with its owner being pulled into the take-out by throw ropes, the day concluded with huge smiles and appreciation of the thrills we experienced.

After being submersed into the river community for several months I met a fellow rafter who quickly became my boyfriend and, I thought at the time, the love of my life. We had many wonderful experiences on the river; our first kiss, first R2. On extended trips, I aspired to be his "boat candy" and first mate. Very quickly however, the "love of my life" turned into quite the opposite. I was submersed in heartache, self-doubt, and fear that I was going to miss out on everything related to the river. That poor attitude lingered for a couple of weeks before I began to shape up. I quickly embarked upon a power trip, enriched with self-discovery and independence, and realized I did not need a man to get on the river. I scored an unbelievable deal on a used 14' Maravia extended Spider with a frame! Before pulling the trigger on this boat, I sat in her for a while and contemplated if I should buy it. Questions like "How will I tow this boat in my Honda civic?" and "Will people invite me on river trips?" triggered my doubts. Before I knew it, I had a crowd of river friends huddled around me explaining to me why this purchase should be a no-brainer. At this point in time, I barely knew these people who were guiding me in my purchase, but my intuition was right on when it told me I could trust them. My friendly neighbor and rafting friend, who has now become what I call my River Bestie, shouted, "Audra, I'll help you tow your boat. I'll even shuttle it home for you." My smile exploded as I was immediately reminded of the generosity of river people. My next move was a discussion with the gentleman selling the boat, during which I even negotiated a couple hundred dollars off the final sale price. What can I say, I was on a roll and that boat was now mine!

My inaugural trip in my new boat was on the Grand Jean section of the Payette River in early May. I had zero experience on this stretch and my rowing experience was meager. I eagerly slapped my boat and frame on my "River Bestie's" truck and trailer, my heart pounding with nervous energy. I wasn't quite sure what I had got myself into. A million "What if?" questions flooded my brain. "What if I flip?" "What if I get myself into a situation that endangers others by my lack of experience?"

When we got to the put-in, I timidly strapped down my frame and set up my oars hoping that the configuration was right for me. When I got in my boat I had about three strokes before the first rapid. It was a tight squeeze with a giant boulder in the middle. My experienced river friends instructed me to follow their lines and not go over the boulder. Within a blink of an eye I was entrenched in the rapid. My right oar banged into the boulder because the entry was so tight and the current was pushing into it. My first reaction was, of course, to ferry my left oar and straighten the boat. There was not enough time and before I knew it I swept through the rapid backward, hitting the final wave square with the stern of my boat. Remarkably, I was still in the seat; I breathed a giant sigh of relief and smiled at my friends. My competitive nature took over and I was determined to not let that happen again. The next part of the river was fairly calm with a few technical rock dodging sections. It proved to be great practice to really get a feel for my new boat.

A couple of hours or so into the trip something happened to me that changed my life. It was a rather calm section of the river and I was mesmerized by the iridescent green color of the spring water and the bountiful, lush, green trees bordering the water. I looked behind me, looked in front of me, and smiled at my river comrades who had graciously invited me into their circle. I suddenly got chills and a couple of tears fell from my eyes. At that moment, something magical happened to me, and to this day I still cannot shake that moment, nor have I had a comparable experience. I was suddenly cured of the heartbreak that had capsized my life for the past several months. It took less than a minute and I was sewn back together by nothing other than the intrinsic power of the river. In that moment, I knew that I was going to be all right and that I could pick up the pieces and move on. I often think back about that moment, as it has helped me overcome other inevitable and painful events in life that have brought emotional hardship.

I have now been rafting for five years and I have been fortunate enough to have been invited, and even been the Trip Leader, on several extended river trips. I have run the Middle Fork of the Salmon, the Owayhee, Hells Canyon, and the Selway to boot. I have grown emotionally, spiritually, and intellectually with each trip. Not only have my rowing skills and confidence improved after each trip, but I now have a heightened appreciation and zest for life. My memory bank and picture albums are full of extraordinary recollections. I am so grateful to have been granted the opportunity to be part of a wonderful Idaho river community, and to have been able to spend time on these marvelous and fascinating Earth creations. Perhaps the following quote by a renowned fellow nature-lover perfectly sums up my thoughts and feelings regarding running rivers:

"Many men go fishing all of their lives without knowing that it is not fish they are after." —Henry David Thoreau

Baptism

Norma Sims Roche

It's summer in New England, and to me that means the Deerfield River. It means whitewater kayaking if you know how, or tubing if you don't. All wonderful ways to stay wet on a hot day. But for the biggest thrill with the least skill, it's all about rafting.

The Appalachian Mountain Club schedules two or three rafting trips on the upper "Dryway" section of the Deerfield River, in Monroe, Massachusetts, every summer. These are Class IV rapids: the big stuff. But that's OK. All you need is one experienced raft guide, and everybody else follows that person's directions. Theoretically.

We practice first in the calm water just below the dam. The guide shouts, "All forward!" and we move. He shouts, "Left forward!" and we turn, sort of—some people on the right keep paddling, contrary to his commands. But we get it down. We're ready to go. My stomach flip-flops as we edge into the first rapid. There's no going back now.

We go through several big rapids—not all of them elegantly, one of them backwards, but we don't lose anybody. We vary in strength and alertness, so the guide's best-laid intentions don't always get carried out. But we're having a blast, and we're soaked—the water cannons the guide brought are completely superfluous.

"Now, the next rapid is Dragon's Tooth," the guide says, "and it's famous for that big hole at center left." He points to a roaring mass of foam just behind the pointed rock that gives the rapid its name. "We really want to stay out of there, so when I say 'Paddle,' paddle HARD!"

We nod in agreement and get ready to go. Into the rapid. Over the first drop and past the Tooth rock; now we need to get to the right to avoid the hole. I can see the mass of water pouring over a low boulder and then rushing back in on itself. "Right FORWARD!" the guide shouts. "PADDLE! PADDLE! PADDLE!" I put in as much effort as I can, but as we slip and slide on the wet raft while we try to get a purchase on the foaming water with our paddles, it's not enough.

As the front of the raft plunges into the hole, the impact squeezes air from the front of the raft into the back, and—ploof—my back-seat-mate and I plop into the water.

I'm submerged before I realize what just happened, but fortunately, my mind switches immediately into survival mode. I remember what I've been taught—feet up and downstream! But my head won't stay above water. I'm in a washing machine, and the cycle is set on Cold, but not on Gentle. It circulates me a couple of times, but I manage to catch a breath each time, though I may be getting more water than air. Finally, the hole spits me downstream. There's nothing I can do but go with the flow. The life jacket now aptly demonstrates why it's mandatory as it keeps my head out of the water. I ride the rapid downstream until it ends and it seems worth the effort to swim for shore. A raft eddies out below me and someone grabs the straps of my life jacket and lifts me in. I lie on the bottom of the raft, exhausted.

"Are you OK?" my rescuer asks.

"I think so." Maybe a bruise or two, but no significant damage. I'd better sit up and make my survival more convincing.

"Need some water?" he says, offering his bottle.

"Uh, no thanks."

My seat-mate has been rescued, and she's fine, too. She appears to respond to the experience with a blast of adrenaline—excited, giggling, almost manic. I, in contrast, am sobered. This stuff could be dangerous.

The leader is apologetic about our swim. He says he shouldn't have let it happen. But I figure there's plenty of responsibility to go around. Stuff happens in whitewater.

We're not far from the end of the trip, so I don't have time to get cold. After we've landed and carried the rafts to shore, the leader takes me and the other swimmer down a trail above the river. "Listen," he says, "That's Dragon's Tooth." We can hear it growling well before we reach the bank above it and look down on it.

Once my initial scare is over, I'm pleased and proud that I didn't panic. That's where the real danger would be.

I go back two years later, and we make it through Dragon's Tooth without incident. I have to try again—that's how much I love that river. What falls into it, it carries. The idea of a natural force so much more powerful than we are, and so disinterested in our fate, is strangely comforting. If you fight it, that's when you're more likely to get hurt. Go with the flow, and take steps to keep yourself safe, and you'll probably be OK. I touched it, and somehow, I came out stronger. I was taken by it and washed clean, then sent back to shore with a message. I could think of the experience as my baptism. Having water dripped on your head, or even being dunked in a pond—what's the point of that? If you really want someone cleansed of their sins, throw them in Dragon's Tooth. It'll test your faith—in the river, and in yourself.

Paying Dues in Plastic
A Story of How Rivers Shape All They Touch
Doug Grosjean

Sitting in a room in a home in Michigan, looking out at the snow coming down, seems a good time for nostalgic introspection about spring, water, and my decades spent running rivers on my own, without benefit of a paid boatman as my guide.

Why run rivers at all?

I run rivers for the same reason humans do many things: curiosity.

That curiosity was bred into me from an early age, and is probably just a part of being human. What child doesn't look at a river, and wonder why it keeps flowing endlessly in one direction?

I grew up in Toledo, Ohio. Like many towns, Toledo was located with access to a waterway for military and commerce reasons. All around was the Great Black Swamp. German immigrants drained the swamp, and turned the rich black dirt into some of the most productive farms in the world. Toledo became an international shipping port on the west end of Lake Erie, about 600 miles from the east coast. Imports came in, and American wheat, corn, and Jeeps went out, thanks to the Saint Lawrence Seaway. Before the Saint Lawrence Seaway, there was the Miami & Erie Canal, connecting Toledo to the Ohio River to the south, and Indiana to the west, via mule-drawn wooden canal boats.

Every local waterway was a path to points unknown. Little by little, I explored what I could. I read local history, much of it intertwined with local waterways. I read about our section of the Miami & Erie Canal, of which only remnants remain. I read a story in our newspaper about a local man who canoed 120 miles from Fort Wayne, Indiana, to Toledo, Ohio in just a few days on the high water of spring on the

Maumee River, and I decided I wanted to do that someday too. My great-grandmother gave me a copy of *The Adventures of Tom Sawyer*, a book about a boy who also grew up near a big river with lots of commercial traffic.

I was drawn to water, and was being groomed by rivers, by my place in the world, by history, and by my own curiosity.

Eventually, my older brother, Ken, introduced me to flatwater canoeing on the Maumee in an aluminum canoe. I found it amazing. Quiet, serene, scenic. A single day trip was followed by other sporadic canoe outings, just frequent enough that a canoe was a normal boat to me, infrequent enough to remain special.

I grew up, moved to Arizona for a few years, and was introduced to still more rivers and lakes in the Arizona desert. I explored the dry riverbeds that only flowed after monsoon rains—checking them out by foot, horseback, and truck. I traveled through Oak Creek Canyon, the Salt River Canyon, and the Verde Valley by motorcycle. The Salt River east of Phoenix was normally dry in those years, but ran high and fast in the spring during high snowpack years when the man-made reservoirs outside town were drawn down to make room for fresh water coming in. That meant I could float the Salt River by inner tube on hot summer days. The motorcycle shop where I worked also gave demos of Jet-Skis at several local lakes, so I learned to ride one of them.

At some point, while living in Arizona, I visited the Grand Canyon with family from Ohio. I glimpsed the Colorado River at the bottom of the Canyon through binoculars, and spied a huge yellow raft carrying passengers through a rapid, everybody soaking wet in the hot sun on the river. That's what I wanted! Hiking required too much time and commitment, and it would take years to see the whole place. What better way to see the entire Canyon than from a boat in the bottom, looking up?

I returned to work the following Monday, and told a co-worker about the Canyon visit and my desire to travel it by raft. He replied that I didn't make enough money in a year to do that, and at that time, he was right. I put that goal on the back-burner, but it didn't go away.

Returning from Arizona to attend college in Ohio, I began to take my younger brother, Brian, down the Maumee in our aluminum canoe, just as my older brother had taken me. The Maumee is a wide river, with a very high flow after rains, gradually dropping over shallow ledges down to Lake Erie just upstream of Toledo. The ledges produce nice surf waves at high water, and a small challenge for neophytes like us.

Little by little we pushed harder and farther, running the rapids at high water. On one of those trips we took on a lot of water in the standing waves. The water sloshed back and forth in the canoe and we capsized, resulting in a long swim in the flood waters before being rescued by another canoeist. A wiser man might have taken it as an omen, but I concluded that I needed a boat with a cover, perhaps a kayak, for the kind of boating I was doing.

A co-worker used a kayak for duck hunting. He told me that really good kayakers could actually stay inside and roll a kayak upright in the event of capsizing. Based on my recent experience, that seemed like the boat for me. So … I bought a kayak from the Canoe Shop in Waterville, Ohio. Then I enrolled Brian and myself in a kayaking class to learn to paddle it safely and roll it. I became involved with, and encouraged by, members of the local whitewater club in Toledo. I learned the basics of flatwater kayaking in Olander Park in Sylvania, Ohio, the basics of whitewater on the Maumee after heavy rains, and advanced whitewater techniques at South Bend's East Race (a former millrace converted to a whitewater training course). I also met Chad at the kayaking class at Olander pond. I was 24, and Chad was 10 years younger. We were both shy introverts, neither of us high school athletes. Kayaking came easily to us, while people skills came much more slowly.

I figured that the best way to get good at kayaking was to do it often. Chad and his mother both trusted me to be an adult with good judgement, and kayaking is best done with a companion for safety. So, Chad was my safety net and I was his. In the early days, I'd pick up Chad and his boat in Waterville and we'd drive a short distance to the Maumee River to drop our boats in the water.

We paddled the flatwater sections. We paddled in the estuary in downtown Toledo, mingling with motorboats, sailboats, and lake freighters. We paddled around river islands till dusk, pausing to eat wild grapes from vines that dangled from the trees overhead down into the river.

Eventually we began to experiment in the Maumee's mild whitewater, practicing eddy turns, playing in whirlpools behind bridge piers, surfing river waves and holes. Fear came easy, then a little confidence when we survived a mistake, then humility again after making a new mistake and taking a swim; and the cycle would repeat. I was in love, and, as with every love, a small taste of pleasure only whetted my appetite. I wanted more, a lot more, as quickly as possible.

We both read William Nealy's amusing river maps and cartoon books on kayaking, and American Whitewater's much more serious tomes on the same topics. We tried the things we read about in books—sometimes they worked, and sometimes they took a bit of practice to master. The good thing about the Maumee was that there were few rocks. The bad thing was that the river was wide, and swims could be long. But eventually, the scary swims of a beginner were replaced with successful rolls.

Chad and I were both prodigies, absorbing kayaking skills like a pair of sponges. Easy? That's harder to say. I think most people who put in the hours of practice that we did would also improve quickly. We were paying our dues, leading to points unknown.

These were heady days in my life. These were my college days, circa mid-1980s, studying mechanical design in the evenings while working as a draftsman by day at a local architectural firm, able to see a sliver of the Maumee River out the window from my third-floor drafting table if I looked just right. I was learning in college, learning at work, and learning in my kayak.

The local club frowned on two beginners going out with only each other as a safety net. But the club didn't go out as often as we did, and we were both young and cocky about our boating skills—so we considered their admonitions an annoyance. If they didn't want us to go on River D with them until we had successfully run Rivers A, B, and C with them first; to heck with them. I had a car, could read road maps, topographical maps, and river maps with equal ease. I had my own gear. Aside from being too young to drive, Chad's skills were similar. He was a bit better at reading whitewater, while I was a little better at punching holes (since I was less skilled at spotting them). We could easily do river trips ourselves.

And so began the phase of our **Weekend River Trips**. The plan went like this:

1. Watch weather forecasts on TV for rainfall patterns.

2. Phone calls to each other to see if a trip was possible.

3. Phone calls to the recorded messages that told about river levels.

4. Phone calls to each other to figure out what river was the best choice.

5. Thursday night, load the car with boats and gear.

6. After work, drive most of the night to get to whatever Appalachian river was running.

I'd always been an introvert. But if I wanted to go kayaking, I had to learn to approach groups, size them up, and ask if Chad and I could tag along with them. The choice was simple: learn to be an extrovert, or don't go kayaking. I learned to be an extrovert, to come out of my shell. Whitewater kayaking ripped me out of that shell, hard and fast; a clean jerk.

As an added benefit, kayaking with many diverse groups exposed us to different techniques and equipment, and Chad and I absorbed it all. I'd never been involved in team sports in school. But I slowly found my place among the grand eccentrics who were like me, those who frequented the riverbanks and scouted rapids to figure out ways to get through them on their own. Whitewater boating tends to attract non-conformists with too much confidence and too little humility. After a bit of acclimation, I fit right in.

It was a sub-culture whose language was one of dams and dam releases, reservoirs, cfs, eddies, waves, holes, jets, kicks, meanders, flash-floods, undercuts, strainers, and other river terms that made sense only to whitewater enthusiasts and professional hydrologists. An early 20th century linguist found that the Inuit Eskimos have over 50 words for different kinds of snow. I'm convinced that whitewater kayakers have just as many words for different kinds of water.

After that first summer of kayaking together, Chad took up whitewater slalom racing. When he had time between races, we'd still go boating, and he'd share what he'd learned with anybody who would listen. We both got better due to his racing, but he got better faster.

Every river has its own unique personality, dictated by the geology of the mountains they cut across, surrounding terrain (urban, rural or wilderness), weather, and climate. Because the Gauley River cuts through soft sandstone, every river rock is dangerously undercut, and swims are risky if a boater is swept under the rocks; hopefully the boater and boat emerge safely, but maybe not. Advice: don't swim anything. The Cheat River suffered a huge flood just a couple years before I started kayaking. It destroyed towns and altered all the rapids in the whitewater stretch downstream of Albright, West Virginia, so it had all new rapids that were still under construction, moving around and changing after each subsequent flood. The Lower Youghiogheny had an undercut at Dimples that had taken some lives, and the Upper Youghiogheny had, well … there really isn't any good place to swim there.

The rivers with a lot of whitewater traffic typically had one particularly challenging spot where the commercial photographers would wait to photograph the carnage. The film would be shuttled back to town on a regular basis, everything carefully scheduled so that when the rafters and kayakers got off the river and back to town, proofs were already printed. If you liked what you saw, you could buy it, and the photo studio would print them while you ate supper in town. When you saw a photographer lounging under an umbrella on the riverbank at a rapid, you knew it was a serious rapid. Worst case scenario—hopefully the photos turned out well!

The Appalachians were also mountain laurel and moss, gray skies, lots of rain, drawls and pickup trucks and coal trucks, and frequently cold. Circuitous shuttle routes on roads were not well-marked, and there was acid runoff from coal mines that were not properly sealed when shut down. The Cheat, in particular, was a tragedy. Acid mine runoff had killed all the fish and plants in the river, and was apparently strong enough that after a weekend on the Cheat our paddling clothes no longer stunk. Apparently, an acid solution is hell on odiferous bacteria as well as on fish and plants. I'm not a fisherman, but I viewed wiping out an entire ecosystem on the Cheat River as unethical and immoral. Along with becoming a kayaker and an athlete with an interest in geology, the rivers were slowly turning me into an environmentalist and a conservationist.

A newly accepted theory in geology in those days was Catastrophe Theory—the idea that the Earth's features changed in a series of abrupt disasters: floods, landslides, volcanic eruptions, earthquakes, and meteorite strikes. Catastrophe Theory applied to rivers as well. I could see changes on the river that had been wrought by recent floods. And just as rivers sometimes changed overnight in a series of violent floods, my own skills usually leapfrogged ahead, then leveled out, then leapfrogged ahead again. On one particular trip I bit off more than I should have …

I hesitate to call it a catastrophe, because it turned out OK, but this trip stands out as pure Survival Paddling where my skill level went up dramatically in about 90 minutes' time. We arrived at the put-in for the Cheat around 2:00 a.m. When we arrived, the flow was an ideal 4 feet on the Albright Gauge—but it was 8.5 feet and rising by the time we launched. We found a group to kayak with. As we prepared to launch, the leader gave a pep talk: "We've run this before at about 5 feet on the Albright Gauge, and it was huge then. Today is going to be a lot bigger. If you swim, we may not be able to save you and your boat, so concentrate on rolling upright successfully." Nobody was smiling or making jokes.

We started down. There were large standing waves, starting at about five feet in height, and getting bigger and bigger as we went. The river was one big, brown mass of water, moving quickly, growing ever more powerful and gaining speed as it funneled into an opening between the mountains. It left town fast, on a long sweeping curve to the right. It was the biggest whitewater I'd ever seen in my life. The waves in the first, small rapid were huge, growing to about 10 feet in height and exploding violently. I recalled the guidebook describing the first rapid as relatively easy, and stating that if you couldn't handle it, well … you should hike out.

Chad was in front of me, and suddenly he was upside down. I waited for him to roll, but in a flash he was swimming, and I was towing him and his boat to the large eddy along the right bank. I saw nothing of our companions, only endless whitewater—and then an empty red kayak bobbing along.

We were about a mile and a half below Albright by the time I got Chad to shore. Out of a dozen skilled kayakers, two had swum that first, supposedly easy rapid; Chad and the woman whose red Perception Dancer I'd seen floating by. Other kayakers had pulled her ashore, somebody else had saved her boat, and though shaken, she was climbing back in and planned to continue on.

Meanwhile, Chad was preparing to walk back to town, barefoot. I offered to join him, having lost a lot of enthusiasm for this river on this day, but he suggested I go on downriver, as I'd had no problems in that rapid. The group said they were OK with that, and so with a great deal of uncertainty and fear, I continued.

I had never seen water like that before. Not in person, not on TV, not in training videos. Nothing prepared me for what I headed into. The rapid Big Nasty, normally a series of ledges leading into a huge hole at the end, is usually skirted on a tight, left line. But this day it was a series of monstrously huge holes leading into some sort of strange feature that was shooting water straight up into the air where the huge hole used to be. All but two of us snuck it on the left, over what is normally an island of cobblestones. Those who ran it disappeared into the holes. We'd see the tip of their helmet or paddle or bow as they appeared to punch through and then repeat the process, all the way down.

I'd never run the Cheat before, so I had nothing to compare it to. I'd read in guidebooks that it was a pool and drop river, but all I saw was drops and no pools at all.

High Falls Rapid, normally a series of shallow ledges sweeping to the right with tall cliffs on the left, forced boats onto a line squeezing between two huge holes and leading into a wave that was approximately 15 feet tall. Kayaks went airborne in that wave, then followed down a series of waves that slowly got smaller, finally darting into the eddy below to regroup. In the eddy, those who had gone before were waiting, trembling, exclaiming "Holy crap, that wave was amazing! Never seen anything that big in my life!" One woman opened up her waterproof container of cigarettes and a lighter, and was shaking as she lit up and puffed away, sitting in her kayak in the eddy, her eyes wide.

Another huge rapid, which probably doesn't exist at normal levels, got the best of me. I rolled upright eventually, convinced that the hole I had just been hammered in was drawing me back for a second beating, only to realize that I was clear of it and drifting downstream safely. I momentarily couldn't tell upstream from downstream.

Suddenly the Jenkinsburg Bridge came into view. With a couple of rather long stops for scouting Big Nasty and High Falls, it had taken us about 90 minutes to travel 10 miles. It was over, we had all survived, and nobody had taken another swim. I felt as if I'd won the lottery!

Glenn Miller, a local lumberjack, gave us a lift back to town in his stake-bed lumber truck, providing beer and sodas for $1 each (on the honor system) out of a cooler in the back. My new companions warned me to leave my paddling gear on, first to protect myself from tree branches on the off-road portion of the shuttle, and then later to keep from freezing during the paved portion when Glenn would be driving 40-50 mph on the road to Albright. It was good advice.

As time went on, I ended up boating with extremely skilled kayakers, and it became normal for us to run challenging rivers with people who rarely made mistakes. Going to work on Monday mornings, glowing from the weekend adventures, muscles and joints sore but the soul completely filled, became a fairly normal experience.

With hopes of someday kayaking the Grand Canyon, I sought out high flows in places like the New River Gorge at flood in order to experience big water. Over time, I became more comfortable in huge rapids, while Chad became more comfortable on tight, technical, high-gradient creek runs. Each of us was choosing the type of river that we liked best, but we could enjoy a technical, big-water river together.

The big rivers hammered home a lesson is life and philosophy: The river is all powerful. You can't fight it, you can only work within its limits, given the tools and the strength you've got.

In 1990, Chad and I visited Colorado for a week of kayaking, and learned that western river trips were an entirely different experience. Eastern rivers run high after spring rains, with weather typically cold and dreary, with gray skies. We ran into crowds if we waited until good weather to run. But rivers in Colorado run high when the sun shines bright in the clear June sky, melting the accumulated snow-pack from the mountains. Blue skies, zero humidity, 80-degree air temperatures and 33-degree water; and all your wet gear is dry by the time you tie the boats onto the roof racks at the take-out. Altitude was a little bit of a challenge—I adapted better to high altitude at age 28 than I had at age 18 during a Colorado motorcycle trip. But Colorado became almost an annual destination. There are so many amazing rivers in the Colorado Rocky Mountains that a person would be hard-pressed to experience them all in a single lifetime.

And there was so much variety in the geology of the Rocky Mountains! Hard rock, softer rocks, jagged rocks, and rock sculpted into sensually smooth curves by ages of water flow. Geology on the rivers began to haunt me, and I longed to learn still more about the subject.

Kayaking led to learning other skills as well: CPR classes at the American Red Cross, River Rescue classes with the Ohio Department of Natural Resources on Slippery Rock Creek in Pennsylvania. I learned knots, how to make a Z-drag out of pulleys and ropes and webbing. I played on climbing walls during the off-season, figuring that I may as well use my new-found rope skills in fun ways. I read about physical training, and applied what I learned, so I could be my best on the water. I read about the mental traits of high-risk athletes, kayakers, mountain climbers and hang-gliders; and I learned about myself in the process.

In 1992, my grandparents passed away. They'd always worried about me on the rivers, but now the gloves came off. I ran the Upper Gauley, Lower Gauley, Big Sandy Creek, Upper Youghiogheny, all with a comfortable margin of safety, and enjoyed each of them immensely.

In the summer of 1993, I entered the Mid-America Slalom Series, a series of five whitewater kayak slalom races scattered across the country from Wisconsin to Colorado that paid money to anybody who finished in the Top 10. I was suffering from delusions of grandeur, which were quickly cured when I finished closer to the slow end of the entries than to the front-runners. So, it could be said that racing was therapeutic. I also came away with far more precise river-running skills. Getting my butt kicked five weekends in a row in distant states was expensive, but the experience of boating with the best racers in the world was priceless.

In years of kayaking whitewater, it never crossed my mind to pay somebody to take me down a river. I don't think I would adapt well to being a passenger, after paddling my own craft. Several times on rivers, we saw commercial rafts flip on the same rapids that weren't giving us any trouble, and thanked our lucky stars we didn't swim that often.

As years went by, life intruded. A child. A business start-up. Adult responsibilities. I never stopped kayaking, never sold off my gear; but river trips became less and less frequent, less and less intense. The mind remained willing, but the flesh was … out of practice, at best.

I longed to run the rivers I'd never gotten around to, the extreme runs that would perhaps forever be beyond me: the huge but illegal rapids of the Niagara Gorge, Clark's Fork of the Yellowstone, the 120-mile run down the Maumee River from its beginning in Fort Wayne, Indiana to Lake Erie at Toledo, Ohio, the Grand Canyon, or … Many of my kayaking friends moved on to other activities, or could no longer kayak for other reasons. I began to realize that life is finite, and each of us is given just so many days and so much time.

There's a joke that the difference between a whitewater boater and a US Savings Bond is that after 40 years the bond matures and starts making money. While there may be some truth to that, I find that there is also an inner peace and confidence that comes from a long history of running whitewater. I have fewer butterflies in my stomach when starting other new adventures. I worry less about whether my skills are strong enough to deal with a new river, realizing that odds are good that I'm sufficiently skilled to pull it off, or figure it out on the fly. I trust my knots and ropes, can read a topographical map well, and can live for weeks out of a cooler and a drybag in the desert, or in the mountains. I relish the simple joy of showing people new to the sport the magic that flows into the mind and body when a paddle is placed into moving water and a boat begins to move downstream, becoming one with the river. And I enjoy teaching others about water, rocks, plants and animals that frequent moving water.

Proverbs about water became more meaningful:

> "Still waters run deep."
> "You can never set foot in the same river twice."
> "Smooth seas do not make good sailors."

Rivers have been my muse, my escape, my art, a place of refuge, a place to relax, a place to learn, a place where I've sometimes gotten beat up a bit, and a place to heal. I've seen with my own eyes the effect of water on rock, how it carves them over a long period of time, and I've been shaped by those same waters myself. I've learned to care about plants, and fish, and rocks, and sand. There's an inner peace in knowing that I've participated in one of the oldest, simplest and most beautiful dances on Earth, drifting downstream on moving water. That at the end of the day, I've slid gracefully across the water, and down the rivers.

III
Connections

Three Generations Afloat on the Salmon River
Ashley Lodato

We are, at first glance, a motley crew. Tumbling out of five vehicles at the launch ramp for the Lower Salmon River, with books, cracker boxes, and crossword puzzles spilling out of the open doors, we rush toward each other with greetings and laughter, ending up in a tangled knot of hugs. Gear is everywhere—stowed in trailers, strapped to roof racks, tucked behind seats. Kids are hot and sticky, tired from the long drive to western Idaho. We have yet to rig the rafts, load the gear, and plan our itinerary for our river trip through rugged basalt and limestone gorges, but in our minds the hardest part of the trip is over. We have all made it to the launch; let the games begin.

Fourteen hours after our arrival at Hammer Creek on Idaho's Salmon River, we are afloat: four rafts, two SUPs, ten adults ages 42 to 72, seven kids ages 4 to 11. Just grandma and grandpa, their offspring, the spouses, the grandkids, and eight cases of Sierra Nevada River Ryed IPA. Bright skies, warm water, and 73 miles of Class II-III whitewater lie head. Bliss.

The idea for a three-generations river trip was conceived the previous year, when a select subset of the family reconnoitered the Lower Salmon with great success. "Wouldn't it be fun," we asked ourselves, "to radically complicate the logistics, belabor the decision-making process, and necessitate the securing of larger campsites by doubling the number of people on the trip next year?"

The promise of quality family time triumphs over practicality, and twelve months later we find ourselves with thirteen family members and an additional almost-family unit of four, wrestling a mountain of gear down to the river's edge—all we will need (and more) for six days on the river.

The jumble of dry bags we unload from the vehicles belies the tight organization that has taken place over the past few weeks. Thanks to Google, lists of personal and group gear are easily shared, and meal sign-ups require little more than entering one's name in a cell. We have not only the essentials, but also such luxury items as a lime squeezer, oven mittens, poi balls, and a ukulele. What might appear to be a yard sale is actually a fairly well-oiled machine of precision packing logistics. Or so we like to think.

While not quite an afterthought, the stand up paddleboards (SUPs) were not initially on the list of essential gear. A few of us in the group are whitewater kayakers, most of us have some expedition rafting under our belts, and nearly all of us were, in our younger years, either raft guides or Outward Bound instructors. We'd SUPped a little here and there—on the Pacific waters off Troncones, Mexico, on the lakes and flatwater stretches of the Northwest—but with kids, jobs, and mortgages, none of us were exactly on the fast track to adopt new recreational activities like SUPping. But still, there was something compelling about SUPs, and since we had access to two of them for the river trip we decide to bring them along, just in case someone wanted to try them out.

The friendly competition for time on the two SUPs begins about five minutes after two of the more calculating adults on the trip secure them at the launch, and continues unrelentingly until the moment we pull off the river at Heller Bar on the Snake River a week later. With only two SUPs and only a handful of rapids that can't be safely SUPped, even given our collective limited SUPping skillset, the SUPs are in high demand from dawn 'til dark. The kids commandeer them in the eddies at camp the moment we land and are out on them again as soon as they wake up the next morning. As we load the rafts, the kids holler "I call a SUP" the way my friends and I used to call "Shotgun!" to nab the front seat back in high school. The adults try to be generous and let the kids have their fun, but darn it—we want our own fair share of SUPping time.

Subterfuge follows. We discover that the way to get the kids off the SUPs is to get them cold as quickly as possible. Thus, we ride them on the bows of our SUPs through some of the splashy Class II+ rapids and get them soaked, necessitating a warm-up ride for them on one of the rafts, which frees us up for some SUP alone time until the next kid begs for a ride. Had we possessed the skills to have the kids ejected into a safe-but-scary hole to take them off the SUP craze for a while and commandeer the boards for ourselves, we just might have done so.

The only person not clamoring for SUP time is Nino, the 71-year-old grandmother on the trip. Although she has since become a lake SUPping fiend, Nino spends much of the Salmon trip crouched in the stern of one of the rafts in what she called her "foxhole." With a foil-covered GoLite umbrella held over her head, Nino has her foxhole sealed up nearly watertight. No foot soldier weathered mortar attacks in a trench with more focus than Nino in her own little rubber pocket of emotional safety.

I SUP my first true rapid on the first day, a Class II rock garden. It is exhilarating—a thrilling dance of maintaining my balance and trying to steer a safe line. At the bottom of the rapid, still upright and dry, I think to myself, "Hello SUPping, where have you been all my life?" I then promptly capsize on an eddy line.

Three days pass in rafting and paddle-boarding paradise. The white sand beaches beckon, the water is inviting, the food is superb, and the kids don't fight. We row and SUP rapids called Rollercoaster, Pine Bar, the Maze, and Bodacious Bounce. We see pictographs and mining remnants. We make Andy Goldsworthy-inspired temporary art installations with polished stones. The kids crack rocks open to reveal crystals inside. We crack beers open to take the edge off the afternoon heat. If heaven exists in river form it is here, along this narrow ribbon of geologic and human history.

It is on the river that we feel most like ourselves. Unencumbered by the small stresses of daily life, we are free to be our best selves. We're interested and interesting. We're patient, tolerant, generous. There are no "to do" lists driving our agenda out here, no emails to check, no bills to pay. We're able to be the people we believe ourselves to be.

Back in the day, back before kids and mortgages, our lives were laced with seemingly huge swaths of free time, when we could disappear into the wilderness for weeks. We paddled the Grand Canyon in the winter, once going twenty-three days without seeing another party on the river. We hiked desolate stretches of Newfoundland coastline. We climbed Joshua Tree's granite mounds until our fingers bled. This week on the Salmon reminds us of those days of unfettered freedom, of the discovery of wild places and, more importantly, the people we could be in those places.

Before and after this week we are, of course, fairly mainstream adults. We're parents and community members. We serve on non-profit boards and volunteer at our kids' schools. We are acupuncturists, teachers, non-profit administrators, and small business owners. We're fortunate; we all love what we do. What we do, however, is not who we are. Our jobs feed our families, but expeditions like this one feed our souls.

When Mike, who is allergic, gets stung by a wasp at lunch on the third day, we are reminded of just how far we are from civilization. Although this stretch of the Salmon is not particularly remote, we're still pretty far from help by most standards. An evacuation would take at least half a day at best, and at worst might take too long to successfully reverse an anaphylactic reaction. We give Mike Benadryl and get an Epi-Pen ready, and he eventually recovers without incident. Still, it's an unsettling reminder that we have chosen to take precious cargo—our children and our aging parents—on an adventure that is not without potential consequences. It's a risk, indeed, but one we take without hesitation.

"What did one paddleboard say to the other paddleboard?" my eight-year-old asks us one morning. Without pausing for our guesses, she answers her own riddle: "Sup, SUP?" It becomes the catch phrase for anyone on a SUP for the rest of the trip.

Four-year-old Una discovers that if Uncle Jon paddles a SUP and she hangs onto the back, she can cop a bit of a fast ride, a little like inner tubing behind a motor boat. "Paddle, paddle," she screams through her laughter, her tiny body nearly skimming the water's surface in the SUP's wake.

Although the Lower Salmon is a family-friendly river, there are a couple of rapids that give pause for scouting. We pull the rafts up on shore while we look for our lines, then attempt to replicate these lines once we launch again. Nino tends not to scout, referring instead to a copy of the river guide that is located on each raft. One formidable drop, Slide Rapid, looms legendary, as it becomes unrunnable at higher flows. No matter how many times we reassure Nino that Slide is going to be a breeze at 6,000 cfs, she's not going to believe it until she sees it. Or rather, until she's safely through it, having not seen any of it from the foil-topped safety of her foxhole.

Slide Rapid is not only a breeze, it's almost disappointing. The monster wave train, ugly holes, and boiling eddies that characterize it at higher levels are non-existent. I SUP through Slide Rapid with a kid on the bow of my board. Never one to take chances, Nino crouches in her foxhole.

Near Cooper's Ferry we visit an active archaeological site. A crew from the University of Oregon carefully excavates a Nez Perce summer camp and painstakingly sifts through the dirt, seeking artifacts that shed light on the culture and practices of these migratory people. I think of our conversations along the river after dinner, listening to the water's whispers, as we sift through the stories of our family and friends and discover each other anew.

Four days into the trip the skies blacken and we see the first flash of lightning. Pulling over to a sandy beach, we set out lunch and wait for the storm to pass. Pass it does, but only after a menacing round of thunder and lightning and about 30 minutes of driving rain, with raindrops so big they hurt when they hit.

Two people take shelter under the lunch table, another dozen huddle under three sun umbrellas, trying in vain not to touch the central metal pole, and the stragglers hold the largest SUP over their heads, the way you see street vendors in the third world hunched under sheaves of newspaper during the monsoon season. It's kind of fun, as long as we don't think about the fact that somewhere between 6000 and 24,000 people die each year from lightning strikes. "Ah well, those morons got hit because they didn't seek shelter during storms," we think, trying to convince ourselves that our flimsy patio umbrellas constitute "shelter."

Such storms usually scare the crap out of me, and although I am able to maintain bowel control during that one, two of my nieces and nephews aren't so lucky. My brother's kids can't wait so Zack has to unstrap one of the groovers from the raft and carry it up to the sodden beach so his kids can answer nature's call amidst what is most likely the biggest thunderstorm of their lives.

After 53 miles, the Salmon empties into the Snake River, which has more volume and more people. A typical weekend brings fleets of jet boats and weekend partiers roaring up and down the river, the sounds of their motors and music masking the trills of the canyon wrens we heard upstream. The storm seems to have kept the usual crowds away, however, and we are able to find a beach to camp on.

Although we have to excavate a flat site in the sand for one of the tents, the effort is well worth it since we soon learn from the little girls on the trip that the Mossy Step Café is open for business. The café, which soon becomes renowned for its precarious location high on a slick, moss-coated ledge and its aggressive sales tactics, offers an inventive menu of Yucca Pound Cake, Slide Rapid Sliders, and Stickleberry Cupcakes. The 8-year-old girls run the café's kitchen, while waitressing is handled by the 5-year-olds. When we tire (all too quickly for the café staff's tastes) of the mind-numbing cycle of ordering and then pretending to taste a sand cake decorated with willow leaves, we wander back to our camp, stuffed full of the contentment that comes from watching kids use their imaginations.

On our final night, we once again seek refuge under our inadequate shelters as lightning dances on the ridgetops directly above us. The wind is so fierce that it threatens to lift our pop-up kitchen tent into the air, despite the big rocks anchoring it. We grab the tent to keep it from flying away as bright bolts of electricity, that look as if they could have been created by the Disney special effects department, somehow avoid striking the eight-foot lightning rods we're grasping.

When the storm passes, the light is golden and almost electric, casting the dry hills above us in an other-worldly glow under a still-black sky. Our chests are tight; with relief, yes, but also with sentiment. I've had other moments like this before: on glassy lakes in northern Maine, in high meadows watching alpenglow blush and then fade, under velvety desert skies looking up at a carpet of stars. Always during the hush of sunset. At such moments I've felt an almost nostalgic ache as I wonder if life will ever be so beautiful again. Nights like this one remind me that yes, it will be, and it is.

The deluge has been long and prolific. Water begins to pool on the parched earth around us. Rivulets form and trickle down to nearby gullies, turning dry drainages into muddy streams, which surge down to the river carrying debris. Overnight, the water level rises by 1000 cfs. Nothing dangerous, hardly even noticeable to the naked eye. But the river is now far more full than it was when we launched a week ago; it is completely replenished. And so, it turns out, are we.

On the Alsek-Tatshenshini Friends, Family and Fruit (or Not)
Monica Gokey

If you find yourself explaining to a Canadian border patrol agent why you're traveling from Alaska to British Columbia with an ungodly amount of food, don't bring up the apples. At this point in your trip, apples are closer to derailing your Alsek-Tatshenshini adventure than any of the forthcoming rapids.

Suppress your inner Snow White. Forgo the apples.

The same goes for firearms. Yes, the Alsek-Tat is chock full of bears. But you'll be fine with bear spray. Do yourself a favor: don't Google stories of plane crashes that've happened because canisters of bear spray inadvertently discharged mid-flight. Whisper to yourself that you'll remember to put the group's bear spray in the newest looking ammo can on the bush flight out.

For all other trip necessities, you're best off investing in the guidebook. Never mind how much the environment may have changed since the book was published. Consider it an educational experience in how much glacial rivers change year-to-year. The guidebook is simply that: a guide.

From there, the rest of your Alsek-Tatshenshini story is yours to write.

My story is bigger than me. When I sent our Trip Leader a deposit for the 10-day trip, I unknowingly committed two people to the voyage—myself and a little stowaway riding along in my belly. My oldest son is two now. And I still consider the Alsek-Tatshenshini our inaugural "mom and kid" adventure. (Despite the wishes of my river mates, we did not end up naming him "Tat.")

Our trip started in Juneau, where everyone met aboard the ferry that carried us north to Haines. It started the way most river trips do: you catch up with the friends you know and eagerly gawk at the "unknowns" who'll be your dear friends by the end of the week. River trips do that to people—especially this river trip.

By the time we hit the put-in I was four months into my pregnancy. My body was still the same—but I had enough little aches and pains (namely in my back) to remind me that I was, indeed, growing a tiny human inside.

This caused me to do things like say "Oh shit" with marginally more vigor after hiking up on a hot, steamy pile of bear scat. The Alsek-Tat runs through some of the most dense grizzly bear habitat in North America. But despite the abundance of bears, they've encountered relatively few humans and don't equate our kind with food yet. So they skedaddle when the bipeds come ambling in.

My pregnant body also afforded me restless sleep (training for the real deal)—which meant I was awake at the wee hour when an earthquake jiggled our camp for more than a minute. Again, I thought "Oh shit," before listening for others and realizing they enjoyed this seismically sweet lullaby in their sleep. So I hauled my increasingly rotund self off my Thermarest to check on the boats in case the quake triggered a rapid water level rise. It didn't.

At Walker Glacier, the sound of ice sliding jiggled my bones before my ears registered the full acoustics of the noise. I felt it in my belly and wondered if the baby felt it too. It was menacing—like the whole glacier was combusting. But we weren't in harm's way. It was practically a sliver of ice. Just Nature flexing her big muscles.

My river mates took delight in my pregnancy and shared their own family stories with candor.

One couple remembered watching their son navigate an oar-rig down a must-make move for the first time on a multi-day river trip. A friend of his was on board. They watched, gripped with "what ifs? He nailed his line, as they knew he would.

A father-daughter duo recalled how the kids in their family all used to hum the Indiana Jones theme song as their family raft approached rapids, eventually reaching a crescendo as they dropped over the horizon line.

And still another of my river mates shared a story of losing a child in its sleep. "How do you recover from that?" I asked. "You just do," they said. My throat went tight at their willingness to share.

River trips take a bunch of strangers and make them intimate friends.

For most of the people on our trip, river trips were very much the fabric of their children's upbringing. I aim to follow that example. When my son is old enough to ask about the Alsek-Tatshenshini, I'll tell him it's one of the finest river trips in the Far North. The Alsek-Tat is wild in a way the world is getting low on.

Two countries. Ten friends. Dozens of glaciers. Hundreds of bears.

And—depending on the mood of the border agent on duty—zero apples.

Ski Ties and NRS Straps
Tying a Family Together
Marci Dye

Our family has two seasons: Skiing and Boating. Why do we boat? For the same reasons as "Why do we ski?" It is truly why we live.

Skiing isn't just skiing ... Boating isn't just boating.

The youngest gets a chance to paddle or row and to learn from his mentors, his older siblings. The cautious kid normally, he sees a different challenge by taking on the river and commanding the boat. Once there, that cautious, shy kid from school floats away. The focus, the adrenaline, the success all boost that kid to take on the river with confidence and pride. Future oarsman in the building, he reads the water the way a young child picks up computer skills ... seemingly by second nature. Oh, what a way to learn, and learn early.

The middle daughter is the athlete, the straight A student, the focused ski racer. She would rather not be on the oars. She wants her own small vessel, whether a paddle board on the long flat stretches, or the IK through the whitewater stretches. The ski racer shows through, using the strength, endurance, and mental process of picking beautiful lines with grace, seemingly by second nature.

The older siblings have chosen their professions ... and have dedicated their young adult lives to river guiding. The older oarsman, who battled ADHD issues through school, struggling with reading and grades all the way through, found his soul on a commercial trip on the Middle Fork one summer ... and never looked back. That kid grew into a master of the river, able to take on any river scenario with comfort, confidence, and grace. He and the river have connected thoroughly. And that shines through when he guides, able to provide his clients with the thrill of an exciting trip on the water, but with the comfort of a relaxed and safe feeling. His accomplishments also seem to come by second nature.

Now, the dad of this crew. He was neither a Nordic skier nor a boatman growing up. His love for both has not been second nature. But watching him dive into each, with the technical and analytical mind of an, "ahem" older person, he manifests a different attraction. He loves reading book after book on the perfect "how to," loves to take the frame apart again and again to get it "just perfect," and pours over equipment magazines to find the dream set up. His skills as a perfectionist wax-technician for ski racers shines through with a focus on the technical gear side of boating. That is his second nature.

Why do I boat? Hmm … I boat to get time on the river. There is nothing like the feel of a boat, the floating, the paddling, the intense times, the quiet times, the stretches of nothingness, and the unseen obstacles requiring quick reaction. Boating is a release, boating is a time of mind-clearing for a mom and a business owner. Time alone on the river with my kayak is my time to release tension and worries and let them go. The river takes them away, downstream and around a bend. Sometimes I half expect to see a stash of worries circling an eddy, but then laugh when they aren't there … I don't worry about the perfect line, or the perfect day, or the perfect river meal. The best days are with friends brand new to boating, to watch their growth, and the melting of their lives into the water. Or to sleep next to my 80-year-old mother in the sand under the stars with our boats tied up close, and then to see the excitement in her eyes the next morning.

Why do I boat? I boat to tie all of these people together, all of these individuals with their different reasons for being there, different feelings, different ideas of the day, to one important goal … to go downriver. It's as simple as that. And then, in the winter, we ski! Also, as simple as that.

Our lives are tied together with ski ties and NRS straps.

Ten Things

Linda Lawless LaStayo & Paul LaStayo

Ten things a newbie private boater notices about family river trips:

1. The most experienced one in the group has the most rag-tag stuff.

It is a guarantee that the boat with the shiniest, newest, matching gear will be the last one rigged. Watch the guy with the mismatched oars and you will learn something about rigging a boat quickly and efficiently.

2. Tents; you are wise to bring them, but un-cool to use them.

There is a bag for them all. They are purchased with the intent of using them. Each owner is quick to talk of their tent's merits and faults, but God forbid they actually get put up! It would take a monsoon to get the guy with the mismatched oars to pitch his.

3. Cook crews get competitive.

Each night the meals get more elaborate with appetizers and pre-dinner cocktails. The guy with the mismatched oars brings a Dutch oven and bakes a chocolate cake on his night.

4. There is always a small kid that no one seems to be responsible for.

This is the kid who is protected by the river gods. He plays with fire, falls in the river repeatedly, and never, ever wears shoes. This will be the child who causes the adults around him endless moments of fear, but will go home without a scratch. Of course, his parents are completely oblivious to the danger he is constantly in and never seem to know exactly where he is. He is never in their boat.

5. Boat boxes create awe and desire.

There is always a 10-minute river box admiration session during rigging. Utilizing its entire capacity is as important as the size of the box. The guy with the mismatched oars never has matching boxes, but the items within are strategically and meticulously organized. His always have multiple river company logos on them and makeshift wooden handles.

6. The location of the absolutely best groover spot seems very important.

According to some, enlightenment has occurred when using a groover in a heavenly location.

7. Kids have reason to be both proud of and embarrassed by their parents.

Proud: organized, great food, childlike enthusiasm, and skilled river abilities.

Embarrassed: nudity, drinking, and really stupid stories told over and over again.

8. The volume of beer seems exorbitant at put-in but is a scarce commodity two days before take-out.

There is never enough beer on a summer trip. Even when it seems like every boat has twice the amount needed, that last beer is gone on the beginning of the last day. It is downhill from there.

9. The coolers; do you drain them or let the water remain?

A randomized controlled study is needed and no one seems to agree on this matter.

10. Tarpology is a science studied and perfected by very few.

—except the guy with the mismatched oars who builds a sauna with hot rocks and tarps.

Where I Belong

Beverly Kurtz

Running rivers is hard. For those of us who are ordinary people, not the sort of bigger than life devotees who live and breathe the river and make it their home, it is very hard. I'm talking the average boater—the ones with a mortgage, a nine-to-five, maybe a couple of kids, certainly a pet or two. Those of us who live a reality far from redrock and the roar of rapids. It's hard for us ordinary folks to find time, hard to gather a crew, hard to organize logistics. It's hard to accumulate the equipment, hard to learn the skills, hard to get the permits, hard to arrange to be away, hard to get there. So why do we do it?

I started running rivers just out of college when I worked as a seasonal archaeologist for the BLM in Grand Junction, Colorado. An experienced and generous co-worker took my best friend and me down the Green River through Desolation and Gray canyons on a week-long lark. We floated on inner tubes, played on the beaches, and thoroughly enjoyed ourselves. We were clueless. Without realizing it, I had tasted something that would change my life. That was more than 30 years ago. Over those years, spending time on rivers has become central to my existence.

When I first met the man who shares The River with me now, we were playing the "get to know you" games that new lovers play. He asked me, "What makes you happiest?" and without a second's hesitation I replied, "The River." He told me later that when I spoke those words, my face lit up and I seemed to sparkle. And he wondered what I meant. He thought it odd that I didn't say, "Going on a river trip" or "Rafting rivers." Rather, I stated it as though "The River" was a living entity that shared my life. And so it is.

The River isn't just a place to me. It is a state of mind and a way of being. It's not a particular river, or even a specific group of people, although the people are integral to the experience. The River is a plane of existence separate from the rest of my life. It is a physical presence to be sure … one made up of contrasts. Blistering sun, icy water, razor sharp stone, velvet sands, stinging rain, feathery willows, hurricane winds, dancing breezes, pounding rapids, glassy pools, silent nights, shrieking laughter. But although those images are accurate, how does one explain to another person who is not as blessed as I to have been there, what it means to run a river? Why do we river rats spend all of our money and all our vacations on rivers? Why are we so passionate about our right to be there? Why isn't it just as good to pay someone else to take us down The River?

What makes running a river trip hard—and why is it worth it? Even after many years I'm not sure how to explain this. Perhaps if I describe what it is like to put together and run a river trip, I can share something of what it means to run a river, on my own, with my own kind.

Getting a Permit

Obtaining a permit is an exercise in bureaucracy and patience. Years ago, I could just call up and get permits a few months or even weeks in advance. But river running has grown in popularity. This is a good thing—the more people who "get" The River, the more likely we can protect it from those who don't understand. But it is now very difficult to get most permits. If I am getting my own permit, I will be signing up myself and a group of friends to an activity that will take place sometime in the future—anywhere from a week to two years hence. I need to identify lots of details like where and when we will put in and take out, how many people will be in our party, how many and what type of boats we will be using. Committing to this requires access to appropriate resources, as well as confidence in one's abilities to plan and manage.

If I can't get my own permit, or don't want to be the permit holder, the alternative is to get invited on someone else's permit. This means learning the system, networking, marketing myself, and making sure that I am always a good participant on other people's trips—you are more likely to be invited if you have a good reputation. Many folks find their own marketing niche; I'm a good organizer, I have tons of experience, I have a huge boat and will carry anything, I'm an outstanding cook, I have a margarita machine! One must be careful that you are marketing to the right group though, since the people you are with will fundamentally affect your river experience.

Selecting a Crew

The people make the trip. If I run my own trip, I get to choose with whom to share it. This is one of the biggest draws to doing non-commercial trips. If I am on someone else's permit, the pressure is off … I just have to deal with whomever they invited once we get to The River. But if I am the permit holder then I need to decide who to invite. There are the people I "owe" since they invited me on their last trip. There are the people I trust because they've been with me through thick and thin. There are the people who have interesting backgrounds who I'd like to get to know better. There are the inexperienced people I want to share The River with. There are the people I'd like to include because of specific skills they have; EMTs are a particular favorite of mine, as are physical therapists, musicians, and anyone with culinary skill!

In deciding on my invitations, I have to consider who will get along. Just because I like or respect all the folks I'm inviting, I must think through the dynamics. Will that childless couple really enjoy 18 days with a young river princess? Perhaps the wild and crazy nudist will not mesh well with the introverted environmentalist I am introducing to The River. Of course, once I've decided who will make up my ideal group, the realities of scheduling may blow it all and I'll end up with a crew of people who are just a big question mark. It's good to know, however, that after 30 years I've often found that the groups that didn't sound ideal in the beginning, ended up being the best crews of all. You never know what magic The River might work on people.

Planning and Packing

For most of us ordinary people, a river trip is our major vacation for the year. We want our time on The River to be fun and stress free—and organizing things ahead of time will help meet that goal. There is a lot of work to be done on river trips. Setting up camp, selecting a groover site, cooking, and cleaning up are all group chores that need to be shared. Part of the fun and bonding that happens on non-commercial river trips is learning how others do these things, inventing new ideas, and working together. Pre-assigned chores and responsibilities simplify the daily routines. Everyone knows when they are on duty and when they can kick back. You can deal with all kinds of disorganization on a three-day trip, and you can put up with just about anything for a week. But for a long trip, or for peace of mind on any trip, assigning things ahead of time introduces a semblance of order into what can be a chaotic environment.

Taking the time to plan equipment and menus, to buy the right stuff, and to organize how it is packed so you can find it again weeks later, is no mean undertaking. Weeks, or even months before a put-in, the Trip Leader needs to decide who will provide which equipment and what meals each person will plan to ensure that all the bases are covered. It's important that the group has everything they need—but equally important to eliminate duplication. After all, everything does have to fit on the boats.

Packing is an art. Rafting equipment is large and heavy and, over the years, gear seems to proliferate. Most of us gave up backpacking many years ago and we love our river gadgets. So—everything goes. That battery-operated lime juicer just has to fit in somewhere. And of course the stuffed beaver that graces the bow of the boat is critical to a successful run of Lava. Regardless of how long your trip is to be, one fact always emerges … once you load the truck or trailer it is always completely, totally full. How can it be full for a three-day trip when we can carry everything in the same vehicle for an 18-day trip? Go figure! Somehow though, it all fits in and it's time to hit the road.

Getting to The River

Caravanning with my fellow river rats to the put-in is fun and introduces a degree of safety. It also can take forever. A quick stop at a grocery store or trading post can turn into an extended visit. The intent may be to just pick up something for breakfast, but somehow everyone spreads out under the fluorescent lights and soon we are all sucked into a vortex of indecision. Did we bring enough trash bags? Should I buy some more fruit? WHAT DID I FORGET? Hours later we all emerge, wallets thinner and plastic bags bulging with items that we don't really need and that won't fit into the overflowing pickups anyway!

Driving to the put-in is fraught with potential delays. Vehicles may break down. Dallying on side trips to interesting attractions or unexpected road construction may add hours of travel time. But finally, somehow, whether it's as a group or straggling in by ones and twos, everyone arrives at the put-in. What a relief!

Put-in and Shuttle

Put-ins are always a bit stressful, especially for the Trip Leader. Is everyone going to show up? Did everyone bring what they were supposed to? Is the river ranger going to give us grief? The mood is light-hearted but with a touch of tension. Lots of sorting, separation of piles, head scratching, and a general triage occurs as equipment erupts from the depths of pickup beds. Then there are hours of hauling and pumping and strapping. But at some point the Trip Leader finally shouts "SHUTTLE!"

I like being a shuttle driver. As I clamber into whatever vehicle I am shuttling and head to the take-out, I can finally relax and think about what's to come. Whether it's two nights on the Moab Daily, a week on Cataract Canyon, or three on the Grand, the anticipation is like a drug. I turn up the stereo and blast out tunes as I rattle down dusty roads, eager for the feel of water under rubber tubes and the searing sun on my face. At the take-out, we all lock up our trucks and jam into the assigned shuttle vehicle to travel back to the put-in. As we chatter and share memories and expectations, I know that in just a bit I will be back where I belong. On The River.

At last ... The River

Being on The River is like a prayer. It calms me. It enables me to put things in perspective. Despite the work and the frenzy in planning and getting there, once you push off from the put-in beach, everything slows down. There is an immediate feeling of relief and release, overlaid with a sense of anticipation and excitement. It is coming home to something familiar and soothing, but always with a promise. The trip to come may prove dangerous or easy, with perfect weather or disastrous winds, breathtaking adventure or much needed relaxation. But whatever is to come, I know it will feed my soul and allow me to remember who I am.

It takes several days for me to leave my usual life behind and completely slip into the rhythm of The River. My senses are first soothed and then sharpened by the lack of modern technology. No ringing phones, blinking email, blaring TVs, or newscasters reporting situations half a mile or half a world away that break my heart. At some point I realize that I'm not sure what day it is. I can't remember the password to my computer—or even what I actually "do for a living." Describing my "real life" to someone while on The River almost always makes me laugh, as it seems so ridiculous in the context of river reality.

A day or two on The River and I am in the here and now. Whether I am stretched under the sun for a mid-day snooze, or hunkered down under the biting onslaught of a surprise desert shower, I can actually feel where I am. This sense of living now, experiencing every moment, tasting the air, feeling the stone, touching life is what draws me again and again. There is no tomorrow, there is no yesterday. I am just here. I open my mind to senses dulled by my fast moving, goal-oriented other life. I see, I hear, I smell, I taste, I feel. And doing so, I am happy.

On The River everything is simplified. Time is measured by side canyons slipping by, rapids descended, shadows lengthening. Decisions are fundamental. Should we camp? Do I want to eat? Do I need to pee? Have we scouted enough? Will I hit that slot next to the big rock? Some of these decisions could have major ramifications. But most are simple and straightforward. Some you make alone. Some you make with the group. Give and take, think of what's best for the group, share your ideas and knowledge. The harsher the conditions, the fewer games are played, and the more people reveal themselves.

As I said, The River is a living being to me. As with every living being, it is affected by whom it is with. I can withdraw from the group and experience The River on my own for some period of time. Sitting on a rock, contemplating space, time, relationships, or oblivion is a solitary endeavor. Floating alone on a boat, feeling the current and letting my mind drift, allows me to reorder priorities and focus on what is important. It's an opportunity to consider how relative everything is and to decide what really does matter. This reflection inevitably leads me back to the group of people I have chosen to share this experience with.

The Tribe

The River is there, no matter whom you share it with. But the people who experience it with you change the way you see it. The reactions of people new to The River remind us of what our first trips were like. Knowing grins are exchanged among old friends. There is no joy I know as deep as sharing memories with those I've been on The River with before. My dearest friends, my soul mates, have all shared rivers with me. Our lives are intertwined in a fashion that defies description and in a way that most people, unfortunately, will never experience. The interdependency on a river trip can connect people more deeply and permanently than non-river people could ever understand. It is a fundamental bonding, tribal experience that I've not found elsewhere in today's hurried world.

River people joke about the classic "No Shit, there I was ..." stories that we all tell. But it is fascinating to me that we can tell the same stories over and over again, year after year, and never tire of them. The details may change a bit over time, but we don't care. In our hearts, we know what really happened and that what truly matters is that we were there, together. On The River. Sometimes the tales are of life and death, sometimes they are of absurdity, sometimes of beauty. But always the stories warm our hearts as we glance at one another with laughter, fear, and love. We were THERE. We tell it again and again.

The tribe plays. We slow down. We are silly. Where else in our adult lives would we strap life jackets on our butts, grab each other's legs and create a human train to navigate rushing, turquoise water through travertine ledges? Where else would we sit in a circle and seriously discuss, much less practice, a symphony of farts? Where else would we lug small boulders into swirling eddies, competing to walk the farthest under water before dropping our loads and springing to the surface? Where else would we perform shadow plays on redwall cliffs in the light of the moon? We become children again. We laugh. Oh, how we laugh!

We rise with the sun and sleep when we're tired. We climb steep canyon walls to search out mysterious rock art left by the ancient ones. Or we may sit, mesmerized, watching ripples in the water for hours on end while we debate weighty or nonsensical topics. We hike in unbearable heat to magical, hidden places where we splash and play as five-year-olds would. Time has no meaning. We don't know the day. We don't care what is happening "out there."

We respect The River and we depend on one another for safety. Perhaps we cling a bit closer together because we need to remind ourselves of our humanity and our importance in this vertical world where we, as individuals, are dwarfed. Whether scouting Hance at low water or navigating Satan's Gut in flood, the adrenaline gets us through. But it is the shared exaltation when we are all safely below the rapids that is the core of the experience. We did it. Together we are ALIVE.

Take-Out

The longer the trip, the more difficult the take-out is for me. If it's been 18 days on the Grand, my blood has turned silty and I have become dependent on the tribe. I remember rounding the corner to see Diamond Creek at the end of such a trip and watching with complete understanding as a lone kayaker paddled furiously back upstream, only pausing in her strokes to state firmly that she would not leave. Regardless of what we have shared and how close we have become, I know that the tribe will disband within hours of take-out. Friendships and connections will remain, but that particular group, in that particular place, will not again coalesce. It saddens my heart.

Sharp edged thoughts of my other life poke unmercifully into my consciousness. I think of things I have put away and I struggle to keep them in perspective, or to hide them again for a few more hours. The mood is usually somber as everyone shares the sense of finality as we pull into shore.

Take-outs involve lots of hard, physical labor and people are often not very happy. The logistics facing us can be overwhelming as we are jolted from our now familiar river routines to deal with de-rigging, packing trucks, driving home, unpacking, cleaning up, catching up. There may be tension, confusion, orders given, or extended silences while we toil in the sun. But then the mood will lighten as someone throws a bucket of icy water on a sweating back. People laugh as they tease about things that happened on the trip. We smile at one another, sharing the knowledge that we have experienced something unique and priceless. Hugs and promises are exchanged. A picture party is planned—something to look forward to, the knowledge that the tribe will reconnect.

I always go alone to the water's edge before leaving. I look upstream and close my eyes and remember. If I am very fortunate, it is quiet, and I hear a canyon wren. I taste the desert air and I struggle to firmly implant the sensations washing over me in my mind. I will need to call on those memories in my other life. As hard as it is to run a river, the hardest thing of all is leaving The River to go back home.

Re-entry

Thank goodness for pets and a wonderful home. It is good to be there. Breathing the crisp mountain air. Enjoying hot showers. Luxuriating in the unbelievable softness of sand-free sheets against skin and the feel of carpet under cracked feet. Reveling in the rumbling purrs of contented cats and the doggy smiles from our joyful pup. The rest of my "real life" slowly takes over. Back to work, back to schedules, back to unending decisions and interacting with all those people who aren't part of my tribe and never will be. I often harbor a feeling of superiority—these people don't know, and can't know, what I know— and I remind myself that despite my sometimes overwhelming sense of loss at no longer being on The River, I am so incredibly fortunate to have been there.

So, why do we do it?

Weeks, months, or years after a trip I certainly remember what The River was like as it is always a part of me, deep inside. But I spend most of my life in a very different world. Then one day something will happen to bring my longings to the surface. Perhaps I'll run into a fellow river rat, maybe one I've shared a trip with. Or I'll get an email advertising a sale at the local rafting store or catch a documentary on TV about a wild river. Suddenly my heart beats a little faster. My mind kicks into gear. Tears come unbidden. Not because I am unhappy, but because the memories trigger a desire, a need inside of me that I simply can't ignore. Once again, The River beckons and other interests evaporate. When can we go next?

Why do I do it? Because I can. It's what I'm good at. Because if I'm away too long, I find myself listless, wandering, lost. I need to be on The River regularly to balance my reality, to maintain an understanding of who I am and where I fit in the world. I get a tremendous sense of accomplishment from running a river. Being part of a tribe, learning from them, sharing the grandeur, the danger, the laughter, the joy has become integral to my happiness. I depend on The River to help me keep things in perspective, to rejuvenate my spirit, to open my mind and senses, to challenge me. I do it because I must. It is my church, my magic, my source of contentment, my teacher, and my refuge. The River is my home, it is where I belong. And no matter how hard it is to get there, or to be there, I will always go back.

Dancing with the River to the Center of the Universe

Scott C. Ramsey

River running has been my passion and profession for the past three decades. I have found my way on rivers all over the world, and have been blessed to share my love for navigating waterways while qualifying hundreds of river guides over the past twenty years. Being on the river is always my yearning and, fortunately, it is sometimes my occupation.

When pressed to answer why I love being on the river and participating in river trips, the answer is that the river makes me feel whole and alive. Simply put, rivers provide me a physical, mental, and spiritual wellness. Although this array of benefits might seem to thoroughly state what I derive from being on the water, it touches only the surface of the story of why I am a boater who craves being on, near, or in the water.

One remarkable private river trip for me takes place in June, in the early years of the 21st century. I am on the Tatshenshini River (Tat), the headwaters of which lie in British Columbia, Canada. Our cadre of more than a dozen rafters has successfully navigated the rapids in a two-mile section of a canyon, despite the cold onslaught of waves that rise from the surface of the water as they collide with a multitude of rocks on their way to the sea. Some of this displaced water breaks across my lap and slaps my chin, a cold reminder that this water is barely above the point of freezing and is not long from glaciers and snow-capped mountains.

This is just the start of a multi-day trip down a 190-mile-long river that flows undammed to the Pacific Ocean along the open coast near Dry Bay, Alaska. On its journey, it will join its sister river, the Alsek, in roughly 100 miles, and take her name in matrimony. This river system, over ten times the volume of the Colorado River through the Grand Canyon, is the only drainage that carves its way through this rugged, remote country that holds some of the last vestiges of the Little Ice Age and the Pleistocene Epoch.

The Tat is part of the Kluane / Wrangell-St. Elias / Glacier Bay / Tatshenshini-Alsek UNESCO World Heritage Site, the largest protected area on the planet, representing a staggering 24,205,983 acres. This World Heritage Site signifies a multi-national grass-roots victory over mining interests; protecting and celebrating the ecological and cultural importance of the area. The vast park system spans the border of Canada and the United States and is home to the largest brown bear population in the world. Wolves, moose, and mountain goats are among the many animals that also richly populate this immense region. Its pristine character can be summed up by the fact that you can drink the water from the river.

In this wilderness setting, we begin our second day on the river. There are many ideal camps downstream, but for now we let the river decide our destination. The sun has come out to finish drying our life jackets and clothes from yesterday's wild run. The character of the river has begun to change dramatically. No longer a relatively small, heavily forested stream—whose origin looks like that of many western rivers— today the Tat is uniquely Alaskan and Canadian. The scenery begins to open up and the vast background now provides sweeping panoramas of a multitude of valleys. Centuries ago, these vast basins were sculpted by glaciers that dominated this landscape, stretching beyond the borders of Alaska and Canada into the Lower 48. Today the glacial holdouts from this era are still significantly influencing the river, despite being a fraction of their former size.

Each new side canyon adds more water and sediment to the growing river, contributing to its rapid morphology. This combination creates an ever-changing maze, the river dividing into multiple channels, splitting and uniting as it finds its way through the immense U-shaped valley. River rats call this unique feature *braiding*. Navigating a river with this exceptional characteristic is extremely challenging, but fulfilling beyond words. It symbolizes many of the qualities that I love about being on the river. Making the necessary moves to get into a chosen channel requires skill and tuning into patterns. However, regardless of the level of proficiency a boater has previously acquired, successfully negotiating braided sections such as these requires going beyond skill, relinquishing ambition to control the river, and tapping into something bigger. In the simple words of Yoda, one of the great philosophers and instructors of our time, "*We must trust the force.*"

As we go downriver, the added volume from each glacial valley increases the complexity of the river. For today, the river party successfully navigates the maze. We reflect upon our day at camp, where I am reminded that this is a particularly mindful group that seems to balance an effortless flow through camp chores with an elevated level of resonance with this wilderness setting. They are distinctive and dedicated to spending the next ten days focused on meditation, yoga, and overall wellness in this special venue. I am not new to yoga or eating organic food, but I am unaccustomed to this type of assemblage on a river.

One of my friends organized the trip to include a modern-day shaman. At first glance you would not pick him out as such; however, after gazing into his blue-gray eyes, it takes only seconds to sense that this dude has it going on. Several years earlier, my beautiful, in-tune wife introduced me to David LaChappelle, who was leading a workshop that we were to attend. Within a matter of moments of our introduction, David looked beyond my eyes and, as if reading from my soul, began to recite an eloquent poem that encapsulated the entire essence of my being. He had captured parts of me that even I could not have pronounced.

In an attempt to give back to the group on this river trip, David has offered to assign each member an undertaking to work on during the trip. I welcome this opportunity. David identifies my mission as a practice of releasing my will on the river. Initially, this seems strange considering my level of respect for the river. But recognizing David's uncanny and profound insight, I am inspired to investigate this perspective.

After dinner, around the campfire, we chat about the coming day. We break out the maps and discuss our proximity to the confluence of the Tatshenshini and Alsek rivers. Those of us who know the tale, discuss the hydrological significance of the intersection. We explain that despite the size of the Tat, the Alsek we are approaching is twice its volume. The Alsek's flow commonly exceeds 250,000 cubic feet per second (cfs) at this juncture. This is a staggering number for boaters, considering that the Colorado River through the Grand Canyon commands boaters' respect at a released volume of 15,000-24,000 cfs. The sheer size of the river at this point challenges boaters' perceptions and their ability to read water.

Where the two rivers join there is a relatively small bedrock island in the middle of a three-mile-wide glacial valley. Geologists call this type of feature a *nunatak,* a glacial island that has survived the time when glaciers scoured the valley. This island lies in an auspicious spot on the map. The Tat, flowing from the east, joins the Alsek arriving from the north, to head west. During the Pleistocene, the glaciers of the Alsek headed across the valley, toward the ocean to the south to what is called Tarr Inlet today. In other words, this island marks the center of four enormous valleys that form a cross. Boaters who know of this area refer to this as the Center of the Universe.

As in ancient times, river runners have a way of naming things and passing stories down generation to generation, commonly enhancing details around the fire. In many ways, the lore of the Center of the Universe may seem like such a story. Curiously, there are pictographs carved into a granite embankment on the island. They are examples of only a few known relics of this type from the native Tlingit and Athabascans. These illustrations are a series of circles within one another with lines coming out like rays of the sun in the four directions— depicting the center of their universe? Similarly, early native traders came down the Tat in the summer on their way to fishing villages in Dry Bay. In the winter they would drag their canoes over the ice and snow from Tarr Inlet, up into the Alsek drainage to find game. This was the center of their universe.

Regardless of the historical interpretations, this powerful spot has rich cultural significance. It seems to be an obvious place to take this enlightened group, along with our shaman. Considering our proximity to the island, going there is congruent with our flexible itinerary.

There is one issue, however. Regardless of the excitement of the group to experience this sacred spot, the river simply might not go there. Considering the sheer volume and force of the water, we are hoping for a route that takes us there so we can experience this spectacle.

The next morning I wake early to build a fire and, after finishing my last round of cook duties for the next few days, I head to the boats to begin my morning ritual. I love rigging my boat and arranging the various bags and gear in a way that distributes the weight evenly, secures the items in case of an unexpected flip, and provides easy access to things I might need during the day, such as my binoculars or an extra layer of clothing. This tinkering process, often referred to by boaters as dakking, grounds me for the day to come. Donning my life jacket, I brush my teeth and pay reverence to the river by splashing water on top of my head and my heart. My morning ritual prepares me for the final loading of passengers and their personal gear.

We are a four-boat flotilla consisting of more than a dozen people, many of whom have boating experience on other rivers, but only five of us with experience on a river of this intensity. Consequently, those of us with the most experience on these rivers row most of the time. Having boated this river dozens of times, and others like it, for the past two decades, I have been appointed the Trip Leader. The designation of a Trip Leader is required for the permitting process, but also provides a successful organizational structure to most river trips. I am grateful for this opportunity because it grants me the first position down the river, a position I savor.

On the river, as the blood courses through my veins, I am compelled to stand and join the river in her dance. A rhythmical rhumba ensues that emanates from somewhere beyond me. I feel a primal, harmonious union with the river. I surrender in accordance with her lead. Despite the intricacies of this dynamic river, I am present. This exceptional unity restores me and fills my soul. This connection is central to why I boat.

We make our way into the main current. I liken this river system to a train. Sometimes you are on the main line, and sometimes you get off on the country line. Currently we are in the flow, riding the ribbon of light as it courses toward the ocean, making good time. I am dancing with the river, enjoying the feeling of dipping my oars into the water and matching the current's tempo. She is strong and getting stronger.

As we approach the next section, I recognize that we are nearing Melt Creek. It is a crystal blue tributary, coming from the Melbourne Glacier, and is bigger than most rivers that boaters run in the Lower 48. Its electric-azure color is caused by the settling effect of a lake at the toe of the glacier. The build-up of outwash from Melt Creek forces the multiple channels of this river to bend toward the confluence with the Alsek. Our next 30 minutes will decide whether we make it to the island or not.

I begin to work my way toward the island. It is a struggle to fight across the current and find a clear path to our destination. I find myself sitting now, concentrating on the river. It is not easy. Suddenly, as if someone is tapping me softly on my shoulder, I turn around. Despite his location in a boat several hundred yards behind me, David's penetrating eyes catch mine. Instantly I recognize what is happening: I am forcing my will on the river. I am supposed to be an actor in the play rather than the director. The real director exists well beyond me, or anyone for that matter.

I smile, nod to myself, stand back up, and push back into the flow. I decide to relinquish my hold on my desire to control our destiny. Upon reflection, I realize that my drive to show the group this special spot reflects my own ambitions and, regardless of my intentions, does not account for the will of the river. This is less of an ego thing (although ego certainly has its part) and more of a perspective thing. In my attunement and realignment to an eco-centric perspective, I acknowledge the river as a character and conductor of the trip.

There is a moment when I realize the river's verdict. She indeed brings us to the island. After securing the boats and preparing to explore this mystical place, I approach David. His nod is all I need to confirm my experience. Tuning into the force, going with the flow, and taking an actor's role rather than that of a director will become life lessons, ones for which I will always thank David and the river.

To this day, I ponder my assignment from David and its ramifications. The lesson symbolizes a chief reason I love being on the river: its ability to emphasize the importance and power of nature, particularly water. River trips reconnect us to nature in a way that no other type of trip can. River running provides an opportunity to tap into a state of grace that is bigger than we are, filling our spirit and soul. This refueling is what pilgrims have sought for centuries, a connection to something that transcends our human form.

In this respect, running rivers can be a spiritual endeavor, with the added bonus of filling our senses in nature's cathedral. The kaleidoscope of color and sheer grandeur of this landscape endows a feeling of humility and awe. The touch of cold water enlivens and reminds me to be grateful to be healthy and alive. The sound of the river both soothes and invigorates. The smell revitalizes, and the fresh air fills our lungs, bringing oxygen to our blood that flows in us like the river herself. Riding this flow, honoring her rhythm, is a spiritual form of meditation.

My recent life journey has taken me deeper into the world of academia, though my passion for the river and her mysterious powers remains strong. The river continues to captivate me and has inspired the focus of my dissertation. I have begun to explore why there is a special connection with the river and with water. There are lessons that can be learned from river travel that can be brought into our everyday lives on *terra firma*.

Perhaps this connection with the river may even stem from our evolutionary background. After all, our human ancestors bravely crept from their existence in the water to a bold new life on land. In many ways we brought this heritage and reliance on water with us physiologically, with water making up more than two-thirds of our essence. As a *new* creature, we flourished. From a watery world of the womb, we emerged and populated this world. For millennia, civilizations were built along the river's edge, developing socio-cultural relationships that tied us to water. We were connected to water and relied on this connection for survival.

However, over time, as humans began to spread across the land and supplement their lives with advanced technologies, we began to lose connection to the water and nature. Many reflect that this disconnect comes from not knowing where our water or food comes from. Most of us no longer must go to the well or the creek to get our water. Rather, it is mysteriously pumped in from somewhere else. Our obsession with bottled water mirrors this disconnection. Our planet suffers.

Healthy rivers represent a healthy ecology. They symbolize a balance between the heavens and the earth. They epitomize a sense of freedom and purity. We depend on their health for our own vitality and survival. Similarly, the entire planet's health is contingent on the wellness of river systems. Certainly, river running can feed our physical, mental, and spiritual body. But it has the potential to do much more by reconnecting us with nature and rewiring our appreciation for what we find there. These are important lessons in these challenging times. As John Medina summarized in his book, *Brain Rules,* humans have evolved to be at our best when we are outside, in motion, problem solving with others. These sound exactly like the characteristics of a river trip. These types of experiences can bring the best out of us. They can help us get in touch with the courage required to become unstoppable, and with the insight so needed in our world today.

Let's go boating!

A Boatload of Work
Andrew G. Bentley

Why should anyone bother with noncommercial, "private" river trips? It's a simple enough idea to pump a boat, slide it into the river, and start floating to the take-out. However, to say that the list of hurdles that must be jumped to implement this idea is short would be a gross underestimation, particularly as applied to multi-day trips. The challenges are so numerous that it's a wonder that anyone would consider doing it at all. Drawing on my personal and professional experiences as a private boater, a multi-day commercial guide, and a seasonal river ranger, I understand the major challenges faced by private boaters to prepare and run a great trip. In light of these challenges, this essay considers a few scientific theories to explain the behavior of planning and participating in private whitewater boating trips. I have included several haiku as I find that a useful means for sharing specific moments from my own boating experiences that pertain to describing the barriers to, and theories of, private whitewater boating.

Rafts are heavy to transport and awkward to store. Moving a deflated, rolled up raft is like wrestling with a sea lion. It takes creativity, some swearing, and, if you attempt this alone, the risk of throwing out your back (which leads to more swearing). A two-person carry is a much better idea, but still requires a partner not offend by the swearing. Keeping boats in good repair is a challenge—and fixing issues is even more difficult. Having punctured a hole in their raft, many a boater has opened a repair kit with the intent of a quick fix, only to find their glue has evaporated. Or, if one has fresh glue, they must be prepared to plug their nose. Repairing inflatable rafts requires strong solvents known to cause cancer in California—they probably cause cancer in other states too.

To protect certain characteristics of North American river corridors, and to provide positive visitor experiences, there are an increasing number of government resource management directives in place to incentivize certain visitor behaviors in favor of minimizing others. In an era of increased demand for access, regulations have become vital to river managers. For the private boater, this requires understanding a patchwork quilt of management regulations that differ from place to place, and where rules may or may not be enforced by various agencies. As examples:

- Group size limits are commonly enforced, although those limits vary widely from river to river.

- Rules about campfires abound. They are allowed in some places and not in others, sometimes with seasonal bans. Or the collection of driftwood for campfires is banned, even though fires themselves are still allowed. Specialized firepans are commonly required to catch the campfire ashes, and that dictates the relative size of the fires.

- Human waste must be transported out of most US river corridors (thankfully) and some land management agencies dictate the use of certain types of human waste containers.

- The same can be said about life jackets—a specific type of jacket is required on some rivers. God forbid if one was to sew an additional lash tab on their jacket for an accessory—that would be grounds for a ticket on at least one American river. Much of this is a far cry from the standards in other countries, where crafty boaters historically sewed their own lifejackets on home sewing machines.

- To the uninitiated, it may come as a surprise that even campsites on several rivers are preassigned before launching. Due to archeological protection or tribal and private property rights, entire shorelines may be closed to foot travel or beaching of watercraft.

Unpacking stored raft
Rubber heavy drags on ground
Dances on water

Can't afford groover
Five-gallon bucket with lid
Ranger not laughing
Head to toe soap suds
Rafter warned not in hot spring
A ticket written

Oarlock squeak
Interrupts quiet canyon
With every stroke

Government rules are typically bound to a set of regulations governing how private boaters obtain official permission to travel rivers; that is, through a non-commercial, river permit system. For many North American rivers there are a limited number of openings available for those who wish to use their own boats, yet a seemingly infinite number of private individuals and commercial interests wanting access. Thus, non-commercial river permits are a challenge to secure, and even more so during peak times of the warmer weather of the North American summer time. A variety of allocation structures exist to equitably distribute permits to private parties. Each waitlist or lottery system has its own set of stipulations, due dates, and application fees for the private boater to manage. When applying for several river permits, one might spend hundreds of dollars with no guarantee of successfully winning even one. Some private boaters try to "game" the system by applying for access during the less-used shoulder seasons— the colder, less hospitable times of year. On the most popular American rivers that also have adequate early and late season flows, the breadth of dates represented by a "peak period" is growing wider due to this shift of permit application behavior.

Hands clasped in prayer
Grand Canyon trip lottery
Thousands will enter

My lips turn a frown
Head and shoulders droop
12th permit lottery lost

Moonbeams bathe my face
River sand covers my feet
Won the permit game!

Reaching the river is frequently an ordeal. Bound for launch sites, boaters using little-traveled roads with deep pot-holes keep some automotive garages and towing services in business! Some roads have well-deserved reputations for numbing the vehicle occupants and producing multiple flat-tires over miles of washboard. On these roads it is not uncommon for vehicle and trailer axles to break. Drivers on their way to Utah's Desolation section of the Green River are reminded of the challenges of making it to the put-in by discarded and bent rims, shredded tires, and the occasional muffler seen along the shoulder of the road. Some roads traverse under well-worn avalanche paths or, like the road to Boundary Creek in central Idaho, may lay covered under several feet of winter snow until late spring, only to change to wheel-spinning mud that may require a tow strap and assistance from another 4x4 to move forward.

Unlike theme-park lazy rivers that start and end at the same place, traveling on real rivers require arranging reconnecting with vehicles. River trip participants must allow ample time or money to shuttle vehicles between launch and take-out points. Even with good roads, some river shuttles add days of vehicle travel to the trip length, requiring drives of great distances around mountain ranges that otherwise are traversed only by the river. I completed my own vehicle shuttle for Idaho's Main Salmon because of a soon-to-be disillusioned belief it was worth the cost savings over paying one of the local shuttle companies. That logic came into very serious question after the 15th hour of driving, a similar number of cups of coffee, and the realization that there was still another hour to go—and that was after I changed a tire that flatted after hitting some recent rock fall in the road.

Avalanche path
Closed road to river launch
Hand shovels moved tons

Suspension sags
Washboard road, trailer wheel snaps
Axle dragging noise

Much swearing
One spare tire and two flats
Miles from nowhere

Invite 10 friends on a private trip and there will be 10 different preferences for breakfast foods, 10 preferences for lunch, and 10 more for dinner. It follows that organizing the caloric needs for a group on a multi-day trip is formidable. Not only does one need to account for the amount of food and various eating preferences and habits, but securing the food itself takes much time and effort. Multi-day river trips commonly use menu-style planning. A 10-day raft trip will require extensive decision making to plan, purchase, and pack each item necessary to create up to 30 separate meals, not including snacks in-between. The meal planner, or planners, are essentially putting together menus and procuring food much as a restaurant would. But restaurants negotiate orders with standing vendors at significant bulk cost savings, and food is delivered to a loading dock with forklifts, pallet jacks, or hand trucks. Private boaters largely secure these items by local shopping trips done personally.

Private Trip Leaders
Bizarre rules sometimes backfire
Bring your own meat trip

Canned fish on sale
Six sardine-breath filled days
Is not attractive

Cashier's eyes roll
Six stuffed shopping carts
Forgot my wallet

Commercial river trip outfitters have simplified life for individuals wanting to participate in river rafting trips by eliminating the need for them to personally handle the enormous amount of "work" required to go boating. Their extensive services provide specialized vehicles to successfully carry thousands of pounds of equipment and people to the launch point over poor roads, warehouses to store and repair equipment, relationships with commercial food suppliers and wholesale purchase discounts for river equipment, and, perhaps most importantly, deep knowledge on how best to safely navigate hazardous rapids while travelling between campsite locations, each spaced a day's length apart from each other. That a thriving commercial sector is supported by a wide range of populations wanting access to remote wildlands, wilderness areas, or protected scenic landscapes is, perhaps, a testament to the need for the commercial guide industry. An internet search about whitewater rafting quickly uncovers the enormity of the river guiding industry both in North America and abroad. Without the extensive framework provided by commercial operations, most individuals typically lack access to the many structures used to streamline the long list of trip logistics. This makes asking the following question, then, even more important: why would anyone bother with private river trips? That is, why in the face of serious challenges, do there remain thousands of steadfast recreational boaters who find commercial trips unappealing?

Considering this idea, I reviewed several of the online boating forums and found a common thread among deeply committed private boaters, including some who shun the idea of participating as a "client," "custy," or "peep" on a guided trip as if it were somehow antithetical to their existence.

> First time gripping oars
> Captain's chair preference grew
> Passenger no more

Users of online forums are not alone in discussing reasons why private boaters do what they do. Scholars in the leisure, recreation, and parks fields have long considered the motivation for these types of experiences and provide a well-developed line of thinking. The common definition of leisure is "unobligated time where activities occur with no commitment to others." That is, they are of one's own choosing. Other definitions suggest leisure is simply a residual of time left over from paid work and household labor (cooking, cleaning, etc.). Recreation is defined as an activity occurring during leisure time, where one spends time to "re-create" themselves in some fashion. Private boating fits this description well and, according to *Relaxation Theory*, private boaters take trips in order to turn themselves "off" or to unplug from their daily routines.

A necessary condition of this process is that a recreation experience is, by nature, voluntary—a distinction that separates private boaters from professional river guides. Even if a guide freely selects their workplace schedule and their watercraft, thus appearing to act out of their own volition, work is an obligatory activity where time has been commodified in a structure typically dictated by the controls of others.

> Private trip floats by
> Guides watch from their camp kitchen
> Wishing it was them?

While some may cringe to hear it referred to in this manner, at its simplest, private boating is almost mechanical—a means to an end, that shares much in common with commercial trips. That is, it's a tool that moves one across the water to a fishing hole inaccessible and only seen (or drooled over) from afar. It's a way to reach the backcountry in pursuit of autumn game, or to collect antler sheds from the high country in spring. It allows individuals to soak in rarely seen hot springs, gaze upon ancient rock art sites, or to watch wildlife. These endeavors are not the strict domain of private boating trips, and certainly are common to commercial tour operator marketing efforts as well. What *is* very different, and key to the private boating draw, is the high degree of autonomy realized in decision-making about how one's experience unfolds. Private boaters have the ability, for example, to spend far more time visiting particular locations. Whereas commercial operators might spend a few minutes at a natural arch, hot spring, or archeological site, private boaters may choose an extended stay to explore a special place. What is more, private boaters are able to decide on a whim to stop the trip for an hour or more to watch a herd of bighorn sheep negotiate a steep cliffside. With the exception of a completely customized expedition, this level of autonomy seldom exists for clients or guides of commercial trips. For example, when the fly fishing heated up during a spring float of Idaho's Middle Fork of the Salmon, my whole trip spent an additional two hours at the beach to allow anglers in the group to enjoy it.

> Bighorn silhouetted
> Stoically eyes me floating
> Unconcerned

Rainbow takes the hook
Dancing rod bends double
Line sings taught

Trout biting fiercely
Every second or third cast
Thirty-six by lunch

Boaters are, by nature, problem solvers. They like the sensation of making decisions and overcoming challenges. Each day, a river trip presents thousands of decisions, chief among them the navigation of watercraft, guarding group safety, and coping with difficult environmental conditions and weather events. Excellent boat captains will simultaneously balance their efforts to read river currents and scan for hazards. They can instantaneously flick a wrist to shift their boat position to avoid pour-overs, while maintaining appropriate following distance from other watercraft or the shoreline. They are (hopefully) prepared to be of assistance whenever needed. In a strong metaphor of community, they set safety and will run first or last as needed, according to the skills and needs of the group. These needs serve to drive the behaviors of private boaters.

Optimal Arousal Theory suggests that individuals seek complexity or novelty that is neither too boring nor anxiety producing but is psychologically fulfilling. The balance can be hard to find. Some boaters find optimization through opportunities to practice craftsmanship. The online forums abound with user-submitted photos reflecting great pride in customizing their particular watercraft with various accoutrements; from store bought drink holders to home-built, custom cut, plywood decks, to welded frames made in home shops, to bimini covers typically seen only on power craft. Others take great care in the trim of their watercraft, and direct their passengers to sit in particular locations to avoid unbalanced loads and a subsequent tracking effect. Some particularly enjoy the challenge of a well packaged gear pile that is rigged to flip. Still others spend a great deal of time considering and executing what they believe to be an excellent camp kitchen layout given particular campsite parameters—best view to the river, access to the shoreline, etc.

Decisions, decisions
Friends, meals, hikes, gear and camps
It's why I boat

Bank full current
Loosens rocks and dirt
Roots lose their grip

Moist smell of fresh dirt
Sweeps my nose cavity
Flash flood coming

Four days pelting rain
Ponderosa pine floats by
Rafters grow concerned

The freedom to be unbound from the structures inherent to guided trips presents private boaters with an intrinsically rewarding experience. They can come and go as they please. They can choose to engage more in activities that optimize their interests to reach a heightened mental state, and less in activities that don't. When one becomes enmeshed with the experience to the point that the lines blur between time, space, and self, the activities of private boating present a prime opportunity to experience the mental state of *Flow*. Noted positive psychologist Mihaly Csikszentmihalyi described the experiences of *Flow* as those where the level of challenge appropriately meets one's physical and mental capacities and limits, and feedback about the experience is immediately knowable, such that reacting to changing situations becomes effortless, or even graceful. These experiences merge physical action and environmental awareness where temporal needs, concerns, and even sounds may diminish. Individuals commonly reflect that they feel an almost laser-like focus when captaining in stiff whitewater where the task of piloting a raft demands undivided attention. In this state there is heightened situational awareness and a fusion of physical action with personal skill. Stories of these moments are not uncommon around the campfire as boaters describe how movement became effortless, time slowed or felt like it stood still, and the mind became one with the grip of the oar, the blade, and the current. It is the rare commercial passenger who gets to experience this extent of merging events, let alone to row a boat in whitewater. For some private boaters it may be as simple as that—they organize their own trips because they want to be at the oars.

Optimal Arousal Theory could stand alone as reason to participate in private boating trips. However, the arousal occurring via private trips for some may provide experiences lacking elsewhere in their lives and, in this way, is *Compensatory Behavior*. As experienced boaters know, private boating provides a whole other world to simultaneously create and explore. Buoyed by incredible natural scenery, social structures exist that may be quite different from one's daily routine. These may provide radical clarity or autonomy compared to their roles and lifestyle back in the workplace or home. In this way, the river may appeal to private boaters in that it allows the opportunity to extend a locus of control in ways where one is otherwise limited. While these points may be similar for commercial trip clients, the level of responsibility and engagement required of private trip members is potentially magnitudes larger.

> Dragon's Breath
> Lighter fluid filled raft pump
> Sprayed across campfire
>
> Licking campfire flames
> Reflected by gleaming guitar
> Catches my eye
>
> Flood stage current
> Unpredictable rapids
> First time raft flip
>
> Friend Beth fell from boat
> Spring highwater long cold swim
> Could not self-rescue

While these theories provide important insight to the attraction of private boating, they do not exist in a vacuum. That is, the reasons one is drawn to organizing private boating trips coexist, depend on, or influence one another. This melting pot of explanations come together in the setting itself of the river. All boaters have in common an implicit acceptance that spending time outdoors is an excellent way to spend a few hours, a day, a week, or even a month. By default, boating requires interaction with nature in ways that are quite profound. For many, just standing at a serene section of water along a riverbank has a calming effect. This "feeling" has gained the interest of environmental psychologists and is well documented. While most folks won't need to remember *Attention Restoration Theory* by name, it provides a coherent explanation of why spending time on the river is good for us.

The theory suggests that humans have the ability to direct their cognitive capacity, that is, their mental energy (known as *directed attention*) to tasks requiring concentration. This explains how, even when temptation is high to disengage from a task at hand, we can tune out distractions to get work done. However, the human ability to focus attention in this way can be compared to a car's gas tank. One can only focus on something so long before needing to refill or recharge before the tank runs dry. To maintain a high level of human health, we must mentally restore our capacity for cognition at regular intervals. Hundreds of rigorous scientific studies of thousands of individuals suggest a striking pattern that runs across gender, race, socio-economic status, and nationality. That is, we experience gains in mental health when we spend time interacting with natural settings, from simply viewing photos or even listening to prerecorded nature sounds, to actually visiting natural places. However, the *type* of nature setting matters. The largest increase in mental restoration tends to be associated with natural settings where there are few human developments. Even though the world has become increasingly urbanized, scholars believe that these places help us feel a connection to evolutionary roots deep inside us. They call this important construct *Being Away*. Most importantly, the landscapes most strongly associated with positive mental health gains include views of water. This connection with nature helps explain some of the popularity of the well-known photographs taken of the five mile section below Nankoweap in the Grand Canyon. While not a substitute for experiencing it in person, even photos of this river vista capture the calming, yet powerful effect inherent to the setting.

Moonlight casts shadows
Of boats tied in the eddy

Floating in snowstorm
Shoreline moose under spruce boughs
Our eyes meet

Silent smooth current
Cicadas call out
Water drips from oar blade

Lounging on beach sand
Scratching my wrist I notice
Scorpion falls off

Compensatory Theory also comes into play when looking at how individuals are invited to participate in private boating trips. Commercial operators typically have little control over who comes through the door, and often the only hurdle to get on a trip is possession of a valid credit card and a willingness to use it. However, private boaters go to great lengths to consider who to invite on their trips, and private boating trips are an excellent way to spend time with family and friends. Only on a private trip does one have ultimate control to shape the style or flavor of a float, and that is clearly done through the invitations cast. Where almost scripted responses and behaviors are assumed at home, school, and the workplace, the occasion to float a river is quite different. It allows one a balance to life that might be missing elsewhere. The river can lessen the distractions of everyday life and provides opportunities for learning, to share roles or try on new ones. It can also magnify a trip member's positive or negative character dispositions, and how this may influence the group dynamic is an important consideration. Unless they are the rare client that fills the entire tour, commercial clients rarely know who else might be on their trip until they arrive. For some private boaters, this is a source of stress minimized by carefully selecting their fellow river travelers.

Watching me, friends fooled
Bare hands, grab wild salmon
But I brought from store

Campfire dancing
Guitar inspires courage
Or is it the beer?

Crusty eyes
Crack open with dawn's rays
Too many campfire beers

No more daytime drinks
Says leader losing control
Glaring stares

As evidenced by the existence of several multi-million-dollar equipment retail businesses, government regulations in the form of lotteries and waitlists, and outfitters catering specifically to the needs of private boaters, private boating is without a doubt a popular recreation experience. Putting together our own trips allows us to exercise freedoms, to act in ways unavailable or different from our daily routines, to make decisions and be leaders, or to relax from our normal roles and pressures of life back home. It's a way to spend time with family and friends, to connect with nature, and to recharge mental capacities. Any one of these ideas is likely an insufficient condition to explain why private boaters do what they do, but, taken as a whole, the rationale becomes more tangible. Now forget about this stuff and go boat!

Sunset births campfire
Friends gather, too tall stories
Laughter hits my ears

IV
Adventures

A Boater's Story

Julie Yarnell

Boaters are a unique blend of folks. We come from all walks of life, from different locations around the world. We have different occupations, are of varying ages, and have different interests in life. But once we strap on a PFD and our floppy river hats, we all share a common love for nature and the raw, beautiful power of water. I am a member of this tribe of water worshippers. The passion of boaters inspires me. There is a respect for the waterways that we conquer and a sense of reverence toward nature. We try to leave things better than we found them so others can enjoy them too. There is a willingness to share ourselves and help one another that often gets lost in the daily bustle of civilized life. People boat for different reasons and are often willing to sit and tell you about them. All you have to do is mention a river or ask if they have ever been boating and the stories start to flow like a bubbling river riffle, and gain momentum like a swiftly dropping rapid as epic accounts of river voyages unfold.

My boating story started after my husband and daughter went on a week-long trip down Utah's Desolation and Gray canyons on the Green River with my dad. They came back and shared their river tales about their float for days, and were hooked on this adventurous water lifestyle. My husband decided he wanted to get into boating. He started his persuasion tactics by trying to convince me that we needed to buy an inflatable raft. He worked me like a river slowly carves the walls of the canyon it flows through—slowly, steadily, and with firm persistence. He wound his argument around our current life and said it would be a great way to take family vacations and see cool places. I pushed back, contending that he knew nothing about boating. His persuasions were constant and steady, and he insisted, "We would have great family time and experience beautiful places." My argument: "It's a pretty big investment to get all the equipment ... would we really use a raft or would it just collect dust in the garage?" He began researching rafts and met the father of one of our son's classmates who had been boating for 20+ years. He spent time talking with him, learning and exploring boating. It took a couple of years of slowly wearing me down to finally convince me, but I conceded and told him to start raft shopping. Looking back at my resistance, I'm glad my husband kept pushing to start boating. That first raft purchase was a gateway to experiences that have changed my life. My husband was right; boating has created some wonderful family time and we have visited some gorgeous places. This boating dad he met, named Kelly, is now one of our closest friends. He has been a great teacher, willing to share his boating skills and knowledge, and is always ready for a river trip. We have shared many a beer on the river, enjoying the splendor of nature, and creating life long memories together.

People boat for different reasons. For some, like my husband and son, they get charged up from the adrenaline rush that arises from picking the right line to run through a rapid, crashing through whitewater with hard oar strokes and pulls, and battling against nature with its fierce force of hydraulic power. They relish the fight to keep the boat upright, unswamped, and avoid succumbing to the power of the waves. The victory of conquering Class IV and V+ rapids, with or without a boat flip, generates great stories and bragging rights. Maneuvering a 12-, 14-, or 16-foot inflatable boat through an obstacle course of river rocks and drops like a race car skimming around the track takes some serious paddling skills and, again, spearheads good campfire conversation.

For others, boating allows the experience of exceptional moments called "river time." River time enables people to get away from life's hectic schedules and technology-filled hours. It gives one the chance to take off one's watch and not care what time or day it is. A time to unplug from cell phones, computers, and television and to not be disturbed by constant texts, emails, reminders, chimes, beeps, and buzzes. Most remote river locations offer no electricity, cell service, or internet, so you have time to "just be in the moment" and absorb your surroundings. There is no multitasking to be done or pressure of that next meeting or activity you have scheduled. Time isn't pressured; you are at the mercy of the river and how fast it carries you or how fast you can row. There are a lot of tranquil, peaceful moments to think, daydream, and soak in some of nature's spirit. While floating along, you can hear the calming river noise as it bubbles, flows, and gently splashes against your boat. The warm sun washes its rays down your face, makes you smile and relax while you gaze at the remarkable canyon walls shaped by the power and persistence of river water. A hawk sails overhead, gracefully catching the thermals and gliding through the royal blue sky. Clouds float through the sky and morph into shapes and creatures that your mind and imagination see. River time is perfect to appreciate the simplicity and beauty of nature and just "be" as you melt in and become a part of it.

Others think of boating as an adventure to be independent and self-sufficient, paddling down remote wilderness stretches creating their own versions of popular reality television shows like "Survivor" or "Man versus Wild." River survival includes wars with Mother Nature and her random, up-canyon winds, nighttime gully-washing rainstorms, hot sunny days or cold spring days and nights. Getting pitched and flipped out of boats into rapids, taking epic swims, and struggling through rescues to get back in your boat are part of life on the river. Let's not forget the challenge of cooking gourmet meals over a campfire for the hungry tribe after rowing 20 river miles in a day. Lounging on the perfect sandy beach campsite and celebrating success with riverside beers and cocktails is a tough task after a day on the river, but I will gladly handle this duty. Some of the best meals of my life have taken place alongside a river. Nature makes food taste that much better. There is something about sitting in your camp chair dining al fresco with picturesque scenery all around after a long day outside that just brings out the deliciousness in whatever you have made. The most refreshing gin and tonic cocktail I have ever consumed was not in a swanky, chic city bar but on a desert boat trip. The desert boat bar was a white plastic cooler strapped into the bottom of a 16-foot inflatable raft. The best feature of the drink was the ice chunks chipped from a heavenly five-pound ice block with a hatchet and a screwdriver. Add gin, tonic, a splash of lime juice and there was pure perfection in my lidded plastic coffee mug.

In all seriousness, though, most longer river trips don't have easy exit strategies if you encounter trouble. Once you put in at the remote locations for river trip launches, you are basically on your own until the take-out point—unless you are fortunate enough to have a satellite phone to call for help, which typically requires hike-in or helicopter assistance to get you out if trouble arises. Boaters must be prepared with enough food and water for their trip, be ready for equipment malfunctions, be prepared to treat injuries requiring first aid, and be ready to face weather hiccups, as well as other Acts of God and serendipitous events. After completing a lengthy stretch of river, it is nice to get back to civilization, but I appreciate the "Man versus Wild" time on the river. It lets you know you can take care of yourself and others in primitive situations, and brings an appreciation of the luxuries in our daily life that we often take for granted.

In the beginning, I boated because my husband wanted to boat and wanted it to be a family thing. It started out with day trips that were fun, but it was a whole lot of work to get all the gear together, set up, taken down, and cleaned up for just the day experience. We progressed to a week-long raft trip, which allowed us to explore further and added the challenge of food and water planning. We managed successfully and started applying for permits for longer trips and destinations farther away.

I haven't always been an avid camper but could do a couple nights of car camping in the mountains to feel I was one with nature. I soon found that boating is glorified car camping. It is the "mother" of all car camping. You can pack more stuff into a raft than a car. Comforts that make camping tolerable can be easily loaded onto a raft. Such niceties might include sleeping cots, thick sleeping pads, full size pillows, solar showers, shower stalls, kitchen set-ups, river versions of port-a-potties, corn hole boards and other riverside game entertainment, and probably best of all, coolers packed full of gourmet food and beverages. Our dear friend Kelly introduced us to roll-a-cots which have made all the difference as to how well I sleep in nature. They can be set up just about anywhere—on sandy beaches, stone canyon ledges, uneven rocky banks, in grassy fields, and along the water's edge. If the weather is nice, you don't even need to set up a tent. Cots are comfortable for sleeping, and I don't wake up feeling like I have a rock stuck in my back and am in need of chiropractic services to get my spine realigned as I often did with traditional tent camping on hard, rocky ground.

Some of the best late-night entertainment I have ever seen was not watching "The Tonight Show" on television, but laying on my cot next to the river, looking up at the stars. One memorable night the stars were supremely bright, and I have never seen so many layers of stars and constellations at one time without any light pollution. Above me in its splendor was a pristine, dark sky—a celestial masterpiece weaving a patchwork of stars light-years away into perfect twinkling brilliance, with streams of shooting stars skirting across the sky for added effect. Add a light breeze, chirping crickets, bats flying and swooping in the night air, and the soft lapping of the river water splashing against the sandy bank, and this easily lulls one to sleep. Looking into star filled galaxies above made me realize I was just a tiny, modest speck in the grand scheme of the universe. It was a comical moment for me that made me laugh to myself. I recognized that we tend to fill our lives with drama, stress, and worry that seem to be such big things, but they really are just a small, insignificant part of life. Sometimes nature needs to set us straight and bring things into perspective. Nighttime on the river is special.

Remember I mentioned that boaters love to tell stories? Sit back and let me tell you about my greatest boating trip yet. I'll give you a clue in four words: Colorado River … Grand Canyon. Rafting the Colorado River through the Grand Canyon is on the bucket list of river trips for any private boater. Having the ability to explore one of the natural wonders of the world and to experience its spectacular, pristine beauty and challenging whitewater rapids make it a highly sought-after expedition. There is a limited lottery-draw process to win a permit to float the Grand Canyon. People can apply to the lottery for years before they get lucky enough to draw a permit for the opportunity to experience this great majesty. My husband was invited on a private party trip to float the Grand Canyon. I was excited for him because I knew this would be the ultimate rafting trip. Two hundred and twenty-six miles of river with seventy-plus riffles and rapids to row through, not to mention the spectacular scenery! It was going to be a guy's trip, sixteen of them floating the Colorado River … a testosterone flotilla!

Plans changed a bit and I fell into this trip rather serendipitously. I got a phone call from the permit holder a few months before the launch date. He said there were a couple of openings left on the roster for the trip and asked if I would like to join them. Two women had been invited and I was one of them. If one of us backed out, then neither would go, as the Trip Leader didn't think it was appropriate to take only one woman along on the trip. The initial answer that popped into my mind was "absolutely not." I couldn't. I had two kids to take care of and this meant sixteen days of camping. But, impressively, my brain stopped my mouth from spewing out this reply and my thoughtful, calculated response to him was, "I can't give you an answer in the five minutes of our phone call, but let me think about it and call you back this evening." I immediately hung up the phone and found my husband in shock that I was even considering going on the trip. He was extremely happy and supportive.

I try to encourage my kids not to be scared to try new things even if they are difficult. Stepping out of your comfort zone is challenging, but when you do, there are often times of great personal discovery and triumph as you conquer difficult situations. I have been blessed since I hit my 40's in that I am comfortable and excited to try new things, even if they result in failure. Why not try new things? What have I got to lose? What will I gain? These are the questions I ask myself when I have opportunities to step out and try something new.

My parents are wonderful grandparents and volunteered to take care of my kids if I went on the trip. The next dilemma was wrapping my head around sixteen days of camping. My current camping record was only a week so this was definitely stretching my comfort zone. A girlfriend of mine had kayaked the Grand Canyon for three weeks, so I asked her about her experience and whether I should go on the trip. She said, "The water is really big, but the trip will change your life. You can do it."

My mind was made up—this was a trip of a lifetime and I might not have the opportunity to go another time. I would be crazy to turn down the offer. I felt strong, mentally and physically, and I could do this. A couple days later, it was confirmed. I was in! I was going to raft the Grand Canyon!

Our boating group decided to use an outfitting company out of Flagstaff that would supply all the rafts and boating gear, pack and freeze all trip food, and provide shuttle services to the put-in and take-out for our trip. But we would navigate the river ourselves without a guide. This eliminated a lot of food and gear planning headaches, which I was grateful for after having done some week-long raft trips previously. We just had to bring our personal gear—clothing, PFDs, sleeping bags, camp chairs, adult beverages, and anything else we might want to make ourselves comfortable on the trip.

We drove to Flagstaff the day before we were supposed to hit the river and had a massive gear gathering party in the hotel parking lot the afternoon before our departure. All trip participants were handpicked by the permit holder from his lifetime of friendships. There were people from California, Michigan, Georgia, Colorado, and Canada. Pleasantries and small talk were exchanged as we got to know each other. I had only met three of the sixteen previously, one being my husband. But based on first impressions, I knew some of these people would become great friends by the end of the trip. A lot of us were Grand Canyon "Newbies;" this was our maiden voyage down the glorious, majestic Colorado River of the Grand Canyon. We had excited, nervous twinkles in our eyes. Others had several trips under their belts and tons of stories to tell about conquering this river and its rapids, and one guy loved it so much that this was his seventh trip down the canyon. You could tell the river held part of his soul.

On departure day, a 5-ton cargo truck rolled into the hotel parking lot at noon in the pouring rain. We managed to fill it quickly with all our personal gear, boating equipment, and beverages that we would need for the next sixteen days. Then we jumped into a large van for the ride to Lee's Ferry, the put-in location a couple of hours away where we would start our journey. Upon arrival, we unloaded the truck and started rigging the seven blue, 16-foot inflatable rafts that would be our trusted vessels to carry us down the river for the next sixteen days. Activity on the boat ramp was harried, but somewhat organized chaos for the next couple of hours. We had to get thousands of pounds of food and gear unloaded from the truck, the boats inflated and rigged-up, and then reloaded with this enormous pile that would support us for the entire trip. Our two drivers said good-bye and left us. We were on our own to make it the next 226 miles down the river. That night camping at Lee's Ferry was beautiful! It was a warm night with a brilliant, bright, almost-full moon, crickets chirping, lizards and toads skittering all around the place, and my mind was spinning with excitement. I couldn't sleep. I lay in my cot waiting for the hours to tick by and the sun to rise for our morning departure.

Let me share some interesting trivia about the Grand Canyon. It is considered one of the seven natural wonders of the world and nearly five million people visit annually. The Grand Canyon is on average a mile deep, with maximum rim distances 18 miles apart, but averaging 10 miles apart, and it is 600 yards wide at the narrowest point in Marble Canyon. The Colorado River is 300 feet wide on average and 40 to 85 feet deep. There are igneous and metamorphic rocks in the inner gorge of the canyon that are close to two billion years old. Between 70-80 million years ago, tectonic plate shifts uplifted the region of the Grand Canyon creating the Colorado Plateau, and then 5-6 million years ago the Colorado River began carving its way down to the bottom of the canyon.

The Colorado River is alive with many personalities. You always should be ready for what it might throw at you. As we started the trip the river was flat, smooth, clear water the color of a deep-green glass bottle. But it quickly started to gain some momentum and formed white foamy riffles, waves, and rapid drops that would increase a boat's speed and throw it around as though it were a tiny, weightless stick in the water instead of a 16-foot long, 700-pound raft. Further on, the clear, green water turned into an angry, murky, chocolate-brown color as the Little Colorado River merged into the main Colorado. It never cleared in color except when we passed Havasu Creek, which is another tributary that flows into the main Colorado. Havasu Creek was filled with the most exquisite, crystal-clear, turquoise blue water I have ever encountered in a river. There was an invisible boundary line drawn where the two river bodies met and neither dared cross into the other's space. It was a unique sight. We were lucky to spend an afternoon exploring, hiking, and basking in the beautiful waters of this sacred place long revered by the Havasupai Indian tribe.

The Colorado River is always churning with currents and boils on the surface, as well as hydraulics below that will suck the oars and the side of your raft down if you hit them wrong, or will spin you in the opposite direction you want to go. The raw power of the Colorado River is astonishing. I spent every day gazing up at the spectacular, mile-high, red-brown sandstone and limestone canyon walls with carved spires, hoodoos, and hidden arches up at the skyline. I would follow the walls down to the cracked and angled polished granite slabs and jet-black Vishnu schist-swirled rocks along the waterline of the canyon walls thinking, "This water has carved this canyon with endurance and persistence for millions of years and continues to do so more each day, slowly and patiently wearing the canyon away."

Desert canyons are a favorite of mine. I love the wind and water-scoured smooth walls. Layers of time are visible in the different hues of red, tan, orange, and purple rock. Millions of years of time are stacked in the canyon wall layers, and only the river knows the true story of its journey and how the canyon was formed. Even though this stretch of the Colorado River is highly controlled with dams, specific water flow releases, and reservoirs collecting its valuable water, it still fights to be wild.

It took me a couple of days to get comfortable and enjoy the rolling, bumpy water ride. My death grip on my seat cam straps slowly loosened to a firm grip as we maneuvered and splashed through the rapids. I got used to having 6, 8, 10, 12-foot-high waves splash above me as we plowed down through the depths of rapids and back up. I will admit that I might be a little bit of an adrenaline junkie like the boys in my family after conquering the turgid swells, whirlpools, and rapid drops in the river. I certainly let out my fair share of whoops and hollers when we came through and finished right side up. Trust in my husband's rowing and navigating abilities grew as he feathered the oars to position us in the right lines to run the rapids, and powered through the strong water to avoid upsetting our raft. I really wanted to avoid flipping a raft in a rapid and having to take a swim in this mighty cold river. The water temperature averages around 54 degrees Fahrenheit. We were lucky. We had no flips with any of the seven rafts in our party during the entire 16-day trip.

I did not fare so well one day as I paddled an inflatable kayak. It was amazing powering my way through the rapids with my paddle. Me against nature, and I felt strong. We were approaching a rapid with a 15' drop that was rated an 8 out of 10 for difficulty. I really should have listened to my gut, tied my kayak up, and climbed into a raft to go through it, but I wanted to see if I could paddle it. "Step out of your comfort zone, try something challenging" my brain was saying. Unfortunately, I got sucked into a big hole. It didn't matter how hard I paddled to try to steer clear of it. I was no match for Mother Nature. I was spun into the rapid, flipped backwards and upside down under my boat, and then Maytagged around like a load of laundry for three rotations in the hole. I could not get out from under my boat. I was sucking in quick breaths of air as I surfaced before being forcefully plunged again under water until I was finally recirculated and spit out of the hole. I was separated from my boat and continued bobbing along, getting dunked underwater along the rest of the wave train until the water calmed. It truly was the most terrifying experience of my life. The sheer force of the water was incredibly strong, and I had no choice but to float along for the ride. Amazingly, I remained pretty calm throughout the experience. Traveling through the water with no control was a bit surreal, but peaceful at the same time as water gurgled in my ears and I watched the waves moving above my head. Thank goodness for a very good PFD that kept me floating towards the surface. I'm sure the megadose of adrenaline coursing through my body helped me survive and maneuver through my "epic swim" as well. I was so relieved to grab the rescue rope tossed to me and be hauled into a raft downriver. This experience will be with me the rest of my life. I stepped out of my comfort zone. I failed, but I also succeeded because I survived.

This Grand Canyon trip was the first vacation where I truly lost track of what day it was, and it didn't matter because I was on my favorite time measurement of "river time." Miles rowed and awe-inspiring scenery filled my days rather than e-mails, deadlines, and hectic schedules. Completely unplugged … no TV, computer, cell phone, iPad, or children. No connection to the outside world. I had nature's serenity and beauty to soak up to recharge my soul as we floated through the canyon. We had some spectacular hikes up slot canyons made of layer upon layer of colorful, compressed dirt and rock. We found crystal clear pools and refreshing waterfalls that we sat under to let water pound our bodies and heads; waking us up and letting us feel we were alive with the power of nature. One afternoon was spent in a hidden oasis in the desert with green trees, bushes, and ferns cascading down the canyon walls, a place to take a rest and appreciate just being alive with all the untouched beauty around us. Our worries melted away and "just being" was enjoyed and embraced.

As I mentioned, food on the river is delicious. There's something about camping and cooking outdoors. Food just tastes so good. The canyon views of our outdoor dining rooms were stunning and different each day and night. We dined on three-course meals, sipped chilled canned beer or cocktails, and engaged in fine conversation about the events of the day, challenging rapids, narrow escapes, and the wonders we saw around us. Friendships blossomed as we spent more time with one another. The canyon had us under its spell and was working its magic on us.

I finished the camping marathon with flying colors! I camped for sixteen days and I actually missed it after I got home. I became extremely grungy (without my normal daily hot, soapy shower at home), wore dirty clothes for days, took baths in the brown, silt-filled river, and styled my hair by putting on a baseball hat. Getting down to basics was just kind of nice. Solar showers, camping soap, a razor, some deodorant, and lotion were a godsend to make you feel a little more civilized during the trip. My existence became very organic as I became one with my environment, and nature became one with me. Sand and dirt seemed to find a home in every crevice of my skin, and in every dry bag, sleeping bag, clothing item, and pair of shoes I took on the trip. I was still shaking out the Grand Canyon from my things weeks after we had gotten home and cleaned things up.

Since the weather was warm during our trip, my hubby and I slumbered on our cots on sandy beaches, on granite cliff ledges, and on rocky, alluvial fans along the river. One evening we had a big thunderstorm blow through. As the big, fat raindrops started to fall, we jumped into our "bivy sacks" for shelter and were pelted mercilessly. But it was spectacular to see the sky lit up by lightning and hear the thunder claps rolling and echoing between the canyon walls with loud, monstrous booms. I slept like a baby on my cot during the trip—maybe it was the fresh air or days filled with constant physical activity. It was such good sleep! It took me four nights to get a good night's sleep in my bed after I got home. I really missed my cot, the soft canyon breezes, and the magnificent, star-filled sky.

Our last night in the Grand Canyon was bittersweet. We had a beautiful, mottled purple-pink sunset to cap the day. On one hand, I was excited to head home, see my kids, and get back to my comfortable life; but on the other, sad to leave the simplicity and raw nature I had come to love and appreciate in such a short time. In only sixteen days, I had a transformation. I stepped out of my comfort zone and was rewarded ten-fold by this experience. What a gift this trip was to share with my husband. It was one of the best trips we have taken together with lots of time to talk and really pay attention to one another without life's interruptions. I enjoyed simplicity and found inner calm. I met people who were strangers at the beginning of our trip but became special friends by the end. We laughed and enjoyed each other's company and became joined together as we meandered through the canyon and into stories we would be able to tell. We shared an intimate trip not many people get to experience. No trip would ever be exactly the same as this one because it was my first time down the Grand Canyon, and I would never be the same person I was when I started this adventure.

We finished off our trip at Diamond Creek on the Hualapai Tribal Reservation—having completed 226 miles of a remarkable river adventure. It ended much the same way it started, only in reverse. We climbed off our boats, pulled them out of the water, and this time unloaded, took apart, and deflated them, thus bringing our trip to an end. The shuttle vehicles arrived to pick us up and we piled everything into the back of the truck and piled into the van to head out on the bumpy, rocky road to the canyon rim. The shuttle drivers told us that we were lucky we were able to get out. The same thunderstorm that had rocked the canyon walls and pelted us with fat raindrops had flash flooded Diamond Creek and washed away the road that leads out of the canyon. The Hualapai had just been able to clear and rebuild the road two days before we arrived. As we inched our way up the only access to the top, we saw rocks the size of cars that had been pushed aside by heavy equipment when they reopened the blocked and destroyed road. This was another testament to the power of water and Mother Nature.

The ride back to Flagstaff was pretty quiet for the most part. I think everyone was thinking about the trip and we were all lamenting that this was the end. I sat reflecting on my "Grand" adventure. My friend was right; this trip did change my life. The Grand Canyon is a natural wonder of the world, full of secrets we will never know the answers to; ancient, sacred, harsh, and beautiful. It will capture a part of your soul if you open up and let it in. It now holds a piece of mine. The "Grand" as I fondly call it, is truly grand!

Why do we boat? Greek philosopher Heraclitus said, "You can never step into the same river; for new waters are always flowing on you. No man ever steps into the same river twice, for it's not the same river and he is not the same man." Each boating experience is different and that is what makes boating magical and special. Every time I boat, I discover something new. A river is a dynamic, ever-changing force that creates new paths and lessons each time you experience it. For me, boating is soul capturing, beautiful, raw, challenging, and something that has changed my life. For another person, it may be something entirely different. There is no wrong answer to the question, "Why do we boat?" The important thing is to enjoy boating on your quest to discover your own answers.

Two Paddles and a Pedal
Pascal Girard

"Are you bringing your spare paddle?" David asks while he fights to get his drysuit's latex gasket around his head.

"Nope."

His head pops out of the gasket with a puzzled look. We are about to paddle the Neilson, a Class IV/V river that runs deep into a canyon with very few exits.

"I've never lost or broken a paddle, I'll be fine. Besides, I'm bringing my camera and the extra paddle gets in the way."

David is one of the most safety minded people I know. Under no circumstances would he let any other paddler be as reckless and stupid as me. We have been paddling together for many years and, although my arguments are poor, somehow he knows I am right, or at least lucky. However, I can clearly see that he disapproves as he stuffs his spare paddle in his canoe.

I met him fifteen years back after moving from the city of Montreal to the town of Granby to get closer to my soon-to-be wife. I was new in town and did not know anyone. David owned a boat shop and, being a paddler, it did not take me too long to find my way to his store. The second-best thing after being on the river is being around boating gear. It is a boater's delight to be studying the paddles, feeling the chines and rockers of boats, trying on new helmets, and even admiring the colors of PFDs. A boating shop is an off-river gathering ground for people who share the same passion. This river passion is such a connecting force that mere strangers become friends. Simply put, river folks understand other river folks.

David and I quickly became friends. We would spend hours exchanging stories about river trips and adventures while I often gave him a hand outfitting his clients' boats. In time, whenever he was away he left me the keys to his shop so I could tend to his clients. The store had to be open in prime paddling season, which always tore David apart. Finally, he sold his business, preferring to be paddling a boat instead of working on one. I was saddened to see him sell his store, but at the same time I knew he would have more time for rivers.

A great paddling buddy is like gold. Every year, we leave our wives for a few days to discover a river that we have never paddled. Finding a new river is just so much fun—I really enjoy studying a region's watershed, reading guidebooks, and finally choosing a river with a water level just in reach of our capabilities. Exchanging information and stories with other paddlers is one of the more pleasant way to learn about a new river. After more than twenty years on rivers I have yet to meet a paddler who is not keen on sharing their river experiences. True passion is always shared; it's bigger than you are and should not be contained. Trading river experiences is like trading baseball cards, except everyone wins. The storyteller gets to relive his account and the listener gets precious information. Hearing "You would love that river!" always inspires a new plan and a new dream.

David and I enjoy hucking 30-foot waterfalls, surfing our local waves, getting our sinuses rinsed in big water, and paddling for our lives on flooded rivers … but our favorite activity is creeking: descending very steep, low-water whitewater.

The sky was clear, but a slight breeze in the air made it cool for August. I decided on my drysuit over my wetsuit as that gentle wind would certainly wear me out in wet neoprene. The river was low but still very much runnable. The Neilson is a prime creeking river, cascading deep into a canyon with uninterrupted drops of lovely moss-covered boulders. It is a favorite amongst extreme kayakers at high water and a nice challenge for OC1 boaters at a lower level.

It was our new river of the summer and I was excited to finally see it for myself. Working as a part-time photographer, I am inclined to go first so I can have the opportunity to photograph my fellow paddlers as they follow me down. Our routine was simple; scout together, I'd go first and then David would go while I snapped away.

And so it went for the morning. We were taking our time choosing our lines, enjoying the light and the scenery. Scouting a new section is always a challenge that I enjoy. Being a full-time math teacher, I love problem solving, and scouting is all about solving a standard equation:

Angle of your boat + Number of paddle strokes + Location of eddy + Timing - Risks = A Great Run (or NOT if the result is negative!)

It's an equation that is always summed up in, "So what are you planning to do?"

"I'm gonna boof that rock and land into that eddy, ferry river right and make that line behind that boulder."

"Don't miss the eddy, you don't want to go over that lip. I'll wait here with a throw bag."

I boof my boat into the eddy, throw my paddle over, ferry river right and, with a sense of accomplishment, peel out into the line. My maneuver is greeted with a "Whoo-hoo! Good job bro!"

What is even better than running a great line is seeing your pal run an even better one. Competition between friends disappears on rivers; there is no way I would want to see my buddy miss a line and get in trouble. Rivers bind us together. A partner in trouble means you are in trouble. Seeing a friend make a great line is just as exhilarating as if you had paddled it yourself.

David clears the boof and lands into the eddy with a light thud. Like a dancer, he spins around his paddle, throws a cross stroke that shoots him river right, twirls once more around his paddle, catches the river's main vein, and dashes out with a pleasing swoosh. Like an artist, he used his paddle to paint a beautiful line on this flowing canvas.

"Dude, that was clean!"

What I love about paddling little canyons like the Neilson is that unless you rappel down you wouldn't ever be able to see the canyon to appreciate its beauty. Paddling this river is, in my mind, the better way to experience this exclusivity.

We were entering an intense section of the river and scouting was getting harder because of the size of riverside boulders and the distance between them. I wedged my carbon paddle in a crack so I could use both my hands to climb a very large rock. Some light-greenish algae made me lose my grip and my foot slipped; just a tiny slide, like on a kiddies' plastic slide: CRACK!

I'm sure this crack echoed all over the canyon, I bet the entire universe heard it too. I paused for a few seconds thinking that it would go away, that if I didn't look down all would be fine. I just lay there completely motionless for a split second that seemed like minutes, eyes tightly shut. Then everything dawned on me and I understood things that never mattered to me before: I'm an idiot, a big idiot! How could I be so stupid and only bring one paddle on this type of river!

I held up both pieces of my paddle for David to see. His expression was screaming loud and clear: "Are you kidding me?"

He boulder hopped toward me and with a grin let out, "So you've never broken a paddle before?" Then he kindly went back to his canoe and handed me his spare paddle. It was a plastic blade, but down here it was my plastic savior. My bruised ego and this plastic blade kept me going the last two kilometers to the take-out.

An eight-foot drop got us out of our boats for a scout. The river crashed into a hydraulic. David normally would have jumped such a drop, but he didn't like the looks of the hydraulic and decided to portage it. I knew I could clear the hydraulic with a strong boof, so I decided to go for it. I placed my canoe perfectly in line, and then came the moment to make that last powerful stroke to boof. The plastic blade flexed more than expected and I didn't fully clear my obstacle. Part of my boat landed out of the hydraulic, but I felt that invisible hand tug me right back in. I started to side-surf. I braced and tilted downriver to keep myself upright. My gunwale caught in the wall of water coming from the fall and sent me rolling a few times. I was thrown up and down and side-to-side with a few rolls in between. No matter how badly I was being trashed, I stayed in my boat.

It kind of amazed me—I was really hanging in there! I let out a cowboy "Woohoo!" But the feeling faded when I realized the hole wasn't letting me go. Like a cat playing with a mouse, I was getting slapped right, left, and center, but I wasn't going anywhere.

"Jump out of your boat!"

David was on a rock with a throw bag.

"Throw me the rope!"

I held out my hand to grab the rope, but at the same time I let go of my brace. The canoe rolled, and I was ejected. I managed to hold onto the rope, but I had to let go of the paddle to hold onto the canoe. As David held tightly to the rope the current swung me and my canoe like a pendulum to shore.

I had never before lost or broken a paddle, yet I managed to do both in a few hours. It was quite a humbling moment.

"I lost your paddle!"

"Don't worry about the paddle," David said with a smile that also betrayed a snicker, "So you've never BROKEN or LOST a paddle?"

He was right, I was wrong. That is what makes him a great friend. There was no nagging or "I told you so." I had learned my lesson. When wisdom fails, pain becomes the teacher.

I cut down a branch and inserted it in my broken carbon shaft and held it together with some duct tape. My prosthetic paddle felt more like a saggy, bent shaft, but it propelled me anyhow. There was one serious rapid before the take-out. Thankfully, that last rapid had a chicken line, which I took without hesitation.

There was a thirteen-kilometer bike ride from the take-out back to the put-in and it was my turn to climb on the bike. (Come to think of it, it's always my turn.) It was David's bike. One kilometer into the ride, the bike pedal fell off.

The first thought that came to my mind was, "Ok, God, I believe I get it now." I wasn't upset, I just started thinking that this was a great opportunity for me to ponder on my paddling day. So I did, on foot, for the next twelve kilometers.

Why didn't I bring a spare paddle? I had experience, I had seen people crash and burn. Why did I make a smart decision based on experience to wear my drysuit instead of a wetsuit, but such a poor one on not bringing my spare paddle? And why did I not anticipate that flex in the paddle? Why didn't I check on David's bike beforehand? Maybe I'm getting too comfortable with rivers and sometimes comfort is dangerous. This wake-up call was a good reminder that I love rivers, but I must never get too comfortable with them. Rivers will be rivers no matter what I do. I'm just a guest; wanted or unwanted ... just a simple guest. I don't make the rules, I abide by them. I can't blame the river for any outcome, only myself. Like so many situations in life, the only thing I can control is how I prepare myself and how I react to them.

I love rivers for how they help me appreciate the bigger things in life and how, sometimes, they put me right back into my place.

Author's note: David still wants to paddle with me because now I always bring a spare paddle. In 2015 we paddled the Grand Canyon together with 14 other friends including my family ... we had many spare paddles and oars.

Liquid Addiction
Maile Field

I have a picture of us at Crystal Rapid. It shows a shiny yellow raft standing on end sideways so that everything in the boat, everything that isn't obscured by the crashing white wall of water, is in motion, falling. It's hard to tell where everything is going, but I know I must be falling up. My upper arms are there in the picture, shiny-wet and brown, gripping the lifeline. It appears I am sitting down. But I know that I am falling, falling upstream into the white froth as the boat spins away underneath us.

I had been in the middle of the boat, but in the picture I am almost hitting the left tube. All that can be seen of Lars is the tip of his right foot. The eye automatically travels up to where the rest of him must be: the ankle, shin, calf, and knee. He is getting mercilessly pounded with water within a churning froth into which the boat appears on the brink of being emptied entirely. We dub the photo *Lars' Foot*.

The port oar is invisible and the starboard oar has slipped out of its lock and lies at an odd angle through the picture. The spare oar, still lashed in place, appears parallel to the right tube and out of the way of Lars who, in motion, has become part of the river upstream from the boat. The boat stands vertically on its portside tube.

When I first see the photo I search my memory and it all comes back. I take a huge breath of air as I look and remember. I was about to let go. I was about to be swept under the boat.

I go under, but my head soon hits the underside of the raft. I had been taught to use my hands to walk my way out from under the boat, but I'd never actually done it. "Walking" is what your hands do on the bottom of the boat that is above you, keeping you from air, keeping you from breathing. This might work except the bowline is wrapped around my foot. I kick to free myself, making it somehow tighter. The bowline is a snake, trying to squeeze my right leg into submission. It tightens and holds fast.

I had known Lars about six months when he first mentioned his "continuing interest form." Just another thing on his list of holiday chores. Holding his position on the waiting list for a permit to run the Colorado River through the Grand Canyon meant paying $25 every December. His position on the list was thousands of people away from the top. It would be thirteen years, in fact, before Lars' number came up. By then we had gotten married, had two kids, and both kids had read all the Harry Potter books twice. I had no idea really what the permit was for or about or why Lars even wanted it. But he had waited 13 years for it. "This ride through the canyon, it must be *something*," I thought.

I had learned to command a paddle boat on the rivers draining the Sierras in Northern California. I had built some confidence for reading 2,500 cfs water and felt I could handle a Class IV river. I was nervous, but I could handle it.

The Colorado River, Lars said calmly, was "big water." How big? It looked like it could pick up not only my house but the entire farm, and deposit it in the Gulf of California tomorrow by noon. Instead of the Class I-VI rating scale we use on all other rivers, the Colorado has its own 10-point scale. Each rapid's rating varies with the flow level. I started looking at pictures and saw that this was a whole different thing. My confidence plummeted. No. Way.

One holiday season shortly after Y2K, as he filled out his annual "continuing interest form," Lars said we ought to start thinking about who to take with us. We mentioned it to our friends; we put a list on the fridge. The list grew long. I did not put my own name on that list. Not at first.

But then I found a book on my aunt's shelf. As I read the flyleaf, I remembered my grandmother's voice. "Major Powell," she was saying. "Green River … trading post." I began to remember a story. A family member—a Field family member—had been involved. A woman had been furious. What exactly was the story? I remembered my grandfather's voice talking about a wooden chair in association with Powell and the Green River Trading Post.

My grandfather loved woodworking. He'd made our dinner table, coffee table, buffet cupboard ... of course it would be about the chair for him. He called it a "conveyance." That chair, somehow, was a "conveyance." But what did it convey?

The sketch on the cover of the book, I finally figured out with my aunt's help, portrayed precisely the chair my grandfather had been talking about. A normal, wooden, country kitchen chair. But this chair had been strapped onto a boat. It had conveyed Powell himself on one of the greatest adventures in history. But what sequence of events, sets of circumstances ... how had this happened?

I found other books. My great-great-grandfather, Samuel Ichabod Field, had owned the trading post. And he had outfitted Powell's crews in 1869 and again in 1871. Powell had commandeered the chair from my great-great-grandmother, Louisa. I found no record of how the woman felt about the loss of her chair.

But this tiny link launched me. I kept reading.

Powell alone had a lifejacket, but the other crewmembers survived the river too. They'd had no map, no idea if they might be floating into a box canyon from which they'd not be able to escape. They had no clue whatsoever what they were getting themselves into. And *they* floated safely through the Grand Canyon.

The river suddenly became do-able to me.

While we had waited those 13 years, the waiting list had grown so long that our next shot at it would be 23 years away. I'd be 59 years old by then. We had to go now. I enlisted grandparents to watch the kids. I gave detailed instructions to my farm foreman. I wrote a will. In late spring, 2003, I drove to the launch site called Lee's Ferry, Mile 0.

Mile 1

As soon as we are in the current, things move fast. The Paria (rhymes with Maria) joins the main river, contributing little water but enough silt to change the color of the entire river from a clear, deep green to *café au lait*. I look back at the cliff I climbed early this morning. A few hours ago the ridge towered above our camp, but now it shrinks before the backdrop of the greater Marble Canyon. Riffles bounce the boats around. Everything is fluid, anything can happen. It's a great feeling.

On river left, carefully placed stones support a gradually descending path, an early approach to the ferry landing. The Kaibab Plateau is at the top here. The upper layers of surrounding geology, the Chinle and Moenkopi formations that geologists call the youngest layers of sediment, have already disappeared. We are sliding down into the earth.

The Colorado River drains an area about the size of France spread over seven western states. The watershed is one-twelfth the land area of the United States plus 2,000 square miles of Mexico. The water upstream from the Grand Canyon enables Glen Canyon Dam's turbines to generate electricity enough to serve 1.5 million people annually in a five-state region. Water from the Colorado River quenches the thirst of 40 million people. From Glen Canyon the water runs through Marble Canyon before pouring through the uplifted wonder that is the Grand Canyon.

Unlike the voluminous Mississippi, Missouri, Columbia, Brazos, Rio Grande, Potomac, Hudson, or Ohio rivers, the Colorado hurtles through a one-mile-deep textbook of geologic history, giving it a reputation worldwide as the ultimate recreational whitewater in America, set in a geology classroom.

The river erodes a path for itself, creating a geo-textbook that can be read in the strata it exposes. The reader is always aware that the river even now continues cutting deeper, even as we stare, blink, and stare some more. Until recently, geologists described the process as one of a layer cake being pushed up as someone is holding a knife, the river the knife. But the cake isn't exactly straight, so as a person rides the river downstream through the canyon, the layers are revealed at a slight angle, sometimes jumbled. The scenery ages hundreds of millions of years as the boat progresses fewer than 300 miles downstream. But geologists are now positing that maybe the river didn't take as long as previously thought to cut through all these amazingly beautiful, but soft layers of rock. Theories are swirling again.

Maybe there was a lake created by a volcanic flow that blocked the drainage at about Lava Falls. Maybe the river flowed upstream for a while? Maybe then it broke through the lava, and the entrenched meander re-entrenched in a slightly different place—maybe the Colorado River started in the middle and flowed in two directions.

Things are never as simple as they seem. The millennia washed layers away, then laid down new sediment, placing and removing and then replacing layers again here and there to confuse the geologic canon. The nearly two dozen layers we see are not as simple as they appear and do not catalogue geology with chronologic precision. Where the geologists start to shake their heads and re-read their theories, the place where too-new strata sits on top of too-old strata, they call that place an "uncomformity."

My understanding of geology derives from the trilogy of words my middle-school kids brought home. All rock is either 1) igneous (think "ignite" as in fire or volcanic in origin); 2) sedimentary (sediment, it was laid down like the dust on the kids' soccer trophies); or 3) metamorphic (it got changed under pressure—think larvae into butterflies, metamorphosis). All three classifications of rock are present here. I would spend 17 days on the river with two USGS geologists among us and at the end of that time I would feel I had learned an enormous amount, but I just had the beginning of a glimpse of an understanding.

Within the first five miles, we are through the layers of the Kaibab, Toroweap, and Coconino, through the light brown and into the deep red of Hermit Shale. My Martin-Whitis guide shows the layers, their names, ages, colors … reminding me of studying for an exam in college. But when I look at the walls we are floating between, everything seems fascinating. Suddenly I am no longer in a book.

Mile 5

It settles in on me slowly that there's no going back. A small plane drones overhead, having taken off from the airstrip near Marble Canyon Lodge just above us on the North Rim. Like the plane we are airborne now, committed to our flight. I understand clearly now why the word "launch" is used for river trip beginnings. We are gone from the world we know, in a fluid space, defined by our own actions. This freedom is glorious, the view magic, the overall sense, exalting.

The first few days I watch a sorting occur. People reunite with old friends, get to know new friends, and Newbies learn the lifestyle of the river. The boatmen and women are likewise sorting themselves out, learning whom to follow, making adjustments to rigging, discussing gear innovations. They talk about what recent floods have done to change the rapids. And mostly, it's Newbies asking Repeaters how to run whatever is coming up next. There's a sense of obligation on the Repeaters' part to remain calm. It's just another day on the river. But they use strong words. "That thing will kick your ass."

Mile 17

Although we have run several rapids before Mile 17, the scouting point above House Rock Rapid marks the place I first feel cold in the canyon's 115-degree heat. At this medium flow, the rating on the rapid is a 7. But compared to the two rapids we've been through, Badger (rated a 6) and Soap Creek (rated a 5), House Rock looks exponentially worse. The Repeaters confirm, this is the first real rapid.

We hike, lifejackets still buckled, to a point on river right where we look down on the broiling, white turbulence. I hold my arms tight to my sides. The hydraulic forces below me rage beyond my ability to fathom. I can see that if a human body took the trip through that rapid it could be pounded against the solid vertical wall, not survivable. Would a human being even be visible? We all wear PFDs, but still, how could we possibly float? The sheer power of 15,000 cubic feet of water passing by per second is inestimable, like trying to imagine what lies beyond the stars … but a lot less peaceful to contemplate.

Our boatmen stand looking over the rapid below. Paul smokes calmly, scrawling routes in the air, his cigarette a pencil. We all watch, gauging the hole and what would happen if a boat slid into it sideways. But these Repeaters all stand firmly on the other side of the line between fear and excitement from where I stand. I am scared: they are thrilled.

As she faces this first big rapid of the trip, Peggie, who is married to Brad, asks me which boat I think is the safest for her daughter. Following her daughter's swim at Badger, Peggie is worried. But she's not letting fear control her. I consider carefully. Ricardo's boat is the most stable, but he wouldn't want to wear pants all day and this mom wouldn't want her 13-year-old daughter to have to witness that ... or Ricardo would have to keep his shorts on. Doc is the most experienced of the remaining boatmen. Julia has the most control of her craft and can read the water best. Brad is a Newbie but smart and careful. Lars tends toward the cowboy runs. I advise they ride with Brad, because he cares the most about his wife and daughter—and Peggie would haul Brad in if he went over.

But Peggie chooses Ricardo, even though it means laborious bailing. Ricardo has to put his shorts on but doesn't complain. The look on Brad's face shows hurt but acquiescence. By the end of the day, Ricardo is sans shorts again. I ask Peggie about it later. She says she asked her daughter if it bothered her and it didn't. "There was no weird vibe, he just wanted to be *au natural.*"

The river forms a V at the top of every rapid, whether a riffle or roaring hole like the one in the center of House Rock Rapid. This transition zone is called the "tongue" and forms where the water slips from a smooth, quiet, peaceful stream into frothing chaos. Following that smooth triangular tongue to its tip generally places the boat in the middle of the watercourse, the roughest point but also the point most likely to be free from rocks.

House Rock Rapid is named for a large, house-sized boulder located far from the rapid in Rider Canyon. Here in the main canyon, the curve of broiling water wraps around a spit of boulders, clockwise. So, in this case, following the V would place the boat in the worst possible place—just above the deep hole, which is located about two-thirds of the way through the roughest water. The hole is the dip before an enormous standing wave, big enough to hide a large passenger van. An 18-foot raft has little chance to remain upright, regardless of weight distribution or oarsman's skill, should it smack into this wave sideways.

Riding with Doc means a safer run but a greater risk and a harder fall. Because our boat is first, we are at highest risk as there is no one downstream to throw us rescue lines should something happen. Doc takes a conservative line on the inside of the curve from the hole.

My disappointment sets in as we sail past the big trench, the flushing dent of water that could flip a boat and then spit it out in any direction, either against the cruel Redwall or downstream. It could flip it back upstream for another spin in the giant washing machine. But as we fly past, it looks like fun.

When we are next to the big hole, Doc begins pulling on the oars, drawing us into the eddy to watch the other boats go through. Most of them follow Doc's line at the entry, but instead of pulling right, they go through the wave train, soaking everyone on board but dropping no one in the water. I watch our friends go sailing past, shrieking through the standing waves, clinging with both hands to safety lines, hats flying back or drenched, whitewater at times blinding their view and our view of them.

Then Doc maneuvers the heavy end of his craft out into the current and the flow seems to grab the boat as the eddy gives us back to the river. We ride the roller coaster below the rapid and we are on to the next stretch of river, the next rapid.

Mile 47

Saddle Canyon meanders west from river right through a relatively lush valley that reminds me of hiking in Hawaii. Most of us opt for a hike, while a few prefer a nap on the boats. The trail departs the river with a steep ascent among rocks and scant, desert shrubs.

Soon we are on a dry, north-facing slope that drops precipitously into a lush valley below. Looking back, the Redwall of the main canyon seems another world. I try to wrap my head around the size of it. By maintaining a more or less level course, the path leads us to the valley floor, which has ascended from river level to meet us. We pick our way along a creek bed made surrealistically green by a jungle of vegetation.

Then suddenly we are in Grand Canyon architecture again. Julia wades through a small pool, but I cannot see how she will climb the steep rocks through which the stream trickles. She hands me her water bottle and places a sandal waist-high on the rock. Jimmying herself up, she achieves the ledge about 10 feet up and lies down on the floor above to lend me a hand.

Betsy and Peggie likewise help each other. As we continue upstream the canyon becomes narrower and we have to help each other again at another bathtub-sized pool. The final approach means swimming through a pool, then climbing up one last time to an opening in the canyon wide enough to provide a lounging area. Disney couldn't have invented a lovelier resort, complete with a waterfall shower at the upper end. Although we are not allowed to use soaps or shampoos—or to urinate—within a quarter-mile of these side streams, we all take turns standing under the falling water. I find a white frog on this shower wall, the frog almost as white as my own naked skin.

We trickle back down to the main canyon and the boats—not together but not apart. Soon we are family again, watching each other, watching each boat, tensing as we see each other tackle each rapid, counting heads, cheering good runs.

As fast as the water courses through the Grand Canyon at certain points, so does a slowness take over most of the time we are on the river. "What day is it anyway?" is a common enough refrain that someone had it printed on a t-shirt with artwork of the inner gorge.

A human lifetime, on the spectrum of Grand Canyon geology, is irrelevant. Nearly a billion years after the formation of the Precambrian Vishnu Schist that would drift past our boats in the depths of the canyon, the Kaibab marine limestone began to form. This top layer, that dusted my sandals as I stepped off Navajo Bridge the day before launch, formed the floor of an ocean. It now hosts desert plants.

It is Day Three and I feel a strong urge to get back to my desk. Shouldn't I be doing something? Isn't there something that needs to be mailed? But all I can get worked up about is whether tonight is my turn for kitchen duty. My responsibilities include setting up my tent, sleeping, eating, brushing my teeth, bathing in a remarkably cold river, watching the light shift on the colored walls of the gorge, then doing it all over again. My job is to love this place, that is all.

The Colorado descends some 2,200 feet, crashing through rapids that soak a person so thoroughly she has to feel around to make sure not only her glasses, her clothes, her shoes, but also her hair, teeth, and vital organs have not washed away. A cycle of wet, dry, wet, wet, wet cracks my feet. The cracks in my heels appear similar to the canyon itself. Daily life is not calculating whether the left lane will get me there faster, whether that checkout line is shorter, whether the paycheck will cover the car repair. It's whether the cracks in my feet are getting better, whether four pounds of pasta is too much for 16 people, whether the first light will hit my tent or Peggie's.

Mile 98

Even the commercial trips in their enormous baloney boats scout Crystal Rapid, the second nastiest rapid in the canyon. Some people choose to walk around instead of floating through the rapid, picking their way among boulders, which seems to me just as likely to cause injury.

The maw-like hole that sucks volumes of water from all sides seems unavoidable. The scouting point is a low plain of boulders on river right. But the real threat could also be the rock garden below. By running close to the hole, on its right, Lars hopes to be set up to miss the rocks downstream. We all stand on boulders trying to get a vision of how the boats could safely pass the hole. I am nervous. My gastrointestinal system announces an emergency, which I ignore. The space between the shore and the rapid's gaping maw seems too small for a raft. The hole looks like hell.

The boatmen all talk and point. Julia seems fine, calm and confident. "What's your plan?" I ask her. "I have no fucking idea," she starts out. Then she regains control and says a right run should be easy, but she wants to go left.

Lars gets tired of standing on the hot rocks and turns back to the boats. "C'mon," he says to me, "let's just do it." We do precisely what no one should ever do. We untie and leave before the others are ready. As I coil the bowline, as I have coiled the bowline every time we have cast off from anywhere on this and many other trips, I try to absorb some of Lars' confidence. Instead, this time I fumble with the line and don't tug it as tight as I usually do, throwing the coil into the bow as Lars is already on the oars, eager to go.

I will have to cope with my foot being caught, I reason. There is no way I can pull out my knife and cut it. I kick and finally use my thumb to peel it to my ankle so I can get my lips to the bow and catch a breath. I surface but am too weak to help myself. When I finally achieve the edge and a delicious breath of air, it isn't enough. The bowline has loosened around my leg so that I'm in danger of being separated from the boat. My body is too weak; I need to breathe for a while before I can even reach for the lifeline.

But I don't have that while.

I lunge for the lifeline, but I'm not strong enough in this new, boneless body. I jam my fist between the line and the boat to attach myself to it, then I reach down and clear my foot of the bowline. This process takes approximately two and a half years. When I finally free myself, I try to pull myself on board by grabbing the spare oar. I simply am not strong enough. But in my attempt, I glimpse the boat's topside; Lars is gone. I have to get onboard to row the boat and find him, but I barely have the strength to hang on to the lifeline, much less heave knee or foot up to it.

I look downstream, buying time. I know I will be strong enough to pull myself up as soon as my oxygen level returns. If I can wait that long. Downstream I see rocks, survivable rocks. And no Lars. Then I feel the oar above me move. Lars is climbing on board from the other side but hasn't seen me. As he positions himself to row, I yell his name, which comes out "Shlaw!" and he drops the oars, pulling me aboard in one fast motion. My face hits the cooler and I stay there, lying low so he can work the oars above me. He gains control of the oars and the boat and I try to get my feet under me, my uncooperative feet.

When I sit up and pat my head to signal to anyone who might see that I am okay, I hear a yell, a cheer from shore. The others are still scouting and have seen the whole thing. In fact, someone has recorded it on video tape. Weeks later I watch the boat stand on its side for more than two seconds, as though trying to decide whether to flip or flop back down. At that moment, I am deep in the river.

Lars catches the eddy at the bottom of the rock garden below Crystal and, although I am sure someone else will need rescuing and I have the throw rope ready, everyone else floats through without incident. Ricardo loses an oar and consequently gets hung up on the rocks below, but soon he floats free. As we regain the current I inspect the coffee mug I've retrieved from the eddy. A construction company, no town given, is advertised on it in worn letters. A short length of string ties the lid to the cup. A carabiner, obviously forgotten this morning, or maybe yesterday, or maybe last week, rattles on the mug's handle.

Lars loses his hat in his swim but, strangely, finds a green visor in the eddy, a good visor, like the ones you can get for $40 at REI. That afternoon, eight miles downstream, Betsy, in the boat ahead of us, lets out a yelp of delight, pointing to the water. We are in a place where the water is churning slowly, deeply. She reaches in and pulls out Lars' hat, somewhat out of shape and entirely waterlogged. Lars puts it on for a photograph, but he wears the green visor the rest of the trip.

Mile 148

Matkatamiba Canyon requires agility I didn't know I had. I have seen pictures of this place. Everyone has seen pictures of this place. I know I have seen it in ads for photo paper, on postcards, on every adventure or wilderness-themed anything ever.

Here, water has carved a curved path through stone, through Muav limestone, just wide enough for human shoulders to explore. Again, no competition from Disney. A backpack or fanny pack is essential for carrying your water bottle here because all hands and feet are needed to maneuver a body through. As the side canyon narrows, we must step sideways to avoid the slippery trickle of water, bracing our bodies on the gray, sculpted walls against hands or feet on the opposite side of the narrow canyon.

After a series of challenges that reminds me of gymnastics moves I haven't tried since elementary school, we emerge into a cavernous place where water, I figure looking around me, must have spun in a huge sucking whirlpool. Red walls of limestone form vertical cliffs that tower too precipitously for us to see the top. I sit to stare, so dramatic is the rise of rock above us. This midway stopping point between the twisting climb and the farther reaches of Matkat Canyon forms a natural patio, a place to study the dripping water. A pink redbud screeches at me, lit up by an errant ray of sun against a cold shadow on limestone. All too soon I will be gone from this canyon. I drink it in.

Flagstaff

The boats have been washed, deflated, and heaved onto trucks. Ricardo has donned a t-shirt, rendering him unrecognizable. As I move through a motel room in Flagstaff a few hours after rolling up the rafts, I detect another person, a stranger in my lodgings, through a window to an adjoining chamber. She is dark-skinned and light-haired, thin, moving gracefully with purpose. Taller than me, she moves efficiently about her concerns. She is one of those women I've always wanted to be.

It costs several seconds to convince myself what I see is a mirror, not a window into another world. I've been moving through the room without noticing the mirror. I forgot mirrors even existed. But I am back now. It hits me hard. *Who is that person?*

When we return to "civilization" from the river we are tight-lipped around others; we do not know how to stand in a crowded room. We are changed. I step into the shower and turn the knob to "Cold." I do this for weeks. When I try warm water the first time, I step out feeling unclean.

As our group of friends re-acclimates to culture-as-we-know-it, I realize some people can't understand why I would want to travel through the Grand Canyon on a boat. Others lock eyeballs with envy. But I worry about those who refuse to engage in imagining the trip, those who say something to dispatch any conversation like, "I don't like camping." I read their words to say, "I don't want to hear about it, I'm not interested." I am as incapable of understanding them, I suppose, as they are of me. I imagine these people just go with the flow as they perceive is expected of them, not even noticing the eddy-out from life that a river trip offers. To them, crossing that eddy fence would take a strength on the paddle they're simply incapable of. Incapable until they try. Until it occurs to them to try.

The biggest whitewater, the wildest wilderness, and the perpetual surprise of travelling through the seventh wonder of the world could become a lifestyle. It's taken 12 years, but, by the time I finish my fifth trip, the Grand Canyon has become familiar enough that I no longer feel like a stranger here. Every day still provides discovery, every rapid still thrills, the wrens' descending notes still defy imitation. To call it a "wonderland" is grossly unjust, but the looks on the faces of the others—and I know on mine as well—are that: wonder. Geologists can postulate for another 570 billion years, but they'll never explain how or why the striped cliffs, backlit cottonwood trees and warbling birds make us feel alive.

Georgie White, a woman credited with pioneering the J-rig construction used by commercial boats today, as well as pioneering the sport of whitewater rafting itself, represents to me the phenomenon of the Western Adventurer. Born in 1921, she left her jobs as real estate agent, as wife, as whatever she was doing, to hike and explore the canyons and rivers of the western United States. Her experiences do not compare to ours today. She chose to embark on trips she must have known would be physically daunting, painful, and often life-threatening. But she just kept doing them.

A friend of mine from the East Coast said recently, in a moment of wild enthusiasm, "Let's have an adventure; let's put on some lipstick and head out the door." I knew the kind of adventure she meant was one that would involve meeting good-looking men in bars and not much else. But that is adventure to her. That is the limit many people are willing to do, or to imagine. Go down a river on a raft? You gotta be nuts. So what are the lipstick-adventurers thinking? How can some human beings be so docile, satisfied with so little as a conversation at a bar? Aren't we talking about the mere procreation of the species, this bar-talk? Just sex?

To the boaters who vie for a permit to run the Colorado River every year this is incomprehensible. Life cannot be reduced to a mathematical equation, an analysis of the risk of doing any particular activity. To subdue our passions as humans seems something like sacrilege, something listed by those busy defining what "sin" is. Getting outside and pushing my personal limits seems an obligation, if only to myself. I cannot explain it other than to try to explain the feeling when I've done it. Beyond ecstasy, it's witness to a spiritual place beyond anything any religious leader could dream of evoking. It's somewhere along there with contemplating the miracle of life itself, something up there with comprehending the universe, what lies beyond the stars.

And I recall, wasn't I terrified when I first saw the pictures of big water? The decision to go had changed me. Then I had found someone inside me I didn't realize was there. I had used the logic "If others have done it, so can I" to propel me to the water's edge. From there, the place took over and told me what to do, how to respond to every wave. The canyon taught me to let myself be pulled into side canyons, to stretch my eyes to the rim, to forget what day it is.

I did not know my great-great-grandmother, Louisa Field, but if she were like me, she thought about going down that river with Powell and his men. Maybe she wouldn't have been allowed to go, or maybe the men begged her to join but she refused. I only know that she did love the place—she showed up for the ceremony dedicating the Grand Canyon into the National Park Service some 50 years later. She chose as a young woman to live at the end of the rail line at that time, to run a boarding house at a trading post at the very edge of the wilderness.

Was she really mad about the loss of her chair? Or was she jealous of it? I imagine that if I'd had a crack at joining Powell's adventures, I would have slipped aboard. I wonder that my great-great-grandmother didn't somehow stow away. But maybe I would have taken a look at the ten, mostly drunk (thanks to Grampa's whiskey), mostly Civil War veteran crew from 1869 and decided "Heck, take the chair. Just get out of my kitchen."

Just Another Day on the River
Patsy Kate Booth

A private river trip requires curiosity, kindness, attention to detail, forethought, organization, experience, knowledge, spontaneity, actual river skills, and a dose of common sense. What really helps is an outrageously good sense of humor.

The winter snowstorms blow cold, then go away, melting into the desiccated ground. One hour after the sun heats up the pavement, compost heap, lawn, and rock pile, the snow vanishes. Underground things come alive and so do my hopes and dreams of running the river that lies just a few miles from my driveway. I've obediently signed on with *recreation.gov* to apply for permits again this year and am in a holding pattern waiting for the response. So are thousands of other river rats, all sanding, gluing, and polishing their oars, paddles, rafts, duckies, and kayaks while waiting to hear if they are one of the lucky ones. Who will be the big winner? Most years, I get the "Sorry Charlie" note via email. The last San Juan River permit I pulled was four years ago.

This year I am a winner. The permit is for mid-September and the winter was a dry one. Knowing that the San Juan River bottom shifts and writhes like the serpent god Awanyu, concerns flood in about river levels and campsites. But I forge ahead and make a list of potential accomplices who will drop and run when a river trip invitation beckons. We have run many rivers together so the planning of basic food groups, who cooks when and with whom, is painless. Each group chooses the meals, menus, and the days they want to provide their culinary expertise, with first-come advantages. We will ride the chocolate-milk-thick river for five days. We will camp at the put-in, Sand Island, where we will gear up early morning on Day 1. My campsite guru, Waldon, will determine where we camp each night with a take-out at Mexican Hat on Day Five.

Email discussions go viral among us discussing which craft each person will take, who has the fire-pan, best groover, water jugs, coolers, dry boxes, cots, tents, first aid kit, extra PFDs, paddles, who drives with whom, shuttle, arrival and launch times. Oh, and how much beer and wine will we carry?

The San Juan River is a fairly easy river to float with Class II rapids and an infrequent Class III in high water. The challenge comes in dealing with shifting river bottoms and quicksand shores. The archeological sites, ruins, pictographs and petroglyphs, hiking trails, canyon scenery, canyon wrens to wake you, ravens to pester your food cache and steal your shiny objects, stars to distract your sleeping hours, collared lizards to demonstrate pushups, guitar and ukulele concerts, crackling fires on chilly evenings, hot coffee, cantaloupe, enchiladas, grilled salmon, chardonnay, IPAs and nightcap sips of tequila, all mixed in with the occasional sandstorm and frosty night, make for the ideal river trip among good friends.

The final group of participants finds us with a variety of eleven strong personalities. Mike and Annie are seasoned outdoor people who travel the world when they aren't bagging peaks in the Colorado Rockies. Annie is well aware of the pressures on a Trip Leader (TL) since she worked for me as wrangler and guide assistant during the years when I owned and operated an outfitting business, La Garita Llamas. Our llama treks into Grand Gulch, Collins Springs, and the surrounding areas honed my enthusiasm for rafting through this wild Utah canyon country. Mike and Annie will paddle individual inflatable kayaks so they pack backpacker light. Annie invited her friend, Susan, who paddles an old hardshell kayak without a spray skirt. This creates some rather disturbing problems as the trip develops.

My dear friend and wilderness companion for the past few decades, Peggy, better known in river groups as the Avon Lady, will row her lovely 12½-foot Avon raft. Peggy will carry extra water, some kitchen supplies, and a few dry bags for the kayakers. And she brings a laugh that makes the river gods rise up and listen. Doug, a canoe enthusiast who holds a PhD in wilderness training, is a serious Zen practitioner. He's excited to join this crazed bunch. I'm sure this adventure will become part of his practice as he also volunteers to instruct Dee Dee on paddling techniques in her new inflatable 14-foot canoe.

Sky, a wild man who boated the Grand Canyon with Waldon, has a reputation preceded by endless stories of escapades as an adrenaline junkie jumping out of airplanes and nosing into BIG WATER. He brings his 16-foot Banana Boat cataraft and two ginormous coolers for beer. Dirk, my former husband, lives to row his beloved Hyside 14-foot raft. He generously takes on all equipment for setting up camp; fire-pan, groover, cots, more water jugs, other people's dry bags, chairs, tables, more food and yes, copious amounts of beer. Dirk lives with painful arthritis and has chronic hip, neck, back, and leg pain due to a grueling career as a concrete contractor. Birdie, the blonde, is in her mid-forties, the youngest of the gang. As an expert Audubon birder, she rides on Peggy's boat and entertains her by identifying yellow warblers and flycatchers flitting through the thickets of willow along the bank.

And there is me. Trip Leader. Former outfitter and guide, now in my mid-sixties, leading a simple, 27-mile stretch of river with experienced, loony, independent, headstrong, laughing, strong willed, opinionated, creative, adventurous lovers of rivers and lovers of people who love rivers. My career as a play therapist comes in handy.

All my river trips have been private boating where the TL invites participants and navigates the choppy waters of bureaucracy. A bit of paranoia always exists around what tiny detail of planning was missed. To dance this dance gracefully among friends and river rangers can be a waltz or a jitterbug. This trip was more like a rave.

Broken Rule # 1: Boaters will not sleep on the launch ramp, leaving the area open for early morning riggers. Sand Island has a broad concrete ramp that accommodates at least a dozen large rafts. Sky rolls in in late afternoon pulling a small trailer stacked high with gear—rolled up cataraft tubes, frame, pump (buried) and assorted items in total disarray. As dusk creeps over the viscous, silty river, painting it a golden-bronze-rose, he cracks open a beer and whirls with joy. The last time we ran this river together was to scatter ashes of a close friend who loved the desert San Juan. Sky is definitely in a celebratory mood. As TL, I must remind him that camping on the launch ramp is forbidden.

This news only casts a gleam in his eyes, a twirling bear hug, and an offer of tequila. I see right away that my request/warning has zero effect. Dirk joins Sky in the subterfuge as piles of gear, soon to resemble a yard sale, scatter across the ramp.

Peggy arrives pulling her camp trailer and sets up plastic, pink flamingos at its entrance to encourage folks to enter, have a cup of coffee, and laugh about past antics on rivers. The group sets up their tents while I check lists, fill out the group campsite information, and stab the yellow envelope on the reserved post. Sky and Dirk continue to hoot, howl, sip tequila, and build more piles on the launch ramp. The second and third reminder to set camp elsewhere finally hits and the rationalizations flood forth. Darkness has fallen. The river ranger is not to be seen. Sky insists he will be rigged and packed up before Ranger Ron opens his eyes to his first cup of coffee. My request now comes with insistence and, in retort, Sky hugs me tight, plants a kiss, and turns to continue his sorting. I have a bad feeling about this.

Dawn breaks; quiet, birds flit, a deep breath, somebody boils water, and the scent of coffee wafts on the chill morning air. The sounds of motors, shoes shuffling across sand-drizzled concrete, whispers and a hiccup and snort. The day opens with cloud cover and indecipherable human language and laughter.

Ten boats for eleven people. We have invaded and inhabited the entire launch area. Each of us inflate our boats and line them up—rubber to hypolon. There is a disarray of cots, tent bags, paco pads, waterproof dry bags of all sizes, coolers, aluminum dry boxes, wooden planks, oars, folded chairs, umbrellas tied with rainbow straps, paddles, boat frames, air pumps, PFDs, small water bottles, sandals, water jugs, a groover, gritty black-stained rubber bags crammed with charcoal, fire pans, fresh groceries, cases of beer, a cantaloupe, an empty can of PBR. A damp sarong flaps on a thin branch stretched over the river. We are almost packed up and ready to plunge our paddles to turn downstream.

The river ranger finds me nearly buried under piles of gear. He asks for my permit; his brow dark, like furrows across a rich field. A quick glance and the verbal assault begins regarding rules, safety, and miscreants. I apologize profusely. I glare at Sky who has his head plunged deep in the watery bowels of the Banana Boat, while sucking the foam off his breakfast beer. I assure Ranger Ron I can keep my renegade charges in check. I feel a sinking feeling in my gut, but flash a toothy smile at the ranger who spins and hunches over his official river permit notepad. He walks away. He warns he will be watching us, and he does as our entourage loads and prepares to shove off. We separate from the shore about noon.

The river gauge reads 7,700 cfs. The water is above bank full and at flood stage. The willow and tamarisk lean downstream in the rapid current. Floating debris snags in a side canal formed by the high water. Our flotilla stretches out for nearly a quarter of a mile. There is no way I can keep these cats herded. The river runs fast. Kayaks are out of view and I count all who pass except Susan in her swampable yellow kayak. I paddle to Sky's boat, which sits in an eddy as he waits for further direction. An experienced and somewhat attentive river rat, he senses something awry.

Ranger Ron follows us in his raft and pulls into the eddy where Sky and I count passing boats. He barks a few malcontented statements about always having my entire group in sight at all times. I reply, "Yes Sir," and the ranger pulls away into the current. Sky and I exchange glances of chagrin and he hands me his beer. I take a deep, long pull.

Annie calls out over the swift, red river that Susan has not emerged from the diversion she took into the narrow canal thicket. I paddle aggressively toward the shallows on river right to glimpse her rust-river stained, faded yellow kayak and wait. I'm anxious, angry, and helpless as the other boaters catch in the current and disappear around the bend. Above the roar and rush of river, I hear the crack and swish of broken branches as the willows whine and then split open. Susan appears smiling, twigs caught in her hair and her kayak plastered with wet leaves. A voice from somewhere inside cloaks my anger and I encourage her to please stay in sight of the group. She tells me her kayak is full of water and she needs to empty it before going any further. I nod and paddle downstream to see the red desert canyon open up and a string of boats hanging on the right and left shores. Laughter floats like the companion raven on the bluing sky.

Before we departed, the group discussed places to stop and explore as several paddlers have not witnessed the historical glyphs and paintings on the stone walls in the river corridor. Butler Wash Petroglyph Panel is not to be missed. With the river running high, parking will be a challenge—but Waldon offers to guide us to an embankment where we can crawl from our boats and slither onto the slippery slope tangled with thin willow branches. Everyone except Sky, Peggy, and Dirk cram their boats into the small eddy. Only about four miles from our put-in, we have already forgotten time and are captured by the lure of the ancient ones. Peggy finds a shady spot just downstream of the panel where she watches Dirk row past. Sky's bright yellow cataraft bobs and lightly drifts in and out of a slim eddy on river left.

Each of us muse over the rectangular-shaped stick figures with back humps or engorged phalluses, headdresses with rays of sun or feathers, bighorn sheep, deer, a frog creature, stairsteps, horses, arrows, trails of dots, serpents, and handprints, until we exhaust our limited creative visions. We descend the trail in a row back to the flotilla cluster.

Our first planned camp is at Riverhouse, less than two miles from Butler Wash. The sandstone ruins are a short hike from riverside camping. We will set our tents, cots, and kitchen there for two nights. From camp we will be able to view the primitive rooms and walls of the Riverhouse Ruins that spread under a length of stone overhang, decorated with undulating serpents high on the ceilings and walls. Our layover day offers hikes over San Juan Hill, traversing the old Mormon trail to the monocline edge of Comb Ridge that looks down a dramatic fall into the broad valley of Cottonwood Wash.

Waldon backs his bucket boat into the swift running river, a strong forward pull on the left and back paddle on the right. We follow like obedient ducklings, waving to Sky while Peggy drops into line. We assume Dirk is waiting for us at Riverhouse camp. I scan the right bank for his gray Hyside, or some disturbance in the flow that indicates his position behind the tangled branches. High water has washed out the eddies so I paddle hard to where I think Dirk is waiting. My intention is to grip a limb to secure a place, jump from the duckie and assist him with landing the rest of the group who are coming on fast. But when I get there, there is no gray Hyside. No Dirk. Empty.

I hold onto my limb as the crew arrives. The boats bump and rub against one another. Hands reach out to the closest person to hang onto a safety line, rope, extended paddle, all connected to my rapidly loosening hold on the riverbank foliage. A wave of emotion and a spike of panic run from hand to hand. Where is Dirk and what the hell? I immediately realize our trip plans could fall apart so I encourage everyone to row down to the next open area and reconnoiter. I am certain Dirk will be there waiting. The only sound is water rushing against the boats and splashing the muddy shore.

No Dirk at the next eddy. We paddle downstream searching both sides of the river for his gray Hyside or his red PFD caught in the bushes. Next camp passed. Next camp passed. I shout out for all of us to keep a keen eye on both banks for anything that might indicate Dirk caught in a snag, or is perhaps just holding on for dear life to some flimsy, supple branch. Dread sweeps the group. The earlier explosions of giddiness, raucous laughter, bad jokes, and water fights are gone. We know that Dirk suffers with critical physical pain and his strength wanes more and more with each river trip. I take a deep breath and recall my insistence on including him on this trip, regardless of his physical disabilities and bouts of depression. The river is what keeps Dirk alive.

A large family has gathered at a long beach, waving and yelling as we approach. They say a raft passed by, but they couldn't tell if anyone was in the boat. About ¼-mile downstream from that beach, a young man with a woman and small child row out to us. He reports intercepting Dirk's raft and finding Dirk clutching the safety line around the boat. The young man gave his oars to his wife and leaped into Dirk's boat, grabbed the shoulders of his PFD and yanked him back onboard. Dirk claimed to be OK, so the man returned to his family. And Dirk floated on.

The good news is that the damn fool is alive, but the heat of frustration rises up my spine. We have yet to find Dirk and wonder how much further he rowed. It looks like a 5-day trip will end on Day 2 or 3. Sky talks mutiny, disappointed at a shortened trip, and wants to extend the trip to the take-out at Clay Hills. Not possible. No permit.

I lean into a splashy little Class II rapid and find my smile, yet I still feel tense and curious about where we will find Dirk. The entourage comes to a stop at an island on river left where a couple of fishermen say they saw some guy row past and is probably stopped downstream. Finally, we see him—alive. And I want to kill him!

With a deep breath and long exhale, I sit beside Dirk on a driftwood log and ask what happened. The stress seems to deepen his already sun-dark, wrinkled face. His arms, once heavy with muscles from hard work, are thin and bruised. Trickles of blood spread like river tributaries down his forearm. Loud chatter, sounding like a flock of disorganized geese, sweeps over us and I'm not able to hear his mumbled speech. Everyone has their opinion (imagine that)! Nine faces lean in to hear the explanation.

Dirk rows to the flooded eddy and sees he has little time to bump land, drop the oars, grab the line and leap to the muddy shore. His timing is good, but the oar swings upward and catches a torn hole in his heavy Carhartt shorts and won't release. The raft spins and the force of the oar under water flings Dirk into the drink! He is underwater and reaches up to grab anything, and with the luck of that salty old Irishman, wraps his fingers around the safety line. He is now floating downstream and in the water. His arthritic shoulder grinds bone on bone with excruciating pain. He cannot self-rescue. He takes a breath, looks around and watches land go by. He sees the family on the riverbank, but they don't see him. Suddenly, there is this young, dark-haired man towering over him. He snatches Dirk by the PFD and pulls him into the raft. He asks if all is well. Dirk says he's OK. The man bounds back to his own boat and vanishes. Vanishes.

We all look like fish out of water with our mouths gaping open and huffing for air. Talk of what now, what next and of course, lunch. Disgruntled whispers wash here and there under the raven's caw. But with food, smiles return and we are back on the river. Enough? The trip isn't over yet.

Our camp that night is lively. Some songs, ukulele playing, green chili burritos, a couple of beers and we settle into our first night on the river, with brilliant streaks of falling stars to remind us of how lucky we are.

After a hearty breakfast the next morning we climb on our silt-slick boats and prepare for a few splashy rapids: Four Mile, Eight Mile, Ledge. Dee Dee's eyes bulge open and terror strikes her when she faces what seems the smallest of riffles on the river. She gets advice from Doug on how to keep the nose of her inflatable canoe downstream and we all hoot and shiver in the cold water. We will spend another night on the river, so Waldon rows a bit ahead to find a camp that will accommodate a group of this size. The sun warms my bare arms and I bathe the sides of the duckie, slathering silty water on the red slip that coats everything that comes in contact with this river.

Susan calls across the river saying the last rapid filled her kayak and she can no longer paddle straight with the extra weight. She is now on river left and our companions are in view downstream on river right, pulled over for a confab. As TL I must stay with the lone kayaker. I point my arm to river left to indicate where I am headed to assist Susan. I reach the shore and find some firm ground to pull my duckie onshore. Susan slides out of her kayak and sinks in the mud. "Come to this spot!" I implore, but she ignores me and says the she won't take long as she dips water from her craft with a small water bottle. Susan continues to sink deeper. I alert her to San Juan quicksand and tell her we must get her out now. Susan is tragically stuck up to her thighs, feet planted flat. She is not able to budge. From the other side of the river I hear curses and "What the hell?" I blow my emergency whistle long, over and over, but the shrill sound is muffled by river and wind.

People immediately across the river from us finally hear the whistle and paddle their duckie to the rescue. My gang now realizes there is an issue here. Sky, Annie, and Mike arrive from across the river. We dig deep with camp shovels and long branches, but the quicksand just floods back in. Susan is not able to move her feet and is now feeling the pressure of the quicksand. Annie lays a paco pad over the kayak and Sky holds on to Susan's arms, pulling forward while a team of diggers and jostlers ultimately begin to loosen her legs. Susan is moaning and Sky makes lurid sexual innuendos. An hour later, Susan is free and we all return to just another day on the river.

The half-day float to Mexican Hat is amazingly uneventful. I turn to inhale the rust colored cliffs, dusty, sage scented air, cloud wisps and the landmark balanced rock of Mexican Hat. I observe my pals in reclining postures, paddling drowsily with oars mostly shipped as the rafts sway in the flow, bobbing to the rhythm of birdsong. Was there drama? Tension? Uncertainty? Disappointment? Confusion? Camaraderie? Bonding? Judgments? Decisions? Change of plans? Laughter? Always laughter.

Any day on the river is a good day.

Moments

Josh Case

Moments. A plural noun meaning "a very brief period of time." We can all define how long a moment is—but it is a subjective thing. To me, being a private boater is all about moments. They may be fleeting, but they make an impression on the soul that differs vastly from the moments I spend in "real life"—driving to and from work, actually doing work, handling phone calls and emails. Moments on the river make all the mundane daily tasks of life seem worth it. When I'm not on the river, I spend time reflecting on those moments. Those times when a push or pull of the oars can have such a significant impact on the immediate few seconds to come, as well as on all points thereafter on life away from the river. Boating allows me to live in the moment. Being in the place, with some of my favorite people, just living each moment. Producing the memories that get you through the other moments in life that just don't make you feel as alive as being on the water, running rapids, or just drifting, listening to the canyon wren's songs.

I have not been a private boater for a particularly long time. Then again, boating takes time, money, and skill. I have some of each of these—but probably not enough of any of them to consider myself anything but a novice. I originally decided I wanted to start boating while on an eight-day hike of the Escalante Route in Grand Canyon back in 2009 with my long-time hiking friend Jim. We arrived on Day 3 of our hike early in the afternoon at Cardenas Camp (River Mile 71) and enjoyed the shady beach and cool river all to ourselves for several hours. Late in the day, a party of 16 Canadians pulled in and asked to share our camp. They convinced us it was a good idea by offering us beers. What backpacker would seriously turn down cold beer? We gladly obliged and moved back up behind the river camp to give their group some room.

Both Jim and I were amazed that these hardy souls were on such an adventure. Most remarkable was all the gear they had with them.

As we watched them, more and more equipment was unloaded and lugged across the beach: tables, chairs, fire pans, tents; it never seemed to end. It was a first-class yard sale! Later our new neighbors invited us down for chips, salsa, and margaritas with ice! We declined dinner and ate our freeze-dried meal to save pack weight. We began to discuss how wonderful it would be to do our own river trip, with all the luxuries of home in such a remote environment.

Not long after this hike I began to research what it would take to apply for a Grand Canyon river permit of my own. Due to some of life's unforeseen circumstances, I wasn't able to apply for several years. Fast forward to 2012. I won! I pulled a coveted Grand Canyon permit on my first try. Launch date was March 23, 2013. With a little over a year to plan, I was able to find a group of likeminded people to pull off the "Trip of a Lifetime." I borrowed a boat and the trip was as amazing as I had imagined—I was hooked. Once home, I dreamed about running rapids. I decided I wanted a boat of my own. I decided to price one out that was exactly like the 18-foot Maravia oar rig I had rowed down the Grand. The sticker shock was astounding. I did not have the money to fund my new hobby. So I came up with an even better idea (was it really better?!)—I would build myself a wooden boat. I figured it would be pretty easy and not nearly as expensive as buying a fully outfitted raft. My naivete was starting to show, but I was SO hooked on the whole experience. The action, the adventure, the luxurious camping, the camaraderie. All of it!

I picked up a copy of Roger Fletcher's *Drift Boats and River Dories* and learned all I could. How difficult could this really be? I printed out a full-sized set of Jerry Briggs' *Colorado River Dory Plans* and then set to work sourcing all the materials I would need. A friend and I set to work on my not-yet-named Briggs boat in November of 2013. Spending mostly nights and weekends on the build, we completed the *Sweet & Lowdown* in October of 2014. In the meantime, I ran my second Grand Canyon trip as a boatman in June of 2014. I was so addicted to this boating thing that I was making plans in my head to do a trip every single year until I died of old age or got smarter, whichever came first.

I launched the new boat with a couple of other wooden boats at Diamond Creek, Grand Canyon, for what is known as the

199

"Diamond Down" trip to Pearce Ferry in October of 2014. Tom Martin brought his *GEM*, and Craig Wolfson brought his *Flavell II*. Accompanied by a rowdy bunch of friends in an 18-foot raft, the maiden voyage of my boat commenced. I was just relieved my dory floated, as this was the first time in the water, not to mention my first time ever rowing a wooden boat. I didn't realize I could get even more hooked on boating than I already was—but this put me over the top!

I was fortunate enough that a couple of friends of mine had won a Grand Canyon permit for a launch in March of 2015. I would take the dory. I made several modifications after the "Diamond Down" trip, and do not think I talked, or thought, about much else for a year. I am thankful my wife didn't leave me—fortunately she was also excited to be going on the trip.

I was excited for the upcoming adventure, could not wait to test my whitewater skills in my hand-built, wooden boat, and enjoyed showing it off to anyone who would listen. I loved the adventure, but I had no idea what excitement lay ahead on the maiden trip for *Sweet & Lowdown* through the entire Grand Canyon.

The morning of Saturday, March 14, 2015, dawned cool and clear at Lower Rattlesnake Camp. This was our last morning after a layover day and it was time to move downstream to set up for our exchange of passengers at Phantom Ranch the following morning. It was not a very quiet morning for us, as we had to get up at 5:30 a.m. to make coffee, and then a breakfast of French toast and bacon for the crew. The cook crew consisted of myself, my wife Amy, Steven (the permit holder) and Rachael (the other permit holder). We rocked out breakfast at a respectable pace and had clean up, packing, and kitchen breakdown all completed in a reasonable time. We were able to break down our camp and pack the boat up at a leisurely pace, and were ready to go before the rest of the crew. What I had learned over the course of our first week on the trip in our homebuilt Briggs dory was that packing it in the mornings was a breeze. No straps to mess with. No gear pile to sort through. Everything had a place in the hatches, and once you put the various items in the boat, you just closed the lids and secured the latches. Simple.

The tension on our boat was running high. We faced a big day on the river. I took the time to install a flip line. Just in case. As Amy and our other passenger, Bobby, climbed aboard and we were about to shove off, a feeling of uneasiness swept over me. We were about to go through a stretch of river that I was dreading. Not because the rapids are bigger or scarier than other rapids we would face, but because of the rocks. So many rocks. I knew Hance Rapid was not going to be fun. I knew the line was going to be tight. I was also acutely aware that we had to run Nevills Rapid (75-mile) before we got to the scout at Hance. I was aware of the pour-overs and rocks in Nevills too. I had hit the mid-channel pour-over on my last trip in June of 2014. That was in rubber. This time I was rowing wood.

We ran the riffle at Escalante while a group of backpackers looked on. It was an easy run. Right around the bend was Nevills. I entered left, with the intention of moving back to the middle once I was safely below all of the pour-overs at the top to avoid a final bottom-left pour-over. I moved back to the center too soon. In fact, I moved back center just in time to hit the mid-river pour-over about two-thirds of the way through the rapid. BANG! The boat shuddered as we hit the rock at the top of the pour-over. It was a hard hit on the left side of our boat, about a third of the way down the side. There was more water in my footwell than usual after we got the fore and aft footwells bailed out, but I didn't think much about it.

Shortly after our incident in Nevills, we pulled into the right scout for Hance. Lagging a bit behind the others, we took time to look in the hatch that is directly in front of the rower's seat, and behind the front seat—it was full of water! This was not a good sign. I hoped this was just water that leaked in from the decks. I could not have been more wrong. Amy stayed back and began to pump the water out with our kayak bilge pump while I went up to the scout.

I can't say I was surprised at what I saw from the scout overlook. There were rocks. Lots of rocks. The first thing I said was, "It looks closed." I didn't see a good run for our wooden boat. I saw a mess of rocks, churning water and big holes. I even joked about portaging the dory. In hindsight, maybe it wasn't a joke? I felt ill. Things were off. I reviewed the standard "Duck Pond" run with Dave, one of the more experienced boatmen. Pointing and gesturing, we reviewed the plan: head downstream with a left-shore ferry angle on the left side of the right tongue; pull through the lateral; spin and exit the "Duck Pond" on the left. I didn't see the slot. I just saw a big pour-over. "Watch out for the Toilet Bowl," Dave said. "If you get in it, it should spit you out." I heard all of this. I soaked it in. I knew it was for the benefit of the others as well. Tensions were high. After all, Hance Rapid is rated as an 8 on the Grand Canyon scale of 1 through 10. We headed back down the scout trail to the boats to get ready to run it.

When I got back to the boat, Amy had some bad news. We must have a hole in the boat. As fast as she was pumping the water out, it was coming in and filling the hatch compartment. We began to empty the hatch and bail the boat out. Once the water was down low enough, it was clear we had put a hole, about the size of a softball, in the side of the boat right along the chine. The chine was blown out. Water poured in continuously.

With the help of several others in our party, we were able to tilt the boat up on its side while I attempted a temporary patch of Gorilla Tape over the hole. It would have to hold. The plan was to run down to Cremation where I could make a permanent patch that night. The hole was still leaking, but the flow had been cut to nearly nothing. We reloaded the boat and the crew pushed off.

We were running sweep boat, which meant we were last in the running order. We were the sixth boat to enter, and we followed Chris in. The top of the rapid is a bit deceiving. I could see the big, red boulder that sits in the middle of the river. I could see the smaller boulders in front of it that we needed to be close to as I pulled into the rapid to break the laterals. What was completely disguised was the pour-over that separates the two tongues on the right side. As we watched each boat glide into the rapid, we saw Chris go in hard and drop over the pour-over. "Oh shit! We are too far right!"

I pulled as hard as I could to avoid the "Toilet Bowl" at the top of the rapid. I have since come to learn this hole is referred to as "Emilio's Hole." At the moment we entered the rapid, the front of our boat caught the edge of the recirculating hole below the pour-over. It sucked us in!

We began what seemed like twenty to thirty seconds of surfing the hole, facing downstream. I had lost the oars when we went in. All we could do was high-side and stay upright. Then the front of the boat swung around to the left and I knew we were in trouble. After the boat swung left, I could see flat smooth water coming at us down the tongue. Then the water began to fill up the boat and dip the left side gunwale into the water. I knew we were going to swim. The boat rolled over gently, seemingly in slow motion. I managed to get half a breath before I was surrounded by cold, brown, angry water. I realized right away I was under the boat. I began to use my hands over my head to walk myself out from underneath. I remembered this technique from a safety talk before a previous trip. As I walked myself to the edge of the boat, I realized I was going to surface on the downstream side of the boat. A very bad idea as the boat was pummeling over pour-overs heading downriver. I remained calm as I began to work myself to what I believed was the upstream side of the boat. A much safer place to surface I surmised. When I was finally able to break clear of the boat I surfaced. Everything around me was complete chaos. I did my best to get another breath before I plunged over another pour-over into a hole. Again, I went under. I was getting knocked around. I grabbed a bottle of sunscreen floating nearby. I went through another hole. I crashed into more rocks. At one point, at what I judged to be the middle of Hance, I was able to get to the boat. I knew I should get on top of the boat and out of the water. I noticed my Gorilla Tape patch was gone. I jettisoned the bottle of sunscreen.

It was then I realized the boat was about to go through another hole. More rocks. I pushed off to create some separation. I was determined to NOT get pinned between the boat and the rocks. I went under again. I lost count of how many times I went under. I kept going back to the safety talk.

"Your PFD will keep returning you to the surface."

"Stay calm."

"It will be over soon."

As I continued to swim, my legs started getting thrashed on the shallow rocks on the right side of Lower Hance. My knees were bruised. Then I realized I could stand up! No sooner did I stand up and turn around, did I see our boat, broadside on a shallow cobble bar. It looked intact! Then I heard it. The undeniable sound of wood smashing and breaking apart. Hideous and grotesque sounds of splintering wood. At this moment I realized the boat was heading straight for me! I did the only thing I thought prudent at the time: I jumped as far as I could away from the boat, back into the main current of the river.

Right about this time, I laid eyes on Chris and Ben's boat. I was exhausted. I was laying on my back, letting the PFD do its job. I was just out of throw bag range. I begged for help, to get pulled out of the water. "Chris. Help me. Please. Help me get out of the water …" I pleaded. "I'm trying," he said. Chris had lost an oar up top and ran Hance with a single oar. He was just getting that oar back in the lock when I drifted past him. There was nothing he could do. They were just not close enough to me for an effective toss of a throw bag.

We were quickly approaching Son of Hance, a smaller but still violent rapid just downstream from the main rapid. Here is where I got my first glimpse of Amy. She was lying on her back, holding her PFD by the shoulder straps. She was alive! She was also headed for Son of Hance. I lost sight of her at this moment. I do not remember if she was ahead of me or behind me. I don't remember if I had spotted Bobby yet or not.

Here we go, into another rapid. Deep breaths, into the holes, under water, back to the surface. Get ready to do it again. I am exhausted. I hoped I had the strength to continue to swim back to the surface each time I was sucked under. Finally, it was over. A bit down from Son of Hance Dave pulled me into his boat. I was no use to him. I had nothing left. My drysuit pants had water in them from the ankle gaskets past my knees. I was alive! Where was Amy? I saw her go by me. She was still swimming! Finally, Jeff, Haley, and Jamie were able to get her out of the water. I could then see that Steven, Rachael, and Tags had Bobby out of the water. We all survived! We pulled over on river left above a small riffle. We were now in the Upper Granite Gorge. Bobby was throwing up. I moved from Dave's boat onto Jamie's as quickly as I could. I had to make sure Amy was OK. She was in shock. It was hard to watch. It is an image that will be forever etched into my consciousness. Only then did I notice that the big toe on my right foot was in an awkward position, yanked out from the strap of my Chaco sandals. I was in pain; legs bruised, knee swelling, foot in acute pain. But we were alive. We were in the water for about fourteen minutes. We swam for over a mile and a half. We were lucky enough to live to tell the story.

Time has a way of smoothing over the edges. It seems to be that way with most everything in life. The adventure in Hance Rapid was no different. The rawness of the emotion, the experience, and the aftermath were a bit of a shock. We were left numb. It was a moment that we will never forget. My wife and I hiked out at Pipe Creek, caught a ride to Flagstaff, and towed our empty boat trailer back to Las Vegas. We thought the boat was a total loss. But this story has a happy ending. The *Sweet & Lowdown* was recovered by a National Park Service Swift Water Rescue Team and the Park Helicopter. Exactly a week after our swim in Hance we were back on the South Rim, taking what was left of our hand-built, wooden boat back to Las Vegas, along with most of our gear.

The dory sat in our garage for almost two years in the same condition. It was a monument to my failure as a Grand Canyon boatman. I seemed to have lost my desire to boat. I didn't have any future trips lined up.

Then a funny thing happened in January of 2017. I decided that I could no longer look at the monument of my greatest defeat. It was time to resurrect the *Sweet & Lowdown* from the ashes. The same friend who helped with the original build moved back to Las Vegas and we set to work on rebuilding her. Better than the first time. Learning from our mistakes. After three months of work, we finally had her back together.

Painted. Gunwales back on. She was back in the water a few weeks past the 2-year anniversary of Hance Rapid. Again, launched with the *GEM* and *Flavell II*. This time, a new wooden boat joined the party, the *Music Temple*. It had all come full circle, and my kids were able to take part in the relaunch.

I still consider myself a private boater. After all, I have a whitewater dory sitting in the garage, and a desire to get back on the river. Boating has enrolled me into the de-facto 'boating club' as I call it. I have made so many friends in my short time as a boater. These are people I go out of my way to see when they come to my town, or when I am in their town. I can honestly say some of my best friends were met because of boating, and it is such a small, close-knit community. I have found that boaters will do anything for a boater in need, and I have witnessed this first-hand. The camaraderie on the water, and off, is one of the reasons I will continue to boat. What started out as a way to see more of the Grand Canyon has seeped into most every cell in my body. Boating is an addiction. It is not only a means to travel wild and beautiful places in style, but a way to connect to the land, the water, and the people around us. Boating teaches, and there is very little in the world comparable to the rewards of building a boat, putting a trip together, and setting off with your best friends.

Even now as I write this, I am longing for the smooth waves on a remote beach, sitting on my boat, enjoying the stillness. Craving some soul-fueling MOMENTS! Knowing that we are able to sit here and be in the moment due to our hard work and dedication to boating. That is the real reward for being a private boater. That, and a river-temperature beer at the end of the day. A day unique unto itself, never to be duplicated in time or place.

What It Means

Guy Cloutier

What does it mean to run a river on my own? Adventure. That is the best answer I can give. But let me flesh it out a bit. It means an adventure within nature. I love it and enjoy the company of other like-minded folks. I admire some of the extreme adventurers like Yosemite climbers, but I don't go that far myself. My adventures are more along the lines of climbing Mt. Rainier, swim-packing West Clear Creek, family camping in Hawaii, exploring old mines in Nevada, scuba diving, cross-country skiing Yellowstone, car camping in Mexico, day hikes near home, biking across the USA, canoeing in Boundary Waters, and so on. From my perspective, river trips are about the middle of the range in terms of difficulty, cost, adventure level, and fun. Obviously, I can carry more gear and comforts on a boat than in a backpack, plus expend a lot less energy getting wherever I'm going. But this does not mean a river trip is better just because it is easier. Nor does it mean a backpack is better because I earned my wilderness experience with sweat. They are simply different ways to be there. River running is a part of all those activities that get me out and exploring the natural world. I'll partake in any and all of them, repeatedly, if given the chance.

An adventure usually starts with the invitation. And this starts my anticipation. Life and work is rescheduled so that I can reply, "Yes!" Already I am on the river, if only in my head. Anticipation builds as planning, shopping, and packing for the trip is done and the time grows near. I like to study maps of the area before a trip. Yet I enjoy it even more if we are straying off the beaten path and the maps are poor or not available. Finally comes the travel day from home to the launch site. And the next day is the day before launch, when we put the boats together and pack all that stuff in them. Do we really need all this gear? No, but it all goes in anyway, because on a river trip—it can!

At the put-in we meet the strangers who will likely be great friends once on the river. Everyone ought to consider this situation very high on the scale of lifetime importance—there is a chance that one of those strangers will become your spouse! On such outings, short or long, many of my friends (including me) have met their partner.

Next comes the launch day when we shove off and go with the flow. The adventure begins. It is said that adventure begins when the outcome is uncertain. Truest adventure is embodied in Teddy Roosevelt doing the first ever run of the River of Doubt in Brazil. Unfortunately, these days we know too much before even starting, and certainly have no doubt as to where the river comes out. But there are still uncertainties on the way down the river. It is unlikely but possible I might not make it. If there are no uncertainties, where is the adventure? If I pay somebody to deal with the uncertainties for me, I lose most of that adventure. Lost also is the self-reliant pride to say, "I did it myself." That is why a commercially guided raft trip has little appeal to me, even if it is better than nothing.

The Rio Mayo in Sonora, Mexico, is the most adventurous float I've done to date. A group of us drove to the end of the road in the Sierra Madre, an adventure by itself. We said thanks and goodbye to our friends who shuttled us but could not go along; their help was essential to our trip. The six of us hired local packers with mules to take our raft, kayaks, and gear down while we hiked with them. The trail ends by a small settlement deep down inside the *barranca*, or canyon, our launch point by the river's head. From our research, we knew that we were to be the third known party to ever run this river. Other than that it was doable, we knew nothing.

The adventure part seemed clear and was proven by what went wrong. If nothing had gone wrong I might remember very little about the trip. The best memories are those stories you tell afterwards. A sample from the Rio Mayo ...

The raft was doing great until an oar busted in the middle of a long rapid. With the one remaining oar, the boatman, Wayne, could merely spin us, while I used the broken shaft to push us out, away from boulders that littered the route. Meanwhile the others on the boat unlashed the spare oar and placed it in the oar locks as if we had practice at this sort of thing. Surprisingly, we made it through the rapid OK.

At one point, the botanist eagerly exclaimed "Stop here—what a great place to collect specimens," with a big smile. Then seconds later, as I was tying up the raft to a tree, he came running back and loudly whispered, "Get back in the boat—let's get the hell out of here!" He had stumbled upon opium and pot fields.

We saw only one person in the remote wild lands the whole trip. Below us, he was facing away and shouldering a large leafy bundle near the river bank. Anyone in the area was probably suspicious, so we pretended to look in another direction and made noises to alert him. He immediately hid in the brush, no doubt a good deal surprised to see a party like us gringos near his secret crop field. Sadly, contact with this native was not an option.

Shortly afterwards we saw a truly ugly sight: two military helicopter gunships flying overhead, part of the war on drugs, paid for by you-know-whose government. Luckily, they didn't seem to notice us in the middle of the river. We avoided all sides of this unfortunate conflict as best as we could.

One of our party flipped his inflatable kayak in a rapid and we, the rafters, rescued him. We pulled him out of the water below the rapid, caught up with his kayak, and put him back into it. This hardly seems to qualify as an incident and yet, considering what might have gone wrong, we didn't take it lightly. If there was an injury, all we could do was continue down the river for help, which was at least a few days away.

I'd never tried a hardshell kayak before and got my first chance on a tame stretch of this river. I squeezed into it—boy that was a tight fit! Everything was fine until I came to a swift curve. I struggled to decide, "Which way do you lean when coming to the edge of an eddy fence?" Oops, that was the wrong way—over I went! The rafters came to rescue me. It looked to them that I was panic stricken and trapped upside-down in the kayak with my arms clinging to it from underwater. In reality, I was surprised at how quickly I slid out of the kayak as it rolled upside-down and I grabbed it first thing before even surfacing. I was only afraid of becoming separated from the kayak in the variable current, otherwise the swim gave me no worries.

The natural immersion part of river trips is hardest for me to describe. What did I see and hear and smell and taste? That is pretty easy to explain. On the Rio Mayo we saw rugged canyons covered with a semi-tropical, thorn scrub forest complete with a profusion of flowers. Mostly gorgeous, morning-glory type flowers. It was beautiful. The canyon was rocky and steep, similar to the Grand Canyon, except the cliffs were almost completely invisible, covered with thick, scrubby trees. It smelled simply clean and earthy. We reveled in extreme quiet, silence broken only by the serene nature sounds of birds and the river. We did not see anything super thrilling like a jaguar. That was unlikely, but the possibility was there and that kept us more alert and therefore more alive. Senses were wide open.

What did I feel? That is more difficult to describe. It was wondrous to see it. I was fortunate to have been there. Uplifted. We had freedom from most of "civilization." You know; free to yell, swim, get dirty, throw a rock, take a piss, or whatever comes to mind. Civilization isn't all evil, but some of it is. And in smother-the-earth quantities it all becomes evil. Yet even I enjoyed our first contact with civilization near the finish. One lady doing her laundry on a rock by the river's edge stared at the lead boat like she was seeing an alien, and maybe she was.

But my emotions waxed and waned and changed and sometimes were one on top of the other. I found a human jaw bone in a shallow cave by the river and held it in my hand. In fact, every cave that we looked into near the Rio Mayo had human bones, probably once the common Indian burial style from who knows how far back. In a sanitized life back at home I had not seen the remains of people, unless you count looking through the glass of a museum display or on a TV screen. I felt both repelled and drawn closer, and a whole bunch of churning emotions. I asked myself, "Is it wrong to pick it up?" I was just looking and returned it to where it was on the floor. These bones could have been me in a different life had I lived a couple of centuries ago. Or, in a few years, perhaps about thirty some, I'll be in the same shape myself. A lot to think on. What did I expect from my wilderness experience? The unexpected. And that's exactly what I got.

But we know our human reactions vary so much. Another person could have gone in my place and done all the same things, but not felt the same way. For someone else, the river trip could have been the pinnacle moment of their lifetime. Another, perhaps the James Watt type, would have found it the most hellish week of his life. Perhaps, to you, scattered bones would mean nothing and the stunning flowers would be just another photo op.

All river trips do have one consistently bad part. No one else wants to write it so I will. It is true. It is called "The End." The better the trip, the worse it is when it comes to an end. The reverse could be true as well. In any case, take-out and de-rigging can't be avoided. So we clean up the gear and pack away the lightened food boxes while saying good-byes to new friends. Those friends that might be for life— or perhaps they could have been, but for whatever reason I won't ever see them again. Back to everyday, normal, mundane living—the unreal world.

The Rio Mayo reached the plains of Sonora and the first village with a road. A professor and one of his helpers from the University of Arizona met us there as previously arranged. We gave him our plant presses and he gave us a ride home in the back of his pickup. At times I wonder about those comrades whom I haven't seen since. Such is life.

V
Reflections

A Rocky Mountain Jewel
Timothy Hillmer

When I arrive at the entrance to the Cache La Poudre river canyon near Fort Collins in northern Colorado, my driving suddenly becomes erratic and dangerous, much to the dismay of my passengers. I am usually conservative behind the wheel, almost cautious, but now I swerve back and forth on the narrow, two-lane road, straining to catch a glimpse out the window of any blue-green current sweeping by. I check familiar landmarks on the river, a massive tree at mid-stream or a bridge piling or a rock just off shore, for some indication of the water level.

My wife, Nancy, warns of oncoming traffic and I heed her advice, yet I'm not sure she completely understands my excitement. After all, it's late May in Colorado. The mountain snowpack at Cameron Pass, elevation 10, 249 feet, has begun to melt and the Cache La Poudre is coming back from the dead, its waters alive and kicking with speed.

As a private boater, the Poudre is one of my favorite rivers, a free-flowing mountain stream at the mercy of its snow-covered headwaters in Rocky Mountain National Park. It was declared a National Wild and Scenic River in 1987. By mid-August, the Poudre is usually reduced to a slow-moving creek, excellent for trout fishing, which eventually trickles into the South Platte River. But now the waterway has swelled to peak runoff at 2000 cubic feet per second and the rapids are boiling with white froth.

My visits to raft the Poudre have become a yearly ritual, a tradition as regular as the river's cycle, which sends water lapping each spring into the backyards of the simple homes and cabins that sporadically line the shore. For me there is something about the canyon that remains natural, unchanging, timeless, and I always find hope in these swift waters.

I continue up the road, occasionally pulling over to hop out of the car and inspect a variety of familiar rapids. At one point the Poudre collapses into a furious descent known as Pine View Falls, where a primitive gauge is painted in orange on a huge rock on the far shore. Today it reads nearly five feet, an excellent but perhaps intimidating high water level.

Put-in lies about ten miles upstream. I drive past the Mishawaka Inn, a fabulous outdoor concert venue and bar originally constructed in 1919 as a dance hall by a motorcycle-riding adventurer named Walt Thompson. The Inn's vast wooden deck extends out over the river and allows a splendid view of another favorite rapid, Mishawaka Falls. As we proceed, a series of intimate campgrounds and picnic areas line the road, all within view of the Poudre. Halfway to my destination, the landscape changes dramatically. The steep, heavily forested slopes turn into sheer walls of dark stone, giving the canyon an ominous, shadowy quality. Any remaining homes and power lines vanish.

When I reach our designated launch site, I purposefully drive past in order to inspect a set of rapids called the Narrows which lie an extra mile upstream. Every classic river should have its expert-only section, the part of the run that creates both apprehension and awe just by observing it from shore. The Arkansas has Pine Creek Rapid; the Roaring Fork has Slaughterhouse Falls; the Colorado has Upper and Lower Death in Glenwood Canyon. Viewing the Narrows at high water guarantees the same respect.

Rated Class V+, this two-mile section was described in many early guidebooks with a variety of colorful phrases, all foreshadowing doom: "hydraulic entrapment"; "violent, dangerous, and unrunnable"; "nightmare material with little room for error"; and "the blood and guts run of the Poudre." Although successfully negotiated by expert kayakers on many occasions, the Narrows had never been rafted in its entirety until 1989 when a team from the Boulder Outdoor Center made the first raft descent.

Now, as I scout from the shore, it is hard to imagine that a raft could fit through some of the constricted, undercut slots. The river is steep and crammed with sharp, massive boulders. One thing seems clear to me: to negotiate the Narrows at this water level would be more an act of banzai boating that a feat of bravery.

I drive a mile back to our put-in at Stove Prairie Campground. Our party today is small: Nancy, my sister and her husband from Chicago, as well as a rafting friend from Boulder. After unloading the gear and inflating our 14-foot raft, I lash on the rowing frame, which will allow us to do an oar-paddle combination, a safer alternative when running solo down the Poudre. Then I distribute life jackets, paddles, nylon windbreakers, and wet suits. We climb into the raft and set off down the river. I row from the center while my passengers stroke along the outside perimeter, our paddles and oars quickly flashing in unison as we blitz through the first nameless rapid.

There are certain days in every boatman's life when descending a river becomes more than just a sport, but a mindless, hypnotic ritual of trusting the water's movement and direction and then following its lead. It becomes a dance of sorts, the current spinning the boat around and tugging at the oars as it attempts to gain control, but then easing up into a fluid ride over smooth waves that have a steady, constant rhythm. This is one of those special days and I feel the weight of the previous week, the hours spent indoors hunched over a desk, slide away and release. We move at a different pace with the river as our guide.

There are few eddies or places to rest on the Poudre today. Its streambed has the profile of a staircase in places, steadily dropping at a gradient of sixty feet per mile. In the upper section the rapids are a series of twisting chutes, often boulder-choked, that zig-zag back and forth in a sidewinder motion. Wave trains abound, the bow of our self-bailing raft exploding with foam as we blast through rapids like Jaws and Wallbanger.

Mishawaka Falls sneaks up on us, a sharp bend in the river, and for a moment, we are engulfed by a white violence that threatens to capsize the raft. The entire boat tips to one side as it slides into the angled turn and we hang there for a precarious second. My wife is catapulted from the back by the whiplash force and slams into my left shoulder. I grab hold of her, wait for the raft to slide free, then scramble back to the oars. Suddenly we are through it, the other paddlers standing boldly upright and hooting with joy. Nancy is shaken, the wind knocked out of her, but she's fine.

The Poudre momentarily slows in the middle section, and we float past the Ansel Watrous Campground. It provides a chance to rest, catch our breath, and warm up under hot, blue, Colorado skies. But within a mile, the pace quickens, the rapids begin anew, and we approach the infamous Bridges section of the Poudre.

The current is deceptively pushy as we maneuver our boat through tight passages between the rusty bridge abutments. We proceed carefully and avoid broaching or pinning on the columns. On past trips down the Poudre, I've seen far too many rafts and canoes wrapped like cellophane around the steel girders and cement slabs that rise like sentries out of the sleek current. We cruise through Avalanche Rapid and Cardiac Corner without mishap, then swing around a truck-sized boulder jutting out from shore, and view a horizon line where the river suddenly vanishes from sight.

Just above the brink of Pine View Falls, I stand at the oars and peer downstream. I can see the entire river narrowed into a funnel of dancing, kicking foam. Then the raft is plummeting over a six-foot drop and accelerating into the first wave. The front paddlers are temporarily buried underwater as I feel the bow straining to break through. We bull ahead and hurtle downstream into the maw of the next drop where, once again, my flailing paddlers are slammed to the boat's floor by a cascade of water. I see an enormous gray rock looming to the left like the great humped back of a whale. Then the river collapses on us in the third and final drop, folding the raft taco-style, but allowing us to wash through upright into the calm pool at the bottom.

As afternoon storm clouds roll up the canyon, we move easily through the last few rapids and soon reach the Elephant Rock take-out. The raft is hoisted onto shore just as raindrops spatter the dusty powder of the road. While waiting for drivers to shuttle our cars, I walk down to the river's edge and stand where the current has formed a constantly swirling eddy. I bend down and dip my fingers into the water and feel the chill of glaciers. It is the same thrill I felt as a child when plunging my hand into a tub of ice in order to yank out a bottle of orange pop. I hold it in for at least ten seconds, long enough to feel the cold sting, then pull it out. I've performed this simple task many times before and have often felt the rippling wake of a fish as it glides away.

I think of the Cache La Poudre as far more than just a name. It is water, cool and snow-fed, fanning out over stone and diving through deep channels of dirt and rock. The smell in the canyon is of rainbow trout and moss and black ant and poison ivy, all mingling together into something earthy and rich. River scent. Something worth coming back to year after year after year.

Rafting Through Cancer
On The River of No Return

Jayson Ringel

The road to the Salmon River was slow and tortuous. It was forty-five miles of washboarded dirt that made one slow down and contemplate one's motivations. It was a transition from an outer world of thought and preoccupation to an inner world of love and fear.

I was on my way to Corn Creek, the put-in for a five-day solo raft trip on the Salmon River. When I discussed this trip with others, the common response was to ask if that was safe. Is it a good idea to raft for five days through ninety miles of remote wilderness by oneself? I wasn't sure. But I wasn't too sure of anything as I drove to the river.

It had been exactly five days since my last chemotherapy treatment. Though the treatments were finished, I didn't know if they had worked. I was not sure where I stood in the continuum of living and dying.

I disagree with the notion that whatever doesn't kill you makes you stronger. I felt weak and tired. But adversity does put hardship and pain into perspective. It also made me realize the importance of doing the things in life that I care about. So, when I couldn't find anyone to go on this trip with me, I resolved to raft the Salmon River solo. This new-found knowledge and anxiety swirled inside me as I drove. I tried to ignore it, but couldn't. I realized that river trips are good transitions from one phase of life to another. They help deal with upheaval.

I had been planning this trip for months. Whenever I doubted my planning skills or my ability to run the Salmon River, in my mind I would approach it like an obstacle in the river. With a slight pull on my oar, I'd take a different tack, around the offending impediment.

That was my imaginary river. But this was a very real road and it went on and on. It was taking me away from the safe haven of planning this trip to the unknown reality of actually doing the trip. All the busy thoughts of meal planning and equipment prep that had distracted me from my illness for months were gone. All I had in front of me was the river, and my anxiety.

I landed on the boat ramp and immediately started unloading my gear and putting my raft together. At home, these were individual pieces of equipment; two neoprene cataraft tubes, a frame to lash them together, a cooler of food, and a drybox of clothes and camp gear. It was time to move from imagination to reality to see if my trip preparation was adequate.

The day was hot. The solstice sun bathed the boat ramp in heat and light. I inflated the cataraft tubes and lashed them to the frame. Then I began to load the gear. The more gear I transferred from motor vehicle to river vehicle, the more the tubes sagged under the weight of my equipment, until one tube lay on the ramp fully deflated. It had a major air leak and was useless in its present condition.

The previous Monday, I had my last dose of chemotherapy. People are curious as to what chemotherapy feels like. For me, it felt like a torrential cacophony of whitewater. It started in my head and cascaded over boulders of doubt. I'd ask myself, "Would the chemo work?" "How much would I have to endure?" Then it would plunge into my chest. My heart would become a vortex of anxiety, sucking any hope underwater and drowning it. Whatever survived this would wash up in my abdomen where it would mix and swirl. Whatever didn't physically get projected out of my gut would catch an emotional eddy to be carried back upstream, and sent again through this horrible whitewater.

This occurred every three weeks. I would approach my chemotherapy days the same way I would scout a river rapid prior to running it. I thought if I made a good plan, I could survive the journey.

It reminded me of my Grand Canyon trip of the previous year. On that trip, we would disembark from our boats to scout a particular large rapid. Inevitably, I would say to myself, "That is the biggest, scariest whitewater I have ever seen." Then I would get into my cataraft and run it, hoping I survived. The next day, we would scout another rapid and I would think, "No, THAT is the scariest rapid I have ever seen." This cycle repeated itself every day on that Grand Canyon trip. It repeated itself every three weeks during my chemotherapy runs.

Cancer and the Grand Canyon have a lot in common. Once you are launched into it, there is no going back. There is no upstream exit. There is also no way around it. There is only one path, downstream, and the doing of the thing. Survival is optional.

Chemo brain is a very real thing. The first few days after a chemotherapy treatment, I would be foggy-headed and spent. It was as if the river had released me after swimming through a nasty rapid and I was lying on shore panting, wondering if I had actually survived. It was in this state, on the previous Tuesday, that I had undertaken a major repair of one of my cataraft tubes.

For the longest time, one of the blue cataraft tubes would slowly deflate until it lay limp on my trailer. Try as I might, I could not locate the puncture in the fabric. Then, one day, I noted a small spittle of bubbles emanating from under one of the hard plastic nose cones that protect the front tip of the tube. The cone had a hairline crack that would allow air to escape when the tube was inflated and pressurized.

The repair for this was to cut a ten-inch incision into the tube, reach into the bowels to extract the nose cone, and replace it with a new one. Then the incision would need to be repaired.

Large holes like this are the death of any raft. I would have to hope my repair skills were enough to bring the raft tube back to life.

They weren't.

When inflated and loaded on the boat ramp, my repair patch became unglued. And, so did I. All my self-doubt rained down, my anxiety bubbled forth, my stomach churned. My post-cancer recovery trip was in peril.

On advice from the rangers, I spent the next two days recirculating back into the real world. I drove out the road to Blackadar Boating, a local rafting company where I could find experts in repair. With their guidance, my tube was patched, and I returned back down the road to launch. On the second driving of the road, I felt more assured, but even more aware that anything could go wrong.

Forty-eight hours after my initial launch date, river water washed over my repaired nose cone as I pointed my craft downstream.

This section of the Salmon River, from the put-in at Corn Creek until the take-out at Vinegar Creek ninety miles later, cut through the Frank Church-River of No Return Wilderness Area. It is one of the largest wilderness areas in America, the size of Rhode Island. My vehicle shuttle driver would put five hundred miles on my van driving around the perimeter, while my cataraft would travel ninety miles on the river as it cut through the heart of the wilderness.

The river downstream of the Corn Creek put-in ran low and slow, with just a few minor rapids and bubbly Class II riffles. I felt huge relief at finally being afloat. After being stuck on shore the last few days, I felt uplifted by the river's swaying motion. The Salmon rocked me gently into a blissful, semiconscious state.

My mind wandered back to my chemotherapy. As I let Western medicine's approach to healing poison my body, I read articles on Eastern Mysticism and its approach to good health. I read how it recognizes seven chakras where energy flows into and out of our bodies. The belief is that health and well-being depend on an unbridled flow of the life force in and out of these chakras. As I drifted down the Salmon, I felt it drift through me. I realized I need river time to re-establish a healthy flow within myself.

Like the slow dawn of a new day, the river woke me from my slumber with a noisy, building crescendo. Rainier Rapid, the first significant Class III rapid, was approaching.

White standing waves filled the river from shore to shore. In the center of Rainier Rapid was a large boulder. The trick was to choose on which side to pass the boulder in order to safely row around it. In the coming days, I realized this was the personality of the Salmon. A river with strong flows, difficult rapids, and many boulders.

Visualizing these hazards and skillfully paddling around them is the key to safe navigation. It is a skill called "reading the river." If a boulder rises above the waterline, the river surges white foam against it. If the rock is submerged, the foam is a smaller pile and there is a teardrop of smooth water downstream. But if the rock stands tall against the river, yet the river still flows over it, the plunging flow off the back of the rock creates a hole capable of catching and holding any craft foolish enough to enter. These rocky impediments in the flow of a river present two possible hazards to a boatman: "pinning" or "spinning."

The rocks large enough to stand above the river have huge amounts of water piling against them. Pinning occurs when a raft runs into such a rock. The river pulls the upstream tube of the raft underwater, sending the opposing side of the raft against the rock, skyward. The raft is then pinned vertically in a vice of water and rock. A dangerous and lethal situation.

Spinning occurs when a raft follows a cascade of river water over a submerged rock. The plunging water creates a pool of chaos downstream of the rock called a "keeper hole." Keeper holes have two vortices of spinning water. One is on the horizontal surface. A raft stuck here spins in quick circles and any occupants are at the mercy of the keeper hole's centrifugal forces. The second is a vertical vortex from the river's cobbled floor to its surface. Anyone ejected from the raft gets Maytagged in a spin cycle that may hold a person until they are limp—and sometimes dead.

The Salmon is a maze of these rocky objects. Safe passage required recognizing these objects and steering clear of them. I felt as if I were on a simulated African river safari. Instead of rocks, the grey masses were hippos lying in wait. I needed to discern which were the smaller hippos I could safely approach, and which were the large, angry adults I needed to avoid.

After Rainier Rapid, the river returned to its bucolic flow. I could relax and drift along in the quiet bliss of wilderness beauty. I continued downstream until I encountered one of the many sandy beaches that make camping idyllic on this river.

The camp is called Motor Camp because of the rusty jetboat engine that sits in the campsite. I appreciated the camp because of the fine sand that is legendary in the Salmon River watershed. Particles so fine and clean I didn't even set up a tent that night, just laid my sleeping bag directly on it. The next morning the sun rose bright and early. I packed my few belongings and left Motor Camp behind. Soon the edges of the river were changing. I was entering Black Canyon.

These beautiful river canyons do not just beckon to river rats like myself, but also to structural engineers. The Bureau of Reclamation sent engineers into river wildernesses to evaluate dam sites. They liked what they saw here in Black Canyon. A dam three hundred and thirty-two feet tall was proposed. Looking upon this majestic river, these pencil-neck geeks dared write back to Washington, "… little damage would result from the formation of the reservoir." Luckily the Bureau ignored them, and the canyon retains its incalculable beauty.

Inundation of the river is not just the work of humans. A rapid called Salmon Falls was previously found at the start of Black Canyon. In the spring of 2011, a storm washed debris down a side stream called Black Creek. This storm flooded enough debris into the Salmon to create a new rapid. The resulting new rapid, Black Creek Rapid, dammed the river sufficiently to cover over Salmon Falls Rapid a half-mile back upstream.

Black Canyon Rapid is difficult. I did not want to run it alone. I pulled out of the river at the scout point and waited for another group to catch up with me. Soon a group of ten boats and thirty-plus people appeared. After a brief exchange about which line to take through the rapid, I inserted myself into their lineup. While every other boat pulled into an eddy at the bottom to wait for the rest of their group, I kept floating on. Even when in the midst of a large group, I was still able to maintain my solitude on the river.

I lazily floated the rest of the day, letting my mind drift with the river. I floated past the hot spring at River Mile 22. I had visited it on a previous trip and knew it allowed a good quality soaking. But I was enjoying my solo time too much to stop. So I was startled when I rounded a corner and drifted into Gordie and Nancy.

Boaters keep track of one another while progressing down the river. One reason is to keep track of the competition for desired camp spots. Otherwise, just noticing other people and how they rig their boat will entertain any boatman. I had previously noticed Gordie and Nancy upriver. They now struck me as a good choice to join up with to help break up my trip.

Gordie and Nancy were the classic Western river contradiction; desert dwellers that love the water. Nancy hailed from Moab and Gordie further east into Colorado. Both of them had hair that was well salted. Their stories of boating the great rivers of the Southwest were equally salty. As I was feeling rather inexperienced and vulnerable, I was glad of their company.

After sharing lunch on the beach at Magpie Camp, we headed downriver, continuing our conversation between boats. When conversing in this way, it is easy to lose track of time and space. This inattention makes an easy rapid like Bailey's more dangerous.

Nancy was at the oars of their boat and mistakenly ran over the top of a submerged boulder in the middle of the rapid. Their raft precariously pivoted atop the rock and slid into the keeper hole beneath. Like a rodeo, they were caught on the back of a bull spinning its circles and attempting to buck those river cowboys out of their boat.

Frantically, I rowed to shore. I had seen rafters stuck in these tilt-a-wheel hydraulics plenty of times on YouTube videos, but never in person. I grabbed my throw bag and headed upstream. I figured to throw a line to them from shore and pull them out myself.

It took time to crash through the brush to get back upstream. Pieces of their gear went floating by, but I resolved to rescue people, not possessions. Then Gordie and Nancy floated by in their raft, smiling and whooping. Like a lazy cat holding a mouse, the river had tired of toying with them and set them free.

I scampered back into my cataraft and caught up with them downstream. We fished floating dry bags from eddies. We estimated they'd spun in that hole for four or five minutes. After all that excitement, we were eager to make camp. We drifted until we reached Yellow Pine Bar Camp and pulled in.

Over dinner that night, I told them about my recent journey through cancer. Like any story told on a river trip, it sounded larger than life. River trips make the mundane heroic.

The next day had challenging rapids from the get-go. After a quick scout, we ran Big Mallard on river right, far from the imposing rock on the left. Further down, we stopped where some intrepid fellow had mounted a rack of antlers to a ponderosa tree. This scout of Elkhorn Rapid showed we needed to stay far left, so we did.

The remainder of the day turned into a historic tour of the river. The Salmon River drainage has been occupied by humans for thousands of years. From the depressions in the ground of ancient pit houses next to the ranger cabin at Corn Creek, to historic mines and ranches, evidence of these habitations is strewn all along the river.

We elected to explore the Painter mine. J. R. Painter was from a wealthy Eastern family. Whether he was drawn to the gold ore with dreams of making money for himself, or if that was the excuse to escape to this wilderness, we may never know. Whatever rock he excavated he replaced with his soul, as he is buried here. His tombstone juts up amongst rusting mining equipment.

Just downstream on the opposite side of the river is the private inholding of Sylvan Hart, better known as Buckskin Bill. Buckskin was a wilderness Renaissance man. A graduate school dropout, Bill settled on this spot of wilderness during the Depression. For the next fifty years, until his death in 1980, Buckskin designed and built an odd assortment of living structures. He manufactured his own firearms, molded his own bullets, grew his own vegetables, and hunted his meat. Today, rafters stop to visit the museum that honors his legacy and to buy ice cream from the only store on the river.

As much as I enjoyed their company, it was time to part ways with Gordie and Nancy. They had many more days to spend on the river while I had only a few. I rowed away from them wondering what had made my time with them so enjoyable. Who are the ideal river companions? Why do river trips strengthen those friendships?

Albert Einstein could explain it to me. He'd say no matter how beautiful, a river only occupies three spatial dimensions. Invite others to share a river trip with us and we introduce the element of time. Time spent on the river elevates us together into Einstein's hallowed fourth dimension of relativity. Rafters call this elevated experience "River Time." It is what calls us back to the river again and again.

Escaping Einstein's physical explanation of the world, I again drifted back to thoughts of Eastern Mysticism. I couldn't recall all seven chakras. But I was keenly aware of two of them—as humans we live our lives caught between two forces. The first is love, the force of the heart chakra. These past days of drifting a wilderness river, I was motivated by my love of adventure and exploration. The second force is fear. Eastern philosophy defines thoughts as energy originating in our minds. For months, I had preoccupied my mind with thoughts of trip food, gear, and logistics. Fear occasionally crept in. What if, for all my planning, my preparation was inadequate? What if the rapids were more forceful then I could stand? What if I wasn't good enough?

I knew the planning of this trip had distracted my mind from a larger fear: my cancer. I had distracted my mind from fearful thoughts of cancer with planning a river trip. I fought fire with fire. And in the end, I doused all inflammatory thinking with river water.

A few miles downriver, I passed the confluence with the South Fork of the Salmon. Its sediment load introduces more sand into the watershed. From here the beaches become larger, extending further out into the river, and are more inviting. My last full day on the river was spent languidly drifting through an occasional Class II rapid. I mildly paddled flat water that reflected the overhanging cliffs, trees, and the sky full of building cumulus clouds.

The camp at Sheep Creek appeared just as my weary body had enough of this river time. The beach made a smooth, gentle descent into the water. A slight pull on the oars nuzzled the cataraft's nose cones to shore. I didn't unpack my tent or cot, but resolved to sleep in the sand at the water's edge.

After dinner, the dusky evening turned into night. I crawled in my sleeping bag and lay gazing up. The many stars of the galaxy flickered on, one after another, until there were bright clusters of light above me.

While I hung in the space between consciousness and sleep, I imagined I was laying atop the galaxy. Each individual grain of sand I lay upon transformed into a luminescent star. And all those twinkling stars overhead morphed into individual grains of sand, the sky a beach of light.

That night I dreamed a dream. The river rose and covered my beach. I didn't float and drift away. As it rose, the water engulfed me. It entered my head via the topmost crown chakra. Then it descended and flowed around each subsequent chakra; past the forehead, around the throat, through the heart, over the solar plexus, behind the sacral and exited the base chakra. It was as if each chakra were a boulder in the river. But there was no danger of being pinned against any of them. There were no deadly keeper holes beneath. Instead, I rafted in an effortless flow. My oars never touched the water.

When I woke, the river was back at its previous position on the beach. The sun was filling the canyon with light. I had a sense of calm surrender, a visceral knowledge that the chemo had worked. My cancer was gone. My life lay in front of me, a wire-bound map of time filled with friends, family, and rivers.

I thought, I am a haphazard survivor.

The Timeless and Insignificant Journey of a Day in the Grand

Janelle Dyer

I lie down on my raft from my captain's seat and look up at the rim of the canyon. I feel small and insignificant here. In my other life, the life where I am not on the Colorado River in the Grand Canyon, I might feel these feelings of insignificance in small pieces within fleeting moments; maybe in a really great yoga class or on a peaceful hike in the redwoods. But on the Colorado in the Grand Canyon, it is an overwhelming feeling that lasts for days.

I sit on my cooler seat and lie back. My head and back lean nicely against my stack of dry bags. The slight midday breeze tickles my skin. In response, I close my eyes and breathe in. My mind goes to a place above the rim of the canyon, above the clouds in the sky, and above the earth. From there I look down and see the Grand Canyon. There I am, a little speck on the river. As I notice the speck, I feel like I truly understand my place in the universe; I am small and insignificant. I mean nothing. All I am is a part of the beautiful landscape that surrounds me. Nothing matters. I exhale, and I feel full of peace and calmness that I have not felt since the last time I was on this river.

How can I describe the beauty that surrounds me? It is so difficult to put into the right words. I do not think I can do it justice, but I will give it a try. The towering, polished, red limestone rises above me to what seems like infinity. I peer into the drainages that I pass and see greenery and cottonwoods. As I dip my oars into the water, I drift toward my favorite section of Marble Canyon, Vasey's Paradise. It is a spring that flows out of the limestone into the river. Surrounding the spring is its own enchanted forest. I imagine that fairies would love to live here. I decide that this is a great place to fill water jugs. As I wait for the jugs to fill, I envelop myself in its healing waters. Initially the temperature of the water feels harsh, then the coolness seeps into my skin and I feel refreshed. From my perch in paradise, I watch as the sun lightly touches the red limestone cliffs. I have arrived.

The definition of timelessness is this: "without beginning or end; eternal, everlasting." Today feels timeless. Life on the river begins to feel like the only life I have ever lived. I begin to believe that there was no life before this moment. I forget what "home" is. The definition gets muddled in my mind and I find it too exasperating to hash it out. How could I know what my life was like before this? The canyon is my home now. I have always lived here. I will always be here.

No time in my life have I ever experienced this feeling of timelessness except on the Colorado River in the Grand Canyon. The canyon is magic, it alleviates aging and worry. It makes me feel insignificant, it cures my selfishness and my ego. When I am on the river I become my best self.

Everything is Stardust
Naseem Rakha

It's a weekday, I think. It's a weekday in December in the year 2015, and I am deep in the Grand Canyon, just 30 feet from the Colorado River. Not far above me is a twisted outcrop of columnar basalt. The hardened lava protrudes right and left, up and down. Some of its columns are as gnarled as tree roots, some shoot outward—spines on an urchin, rays of the sun, ion trails cast off by dying stars.

I've been rafting through the Grand Canyon for 19 days now, floating under Navajo Bridge and through Marble Canyon, past sites such as Redwall Cavern, Nankoweap and the Little Colorado, and through 80 rapids, one of which is considered the largest navigable falls in the country. I have eleven more days left on this river trip. Eleven more nights to sleep under a sky wrapped by the Milky Way's diaphanous, silky scarf, eleven more opportunities to absorb all I can from this primitive, bare-knuckled world and the majesty it holds.

There are just 15 people on this river trip, most of us strangers to one another before we met three weeks ago on the night of a Flagstaff blizzard. The permit holder, a Texan who had never rafted the Colorado River, found a seasoned boater who put together a group based on one criteria: a love of the Grand Canyon. Now, we 15 are river mates, working as one unit to move ourselves, a couple of tons of food and gear, and our four rafts, two dories, and two kayaks down 280 miles of winter river. Short days, long, cold nights, frosty dawns—we are a tribe of people isolated by mile-high walls that keep the chaos and distractions of the rim-world at bay. There are no cell signals deep in the Canyon, no interpretive waysides, no Netflix or radios. The last time we saw anyone from outside our tribe was ten days ago, on the shore of Unkar's sandy delta. On that day a haboob—a desert windstorm— hit, making progress on the river nearly impossible. As we fought our way downstream, one person on each oar, we caught sight of a group of brightly clad rafters huddled in the tamarisk, risking the prick of thorns in order to shelter themselves from the assault of the wind-born sand. Since that day we haven't seen anyone but ourselves, so it's easy to imagine we're the only ones left on the planet, but for the slash of contrails against the lazurite sky, and, of course, the daily river surges—tides determined not by nature, but by the power demands of far-flung cities.

I've found no better place than the Grand Canyon to separate myself from the friction of the world. The daily rub of sights and sounds that constantly erode. The news and the neighbors with their needs, always the needs, and the traffic and the crime and the bills and the ills, so many ills, and the Girl Scouts with their cookies, and the Mormons with their missions, and the politicians with their smiles, and all the aisles of things and things and things that end up in landfills, or as plastic islands the size of small countries, floating in a forgotten sea. All of it rubbing until a numbness sets in. And an apathy. And a kind of modern-age depression born from a sense of powerlessness. A weakness so overwhelming that when a personal crisis hits, it is hard to know just how to get up off the ground.

The invitation to join this winter trip came at the right time. My father had died. He died, and there was this hole, you see. A place where my father had been, and now he was gone, and I had no idea how to deal with this loss, this hole, this sense of being plunged into a new and far lonelier world. I needed perspective. I needed quiet. I needed time. I needed to be in the presence of something larger than my grief. So, I accepted a trip to a place that promised to be cold, and dark, and raw—and very, very deep.

I pause in my hike to sit on a ledge above the Colorado. Beneath me, boulders are hammered by cascades of whitewater. The sound is open mouthed and large. I open my backpack and dig out a sandwich and a bottle of water. As I drink, I watch a raven circle and then land on a nearby rock. His eyes are on my sandwich. I smile. Ravens are audacious robbers. I've had one break into my backpack, steal a dried piece of papaya, then fly over me to gloat about it, the pilfered treat hanging from its beak like an orange cigar. "I'm not sharing," I shout over the roar of the river. I bite into my sandwich menacingly, and the bird flies off, going up and up the mile-high walls until he is too tiny to see.

Once, when I was about four years old, my father woke me at dawn. "Come with me," he said. Our family lived in an apartment in Chicago with a view of the Loop to the north and Lake Michigan to the east, and as I followed my father into the living room I saw for the first time how the rising sun poured its color into the lake—rose and peach and orange and maroon. I pointed, and my father nodded. Then he led me out onto our small balcony, and, even now, sitting beside this swift river, I can feel the sensation of standing out there—the smell of the air, the coolness of the spring breeze against my thin pajamas. It felt like we, my father and I, were on the wing of a plane gliding through the pale, morning light. But what I remember most about that morning, what has stuck with me and what I look forward to still, was the sound of the birds—hundreds, and hundreds, perhaps even thousands of them singing to the rising sun, as my father and I stood there, hand in hand, listening.

I pull out my binoculars and scan the layer cake surface of the surrounding rock walls. In my experience, nothing lessens the burden of personal loss more than having it weighed on the scale of geologic time. At Lee's Ferry, where I've begun all my Grand Canyon river trips, the surrounding rock is approximately 200 million years old. Within a mile, the boater has floated 50 million years deeper into the past to reach the fossil-rich Kaibab limestone, created when the region was an inland sea. Eight-tenths of a mile further and the Kaibab is out of reach as the river carves deeper and deeper into the earth, through limestones, sandstones, shales and conglomerates: 1,800 million years of time stacked like bricks.

How long does it take to count to a million?

Eleven days—no eating, no sleeping.

How long does it take to count to a billion?

Thirty years.

How long does it take to count out the years of my father's life?

Less than ninety seconds.

I finish my sandwich, pack my water bottle, and zip up my backpack. The basalt I am sitting amidst is a relative newcomer in this place. It is part of the Uinkaret Lava Field, a series of some 200 volcanoes that reshaped this area from 3.6 million to 1000 years ago. These particular rocks were likely from Vulcan's Throne, a 1000-foot-high cinder cone which sits on the north rim of the canyon, just east of where I am now. Vulcan's Throne is thought to have formed a mere 73,000 years ago—barely a baby's first breath—geologically speaking.

Still, I have to wonder what this place was like back then. How wide was the river? What grew, what prowled, what grazed? What was the first sign that the dome growing on the edge of the north rim was about to release millions of metric tons of blood-red lava into a soon boiling river? Usually, pillars of columnar basalt either stand shoulder-to-shoulder like soldiers, or lie horizontally, as orderly as cord wood. Instead, these distorted stones shout pandemonium, clashing forces, disarray. This is lava that danced with water, curled into its eddies, pooled in its shoals, dammed the river, and was ultimately broken by its inexorable flow. The result is what I am standing next to now; the churning, chocolatey froth of Lava Falls. Its 10-foot waves heave over sharp-toothed boulders, pounding into them with concussive force, icy claws slashing at anyone fool enough to try to make their way through.

Long before any Grand Canyon river trip commences, boaters anticipate the moment they will meet Lava Falls, the most dangerous rapid in the canyon. They study rafting books, watch videos, compare notes. Which is better—entering at high water or low? Taking the left run or the right? What about the lateral waves that wait at the bottom? How do you avoid the raft-eating holes?

Just yesterday, we were rowing toward Lava Falls. A mile upriver, the water was calm. We drifted silently. A half-mile further, the water was still calm. A canyon wren sang. A heron flew by, its arrow shaped body pointing us toward the falls. A few moments later, we noticed subtle changes in the atmosphere. First, there was a shift in air pressure, a tightening around our ear drums. Next, came a subterranean hum that gained strength with each passing moment. By the time we stopped to scout the rapid, the sound had grown into a hungry growl. We hiked along the river's edge, climbed up a cliff, and then looked down. Beneath us was a maelstrom. A chaos. A cross between hell, and whatever lives right next to hell. From above, we could distinguish various routes, but all of them were questionable, and none would be visible once we got back on the river where the water drops precipitously out of sight. A misjudged angle, an overcompensated drag on an oar, anything at all, and a raft, or dory, or kayak would be swallowed by the waiting falls.

Wordless, we trudged back to our boats, made sure all equipment was secure, tightened our life vests, and one by one left the shore and drifted toward Lava's precipice—until suddenly the red silt water sucked us down a chute, then tossed us into the air. It grabbed at our oars, bludgeoned our boats, knocked us sideways and silly so that all there was to do was to hold on, as thousands of pounds of water crashed on and over and around with a sound and force so loud you could not hear your own scream. Then suddenly, it was done, and the unsatisfied river spat us out, still upright. We raised our arms in triumph, another group of fortunate fools.

We celebrated our successful run with a layover, unpacking the boats in the early afternoon with plans to stay on "Tequila Beach" not one, but two nights. So today, I have hiked back to the falls in hopes of seeing a different group take its turn with the rapid. In the summer months, this would not be a long wait. Commercial trips embark from Lee's Ferry four or five times a day, many of them carrying twice the number of people we have on our trip now. Those summer trips are floating parties, with young, well-tanned and hardy people serving a well-heeled group of tourists who speed through this canyon. Those groups never have the opportunity to do what I have done so many times already on this winter journey: just sit, just watch, just think, just feel. Just hike up a side canyon to see where it might go. Just watch a rapid, or a raven, or the light move up a canyon wall.

My father saw the Grand Canyon twice in his life. The first time was in 1957, when he and some other students from Purdue University, all of them Indian immigrants, borrowed a car and drove from Indiana to California. The second time was in 2006, when my brother drove him across the country to come live near me, my husband, and his only grandchild. My mother had died, and he had been keeping vigil over her memory in their oversized house in Illinois. He would not sleep in the bed they shared, could not listen to their classical music without crying. Every week, he would go to the cemetery and lay yellow roses on her grave. My father, who had just left all he knew back in Chicago, looked into the time capsule of the Canyon, two billion years compressed into stone, and found solace.

I stare upriver, willing a flotilla of rafts to appear. But none do, so I turn my attention to the contoured outcrop I'd seen earlier. It is a couple hundred feet above where I sit, so I strap on my pack and start to scramble up a scree slope to get a closer look. But scree is unfriendly territory, and my footing is poor. I grab a nettle plant to stop a fall, feel its sting; I scrape against a fishhook barrel cactus, feel a spine embed in my thigh. I slip and slide and call myself stupid, but I climb on. Finally, I reach the outcrop and haul myself over its top.

Beside me on this ledge is a dead barrel cactus. The living one—the one whose spine is still lodged in my leg—was strikingly beautiful, with four-inch yellow and magenta spines. But this one, this dead and desiccated one, also has a certain beauty. Its body is ashen and has collapsed in on itself; its spines, no longer alive with color, stick out like rusted nails. In this brittle environment, where decay is so slow, the cactus may have died a decade ago, maybe even more. I know from its size that it had lived at least ninety years—nine decades surrounded by a landscape that dwarfs any imagination of time and space.

Three days before we reached Lava Falls we had stopped at River Mile 136. There I climbed several hundred feet up above Deer Creek Falls to the soft, narrow, and sinuous chamber that makes up its canyon. Deer Creek's gray sandstone walls come as close as 15 feet together in places, and they are warped and layered like the coils of hand-worked pottery. In between, Deer Creek runs diamond clear and melodic. It gathers in pools, then drops. Gathers in pools, then drops again; sometimes visible, sometimes disappearing into even narrower and darker passages. I take time here on every trip through Grand Canyon. It feels sacred to me, this cloister. Almost umbilical. A link from the Earth's very womb to the outside world. I followed the narrow footpath, past thousand-year-old handprints, to a bowl-like chamber wide enough for a few cottonwoods to grow. There I sat and thought about how my father would have loved this place. How he would have pressed me, his geologist daughter, to tell him about its origins. And how it would have satisfied him to know that, for all that is broken in this world, at least this canyon is whole. Then while I sat there, a water ouzel, a dull-gray, robin-sized bird—John Muir's favorite bird—played in a pool and did what it is most known for; it sang and sang and sang. That's when I reached into my pocket and pulled out the plastic pill container. I had been carrying it every day of the trip, waiting for the right time. And that moment, right then, with the sunlight slipping through the narrow gap between the canyon walls, lighting the water, the leaves of the lone cottonwood, the ouzel and its spray, that was the moment I opened the container, reached over, and sprinkled its contents on the water. Some of my father's ashes sank to the creek's sandy bottom, some lapped onto its bank, and some, the lightest, most crystalline specks, swirled around like the numbers in a Fibonacci Sequence, the whorl on a nautilus, a spiral galaxy … and then they just floated away.

I came to the Canyon because I needed time, I needed quiet, and I needed the perspective that comes from these ancient walls. I needed the desert space where the rocky roots of the Earth remind me that all things are temporary. Heartaches, heart attacks, politics, politicians, preachy puritans, guns, laws, dams, disease.

Canyons.
Rivers.
Stones.

"Everything is stardust," my father once said as we looked at the night sky. "Borrowed pieces of light, elemental, fleeting and bright."

Why I Run Rivers
Blair Holman

I sit, leaning back in my seat, pressing my knees outward and my feet forward, stretching as much as I can. As I do, I lift my face up to the sky and breathe in the fresh air of the wilderness around me. My eyes confirm what I smell—trees, birds, fresh water. This is why I run rivers.

I enjoy this slow, relaxing section, allowing my boat to carry me forward, placing my paddle in the water every so often to keep me in line. I take in the sights—the contentment on my friends' faces, the darkening clouds overhead, the mountains that come into view as I pass beneath an old bridge. Breathtaking. This is why I run rivers.

I've always felt connected to water, growing up with it in my sight every day. I spent as much time in and near the ocean as I could as a child. It always brought me a sense of calm and wonder at this universe we are a part of. So going down a river, surrounded by water and feeling the life it supports and gives to the world, I feel as connected and alive as I did watching the ocean's horizon. This is why I run rivers.

As the current picks up, so does the pace of my heart. I start paddling more often and with stronger strokes. Small rapids create eddies behind a rock. I catch one and look up the way I have come. I peel out, back into the faster and faster running water. Everything I do is in my own hands. I boof off a small rock, a smile unconsciously breaking my concentration. I laugh, feeling full. This is why I run rivers.

I paddle down a small drop and as I come through, I see a deer standing tall on an outcrop at the side of the river. I am surprised, amazed by its beauty, its unexpected arrival, its breathing, moving form in the still life of the trees and rock around it. I need to share this moment. I yell, somewhat unconsciously, spurred by my exhilaration of the moment. "Deer, deer, deer," I call over and over to the boater following me. He yells back, "That's a goat." Realization. I laugh at the ridiculousness. I love that it happened. I love the wonders nature gives me. This is why I run rivers.

I take a strong pull on one side to eddy out before a big drop. I feel my heart beating. I feel the cold, the numbness of my hands as I flex them. I feel uncertainty about my ability to make it through the drop without flipping. We discuss, we support each other, give encouraging words as, one by one, we take our turns. My turn comes, and I feel supported, excited, but still nervous. I paddle hard, aiming for the right angle, preparing myself to brace, to work hard, to do what I need to shoot it clean. I drop through, feeling water pulling me to one side, tilting me. I manage to slap upright and keep paddling through the frothy turmoil of the wave. I give a shout of joy—Success! I break into a laugh. I feel triumphant. I share this feeling with my friends, my teammates. We pass around high fives, feeling happiness for each other, as well as a little relief. We are alive, we are exhilarated. This is why I run rivers.

I feel rain drops start to come down. Now water above and below. Now life all around. Our day is coming to a close. I know we will pull out of the river feeling more alive, more connected to nature and each other than when we entered it. This is why I run rivers.

I run them for the pure joy, fear, and success it brings me. I run them for the desire to improve; to do it better, to gain confidence, to be in control. I run them to be outside; for the views, smells, for all of nature. I run them for the company; camaraderie, connection with others and myself. I run them to be near water, to be alive, to feel challenged and to be surrounded by life. This is why I run rivers.

The Pursuit of Vulnerability
Shelby Rogala

We are here / Here we are

There is nothing comfortable about boater butt. There is nothing fun about dropping your dinner in the sand or arguing over shuttle rigs or sipping a yellow-jacket out of your Coca-Cola. There is nothing brave about feeling so terrified before running a rapid that you relieve yourself in the rocks, warm water trickling below the high-water line in a desperate escape act, an attempt at relief that doesn't lessen your panic. There is nothing heroic about pumping boats with cold hands, skipping lunch to make camp early, then missing it anyway, and paddling until dark.

There is no glory in the questions, the details, the boring logistics.

"Did we pack enough salt?"

"Mark forgot the lighter fluid."

"Are you girls on your periods? You should sleep down by the boats. Bears can smell the blood."

"Matt'll be lead boat on this one—follow his line as tight as you can, paddle like hell, don't flip your boat."

"I said run left."

There is nothing tough about rigging boats, running flip lines, drying your clothes on rocks at lunch while shivering around a thermos half full of stale coffee. There is nothing virtuous about choosing to struggle in the downpour with a fly tarp, arguing four ways over which boulder to tie down to, which oar to prop up with, which knot to use, while rain soaks your coals and your clothes and your calm.

There is nothing but the wanting, and the waiting, and the wishing for the permit, the group, the planning and packing and pushing rubber down a wide or narrow or tall or flat or fast or slow corridor, sliding on a surface that would drown you as easily as let you float. There is nothing but the choice to persist, to embark, to embrace our vulnerability. There is nothing, but time.

Space

River time. Play time, work time, sun time, row time, greasy hair time, no recollection of time-time. The hours pass, and I still can't remember if I have been sitting here, on this red Paco Pad in the boiling sun, for half an hour or half a day. Even telling time by the position of the sun escapes my logic until we settle in camp for the night, weaving our way through the twists and turns of the river to a solid location. Only then can I look at the sky and surmise from which direction the sun is coming, and to where it is going. Sun setting means nothing to me on the river, except for a vague hope of having gotten the dishes done in advance of the darkness. Sun rising means more, as it is hard to stay asleep on an awakening river. Camp is an almost well-oiled machine, a natural settling into cooking, cleaning, packing and unpacking, playing, and talking. Time passes no differently at camp than it does on the boats, in that it seems to pass silently, unobtrusively. We are lost in the day, disconnected to the essence of what holds our lives together "back there."

Before camp, before our departure into the wild, before drying dishes by dancing in front of the fire, before boat beers watered down by waves and the smell of brownies rising from a Dutch oven, my perception of time is "hurry up and wait." Unpacking all our gear onto the ramp in a collaborated mess with boats to inflate, kids to corral, and coolers to organize, we are subject to hurry up and wait. "Push, PUSH, push!" Get up, get in the car, drive, drive, drive. Unpack the truck, make a big pile, wander around aimlessly for another two hours as we argue for the 100th time over who carries the groover and who brought the soap. "Get out of the way!" At some point, we watch, frantic in our stillness. "Bring me that cooler ... NOW!" We rush, ten hands doing the job four could handle just fine, while the gear pile never seems to lessen.

Personalities flare and feelings get hurt. Someone forgot toothpicks. We have too much damn beer. There isn't such a thing as too much beer. Well, except for that trip when we left two mesh bags with another group on the way out, because there really was too much beer. Our boats will never be packed. Chuck's is already too loaded down. "Leave the tiki torches in the truck, we don't have space." "Where will this bottle of liquor fit?"

"Hey, guys. Look over there, at that group." We watched them pump and pack two boats—loaded up, tied down, rigged to flip. Ten feet up from the water. Their hands dropped suddenly from valiant high fives to hang limply at their sides. Dry docked. "Go give them a hand, Zack."

Boats cleared, we look back at our own pile. "We're going to be fine," Billy chuckles, as he sits down on his boat to crack open a beer. "Go get the tiki torches, I can rig them here, behind my seat."

Closing the Gap

It's big rapid day. I'm a rookie rowing the Salmon. Today, time passes painfully. This is because I spend the day on a roller coaster ride of nerves, adrenaline rushes, and post-adrenaline shakes. I was told that Big Mallard would be the only rapid at this water level that might give me some trouble, but I can't help thinking it is the only rapid that I feel comfortable with. I can remember the left run, the squeeze between shoreline and hole as if I had rowed it yesterday. Elkhorn, Salmon Falls, Five Mile, and Split Rock are different stories. I have trouble recalling where they are on the river, let alone what runs to take in this flow. All I can think about is the time Maks got his arm broken on the river, or when our dog almost jumped out at Snowhole and we ran left, or how my mom and the other duckyers always seemed to flip in Salmon Falls. I guess that is one of the bittersweet things about being a boat brat as a kid—a very acute memory of just what can go wrong. This may make me a cautious and successful boater in the long run, but right now it's giving me hives.

Salmon Falls run goes well. I hit the sneaker rock at the bottom that Frogg warns me about, but the flow is high enough there is no damage done. We are rewarded a few miles downstream at Garth Hot Springs, where I am able to recuperate and rest for the upcoming rapids. The day passes slowly, quickly, unbearable slowly again. I hit Big Mallard, shipping my oars, and smile with delight when I realize I didn't hit the sneaker or get turned around. Near the end of the day we get to Five Mile, or was it Split Rock? My hands are shaking, my body tense. We pull into camp, I am exhausted. I have done it. I have conquered Big Rapid Day on the Main Salmon, and the gulf between the heroes of my childhood and the guide I want to become shrinks.

The bravado of my first trip wears off quickly. The stress and anxiety about running the rapids doesn't. I still feel it, deep in my core, whenever I hear the whitewater approaching. My lifejacket still chafes my chin, I still drink too much at night. I have conquered nothing, let alone the river. She still dictates where I go, how I get there. She is in charge. She calls to me as soon as the snow begins to melt in the mountains, inviting me to explore her with paddle, tube, oar. I am as vulnerable now as I was on that first day—subject to the currents.

Because

I sit in this discomfort. This wet-bottomed, sunburnt, dehydrated daze. I hear the water running along the rocks, bubbling against my tubes. One oar, resting under my knee, engages in a balancing act with the slowly rocking boat, while the other dips lazily into the water. I feel the current push and pull against the smooth blade, tilting my wrist to increase and then dissipate the pressure. The sun glints off the river ahead, beaming heat and light into my face. On the front of the boat, Hannah hangs off the side, head upside down to watch the river become the sky, trailing the top of her head in the water, grounded through her crown. Mary lays across the bench seat, hat resting over her head, hands folded on chest, toes wriggling in the dry heat.

Behind me, the armada follows and noises of splashes and giggles, shouts, and paddles slapping water drift up in the afternoon breeze. The boats sit on the water like big, lazy bugs. My brother Zack paddles over. I reach for a bottom-of-the-cooler-beer, toss it to him. He holds onto my boat, leaning back, sharing in our lazy, inevitable momentum downriver. My stomach is full from lunch. Camp is some ways off, but the miles between here and now melt into the afternoon, taking care of themselves. This morning we pushed our way through rapids, adrenaline racing, and each stroke carefully placed. Tomorrow will bring another set of rapids, another flurry of activity. Two days will bring the crowded boat ramp, the fighting for de-rigging space, the long, hot drive home.

But for now, we float. We indulge in our vulnerability. We have nothing to overcome, nothing to prove. We hold no pride, no pretense. We are here. Here we are.

I Vote for Wilderness
Duwain Whitis

The sunset lit the west face of the Sierra del Carmen with incredibly brilliant color. I scrambled onto the top of a trash dumpster in the Rio Grande Village group campground in Big Bend National Park to try to get a better photo over the brush and trees lining the river bank. This was my and my son's first river trip in Big Bend in seven years, and I was glad to be back. The drought in the West had drained the reservoirs on the Rio Grande in New Mexico, and the Mexicans appeared to be withholding more water in the reservoirs of the Rio Concho than allowed by treaty with the United States. As a result, the river's flow had been substantially below historical averages since 1997 when we took our last trip. That trip, through Santa Elena Canyon, saw us walking through the Rock Slide, a Class IV rapid in better years, in water that was no more than ankle deep in places. We were forced at one point to unload our two rafts and walk them through on their sides, like mattresses through a doorway. I resolved not to go back until the water was higher.

I'm an engineer, not a writer. One of the reasons I went to engineering school was because it was one of the few degree programs that did not involve writing papers that would be judged subjectively. Math and engineering involve facts that are provable, repeatable, and definite. It is difficult for me to put into abstract words what is essentially a wordless experience. I suspect that is the essence of why I am attracted to roadless places that are away from the world of numbers, telephones, fax machines, email, and all the noise of my everyday life; they have a wordless appeal and are absolutely "real." There is no ambivalence or equivocation in nature.

Regardless of whether I am in a cave in Mexico, on a trail in the Guadalupe Mountains, or on one of the many rivers that we have had the joy of running, the time I spend outside allows me to step away from day-to-day life and live for a short while in a place where there is no brochure describing the comfort or safety of the trip. The permanence of comfort and safety are illusions that most folks seem to accept as fact in their normal lives. An automobile accident, sudden illness, or other calamity can impact us at any time, but most never give the fragility of life serious consideration until it is too late.

This does not imply that I go outdoors for the adrenaline. In fact, I have backed away from some activities that, in retrospect, really were not very hazardous. On the other hand, any wilderness activity involves objective hazards that must be judged, since the consequences of an error can be significant. The consequences of leaving your umbrella in the closet on a rainy day at home are not the same as being unprepared for a rainstorm in the mountains. City living does not require the same level of environmental awareness as wilderness travel. Traveling in wilderness areas makes me take responsibility for myself in a sort of primal way that is not required when I am ensconced in my workday life. As a result, I feel more attuned to my surroundings when I am floating a river or hiking on a trail. At home or in the office, my surroundings often become noise that I block out in order to stay focused on the task at hand.

Big Bend is a special place. Driving through in a car, it looks desolate, forlorn, remote. Historically, it has been just that. A succession of individuals has come to Big Bend seeking fortunes, both legitimate and otherwise. It draws the same type of fortune seekers today; a developer attempting to build a resort in a location where his predecessor failed, *coyotes* smuggling human cargo, and the bigger business of satisfying the United States' insatiable demand for illegal drugs. We once floated past San Vicente, crossing below Mariscal Canyon under the watchful eye of armed Mexicans on both sides of the river. There was little doubt about their purpose, and it didn't involve enjoying the scenery, the river, or a few *cervezas*. We stayed in the middle of the river and kept to our course downstream. I suspect many loads of contraband have entered the United States in the RVs of park "tourists." A father and his child were murdered in the park several years ago, and their bodies were burned. He may have seen too much, or, more likely, been involved too deeply. There appears to be a code in Big Bend, and most folks there know it well: Don't ask, and don't put your nose where it doesn't belong.

Floating the Rio Grande offers a sensory experience unlike many others. The vegetation of the Chihuahuan Desert is unique. It can appear lush, even though the plants are adapted for the harsh dry environment. The broken limestone of the canyons provides a multitude of footholds for lechugilla, sotol, and other plants to take root, and the visual effect is contrary to what you may expect in a desert. The sensory experience expands after a rainstorm. The first effect is immediate as the smell of creosote bushes permeates the air. The olfactory and memory centers of the brain are closely associated, and smells often trigger strong memories. There is nothing that smells quite like creosote after a desert rainstorm in the hot summer. I occasionally bring a creosote branch home for its aroma, and it takes me back to the river every time I waft it near my nose. Summer rains also bring out an abundance of wildflowers. The desert explodes to life with the color of the flowers seeming more intense against the subtle hues of the normally dry landscape.

My wife, Barb, and I met through the caving club at Texas A&M University many years ago. I had done some backpacking and was looking for opportunities for outdoor recreation. She had been active in the University of Texas caving group before relocating to College Station to pursue her degree there. We went on a number of caving trips together, became friends, and ultimately married. Children soon followed and we discovered that caving was not a family-friendly outdoor sport.

Our river life began when we stopped by a caver-friend's house one Saturday afternoon. He was having a yard sale, but it was late in the day and there were several items yet to be sold. One was a battered, old, fiberglass kayak that was ruptured across the lower half of the hull in the middle of the boat. This thing was never going to float again without a bunch of work. As a courtesy, we offered to take it off his hands at no charge so he could get rid of it. He accepted our offer and also gave us a ratty, chewed-up paddle. What a deal! We were in business.

I bought a fiberglass repair kit a few days later and went to work. The result of my effort looked about as skilled as a mud-daubers' nest, but the boat was ready for the river. Needless to say, it sufficed to get us started, but we soon were the owners of a brand-new Perception Dancer. Later that year, we were invited by another caver-friend to participate in a seven-day trip through the Lower Canyons of the Rio Grande. This is an 85-mile stretch of river downstream from Big Bend National Park that is a dedicated Wild and Scenic river. It is mostly flat water with some intermittent rapids, a couple of which approach Class IV. The real appeal of the river is its solitude. It is not uncommon to run it without seeing another soul. I hope it stays that way. (By the way, you probably wouldn't like it. Please stay at home!)

This first river trip was wonderful. We took our two daughters (ages three and six months), and Barb and I took turns in a raft with them while the other paddled. We walked the girls around anything that looked even remotely hazardous. We had found a sport that allowed us to take everything we needed to care for our children, without being chained to a car or crowded public campgrounds. We could stop anywhere to camp or hike, and the scenery was spectacular. We were hooked.

We bought our first raft shortly thereafter. It turned out that one of the rafts our group borrowed on that first trip was for sale. The owner was an avid kayaker who mistakenly bought it thinking it would facilitate more multi-day kayaking trips. The only problem with this idea was that he discovered he could not kayak if he was rowing, so the raft had to go. We bought it without a second thought. It was an early cataraft built by a small, independent boat builder in Texas. This was before cats were in common use. It had black neoprene tubes and a welded frame made from one-inch electrical conduit. It also had a plywood deck. We would occasionally encounter a seasoned river guide who would holler comments like "Old school!" We still rowed that same raft twenty years later, but we finally retired it as our fleet expanded.

Over the following years we ran the Rio Grande in Big Bend more times than I kept count of. In the early years we tended to go for easier, kid-friendly rivers. Barb or I would occasionally accept invitations to go on other, more challenging river trips by ourselves. As the children got older and we became more comfortable with their abilities, we began to run other western rivers. The motivation remained the same—to enjoy the outdoors and escape modern life.

A trip through Boquillas Canyon with my son included a new discovery that made the trip most enjoyable. We had traveled through Boquillas many times since before he was born. His first trip through the canyon, in fact, had been in his mother's womb 16 years earlier. Most of our trips did not allow enough time for much hiking, but we always poked into at least one or two side canyons. There was one canyon that we had tried repeatedly to enter on several trips, but it was always impassable without more effort than we had time to expend. The mouth of the canyon was blocked with thick brush or deep mud, and the cliffs prevented an easy entry from above. On this trip, we discovered that a flash flood had scoured the mouth of the canyon and blown out all of the mud and brush. We were able to stroll into what is one of the most enjoyable slot canyons that I have seen along the Rio Grande. We returned the following year to explore more of it and to climb to a high saddle at a point where it opens up. There we could see that there is more to be seen beyond where we stopped—I look forward to a day in the future when we will return to continue our adventure.

Our country is changing rapidly, and the pace is quickening. I recall that when I was a young child, the interstate highway system was just being built. Major highways in Texas were two-lane roads with no shoulders. Some of those highways still exist in their original form, but they are isolated stretches that were relegated to local jurisdictions when the roads were widened and straightened. Traveling from Houston to Dallas was an ordeal. We now have nationwide fast food and retail outlets that look the same everywhere. A 500-mile drive can be done in one day with little advance planning. It is becoming harder to find stretches of highway where you cannot see any man-made structures other than the road itself, and a parallel railroad or power line.

As the progress of development proceeds, pressure will mount to change the role of wild places in our nation. I discussed these issues with a friend a number of years ago in the context of the debate over the revision of the Colorado River Management Plan for the Grand Canyon. His response, in part, was "...the majority of Americans have morphed into viewing vacations as being theme parks with simulated sensations. They will pay to feel like they had an adventure as long as it can be done in a week (including travel), they are well fed with lots of fat and sugar, do not have to think, and the primary effort is done by others, preferably machines. The commercial outfitters cater to this. It is no different than a cruise, a resort, adventure travel, tour bus, Disneyland, or a sports event. Many Americans confuse watching someone else do something with doing it themselves. I continue to be reminded of the Seinfeld episode:

Fan: 'Hooray, we won.' Seinfeld: 'No, they won, you watched.'"

My friend concluded by writing, "So the decision is whether to use the Grand Canyon and other wilderness areas as a colossal theme park where customers are fed, given rides, and sent home with T-shirts saying 'I Survived the Grand Canyon' for money, or to use it as a wilderness that rewards those who put out the effort to discover it and preserve it. If the area is revenue-driven, it will become a theme park. It is my opinion that we have no shortage of theme parks in America, but wilderness is a disappearing, nonrenewable resource. I vote for wilderness."

I agree with my friend. I would much rather take responsibility for myself and enjoy the wilderness on its terms, than have wilderness become another experience that I pay someone to provide and take responsibility for. If we lose or diminish the ability to get away from the modern world and take responsibility for ourselves in a very basic, immediate way, then we lose something as a nation of individuals who have historically prided themselves as being "self-made."

I vote for wilderness too.

About the Contributors

Walt Bammann has lived in Roseburg, Oregon, since 1970 with his wife of 50 years, Jody. After graduating from Oregon State University in 1966 with a forestry degree, he spent 3 years in the Army as a helicopter pilot, including a tour in Vietnam. He and Jody got serious about rafting in the mid-80s and introduced their 2 sons and, lately, their 2 grandsons to the sport. They played a major role in starting the Roseburg Chapter of the Northwest Rafters Association in 1989 and remain involved. Walt retired as the Human Resources Manager of a printing company and enjoys rafting, traveling, fishing, and skiing.

Andrew G. Bentley, Ph.D. In an increasingly urbanized society separated from nature, Andrew uses river running to connect people to natural landscapes. As a multiday commercial river guide and private boater, he has hundreds of times been lulled to sleep by falling water's white noise and knows its powerful sway. With the serendipitous fortune to have worked with Sheri Griffith Expeditions, Outward Bound, the United States Forest Service, and now as a professor to an academic adventure education major, he designs curriculum and leads distinctive expedition-formatted college field trips with flowing water as a central learning theme.

Patsy Kate Booth called the La Garita mountains home for 40 years. From this remote location, she operated La Garita llamas, an outfitting and guide service providing wilderness education and experiences for children, families, Zen and women's groups. She has run the rivers of the Southwest since 1980, is a published writer, poet and former special education teacher and play therapist. She believes wild places are our most powerful teachers. She invites people to go to the river and fall in love. She lives in Pueblo, Colorado.

Josh Case lives in Henderson, Nevada. He has been running rivers since 2013, and backpacking in the Grand Canyon since the late 1990s. Josh works as a construction project manager, primarily building high-end restaurants and retail spaces on the Las Vegas Strip. He spends his free time raising his three daughters, traveling for live music and seeking new outdoor adventures with his wife, Amy.

Guy Cloutier lives in Tucson, Arizona, with his partner, Jan Staedicke. Nearing retirement, he has been in the home remodeling business for many years. Most of his free time is spent in the outdoors hiking and backpacking, often in the slickrock country of southern Utah.

Jane Dally has worked as an outdoor educator most of her adult life, running rivers and dogsleds, hiking and horsepacking, and mountaineering throughout the Lower Forty-Eight, Alaska and Canada. She first began boating in 1986 when she "left the settled life," as Stan Rogers says, to pursue her passion for wilderness and adventure. She currently lives in Durango, Colorado, where, when she is not working as a child psychotherapist, she can be found floating one of the many beautiful mountain or desert rivers of the Four Corners.

Marci Dye lives in Red Lodge, Montana, just north of the vast wilderness around Yellowstone National Park. She grew up in the mountains hiking and Nordic skiing, and began true river running as an adult with her kids. She and her family own and operate a small outdoor gear shop, catering to the hiking and Nordic crowd. Now with a family of river guide children, who have found careers on the rivers and as ski coaches, she gets out as much as possible paddling the rivers, and skiing the mountains.

Janelle Dyer lives off the northern coast of California. She has been running rivers since she was a kid, but started making it a profession in 2004. She went to school for Earth Science and Outdoor Studies where she pursued a career in science for several years. She is currently becoming a teacher. Janelle is no longer a full-time raft guide, but enjoys private trips whenever she has the chance. Besides rowing a boat down the river, she also enjoys playing music, knitting, painting, and planning her future wedding and family with her partner, Greg.

Hilary Esry was born and raised in the mountains of Appalachia. She has resided, studied, and worked in West Virginia, the Southeast, the mountain West, the high desert Southwest, and the plains of Kansas, but feels most at home in wilderness. An avid outdoorswoman, she began kayaking in 2011 as a means of accessing beautiful places she otherwise might not reach, thus beginning her ongoing love affair with rivers.

Maile Field was born in Hawaii and raised in western Montana. She worked as a daily news reporter, editor and feature writer before receiving her Master of Fine Arts in creative writing (nonfiction) from George Mason University in 2015. She also managed organic pear orchards and winegrape vineyards in Northern California for 20 years while raising two boys, musician Seth Crail and filmmaker Chauncey Crail. She is completing final revisions of her hybrid narrative guide/adventure book about private whitewater rafting in the Grand Canyon. She recently returned to northern California and tries to maintain a travel blog at www.mailefield.com.

Audra Ford currently resides in Boise, Idaho, and has been actively boating and running rivers since 2010. She also enjoys skiing, scuba diving, and taking in all the other outdoor attractions the Northwest has to offer. She works as a client services manager for Clarivate Analytics and is always planning her next adventure.

Amanda Gibbon lives in San Francisco with her husband and son. She loves wild open spaces, both inside and out, spending her work life as a therapist and social worker. Ten years after her essay was written, Amanda was able to return to the Canyon where her now-husband proposed while skinny dipping in the third pool up at Stone Creek. (On that trip, he rowed Crystal.) She hopes she has many more river trips ahead with those she loves, certain to include her familial professional Grand Canyon guides, her sister Jocelyn and brother-in-law Sam.

Pascal Girard is a French Canadian who lives in Quebec's Eastern Townships with his wife and two daughters. His love for rivers started in the summer of 1991 when his father signed him up for a whitewater clinic weekend. He has never stop chasing rivers since then. If he is not teaching teenagers math or paddling a river, you can either find him training hard for his next adventure race or triathlon. He is a longtime collaborator with Quebec's outdoor magazines as a reporter, photographer, and videographer. He has also worked as a radio journalist sharing his passion for the outdoors.

Monica Gokey is a whitewater kayaker who has traveled the world in pursuit of fine river trips. She prefers drop-seats to she-wees, and prides herself on packing a raft cooler like it's the World Championships of Tetris. Off the water, she works as a journalist and cattle rancher alongside her husband and three kids in central Idaho, a stone's throw from the banks of the Payette River.

Doug Grosjean lives and works in metro Detroit, Michigan. He has been fascinated by moving water since childhood, and began running whitewater rivers in kayaks in the late 1980s. Trained as a motorcycle mechanic and mechanical designer, Doug finds solace in whitewater and wild places. Besides whitewater kayaking, Doug has also rowed a raft through the Grand Canyon and crewed aboard a Colonial-era batteau (a whitewater cargo boat) on the James River in Virginia. Doug is currently employed as a mechanic at the Henry Ford Museum in Dearborn, Michigan, while continuing to study art and dabbling in writing and photography.

Timothy Hillmer lives in Louisville, Colorado. He worked as a raft guide during the late 1970s and 1980s on rivers in California, Oregon, and Colorado. He is the author of two novels, *The Hookmen* (Scribner) and *Ravenhill* (U. Of New Mexico Press), and has published a wide variety of stories, poems, and articles. He taught in the public schools for 32 years. Now retired, he is looking forward to rafting in Nepal in 2018.

Blair Holman first got a taste of whitewater kayaking on the Potomac River some years ago, and has since found it again, and a love for it, over the last two years on the rivers of Colorado. She has spent a lot of her time teaching kids many outdoor activities, including whitewater kayaking, through an outdoor adventure company. She loves being outside any chance she gets!

Herm Hoops has been running rivers in the West since 1966. His life has always been associated with water: from bucolic farm ponds and awe-inspiring rivers to the endless ocean, and he's always had an interest in history. The son of Vermont farmers, he grew up on a large dairy cattle and Morgan horse farm, attended the University of Vermont, taught Forestry in Northern Vermont and worked for the National Park Service. Herm and his wife, Valerie, live in Jensen, Utah.

Jeff Ingram saw the Grand Canyon first in 1962 and spent much of the 1960s travelling about in the canyon. Over the next half century he devoted much time to fighting dams. The 1970s were full of Grand Canyon issues, dominated by the Congressional battle to complete the National Park, and the failed fight for Wilderness status. From 1998, the river access / wilderness issue led him to write *Hijacking A River: The Political History of the Colorado River in the Grand Canyon*. That book was the dark side; at present he writes the blog "Celebrating the Grand Canyon," aimed at shedding light on the Grand Canyon as an icon of our present and future environmental consciousness.

Linda Lawless LaStayo and Paul LaStayo find traveling as a pack on rivers, bicycles, and skis rejuvenating from the distractions of their lives in biotech and academics. When not with family and friends on water, dirt, or snow, these transplants to Utah hunker down in the Ogden Valley and Moab pondering whether it is best to drain or not drain the cooler. After a rigorous, controlled study they look forward to sharing their results and why they boat with their grandchildren.

Lloyd Knapp, a resident of Oregon, was one of the original members and instigators of Riverhawks, providing intelligence and direction for their early endeavors. These included the successful lawsuit against the Forest Service that led to reduction of jet boat traffic on the Wild and Scenic Rogue, the cessation of construction of a new, massive, and inappropriate visitor center on the Rogue at Rand, and the paradigm shift in managing the "bear problem" on the Lower Rogue from killing bears to educating the public. Lloyd loved nature and wilderness. He had a hearty sense of humor and accepted the nickname of "Mongo" even though it didn't fit his wise, kind, considerate persona. Not many have been more motivated to enjoy nature, protect it, and create alliances than Lloyd. When Lloyd passed away in 2013, the wild lost an advocate and we lost a very special spirit.

Beverly Kurtz lives in the foothills west of Boulder, Colorado. She has been running rivers since the mid 1980s when she worked as an archeologist in

Grand Junction, Colorado. Follow on careers as a middle school teacher and then a project manager at IBM allowed her time off to pursue her passion for rivers. Now retired, she spends much of her energy fighting dams, traveling, writing, and playing in the out of doors with her husband, Tim, and her river tribe.

Ashley Lodato lives in Winthrop, Washington, at the eastern base of the North Cascades. She started boating in the late 1980s as an instructor for Outward Bound in Maine, Montana, and Texas. She taught high school English for several years, and spent 25 years in the field as an administrator for Outward Bound. She currently works in arts education and as a freelance writer. She and her husband take their two daughters into the mountains, up rocks, and down rivers as often as they can.

Dave Mortenson was introduced to the Colorado River in 1957 by his father, "Brick" Mortenson, and P. T. "Pat" Reilly. They showed him Lava Falls from Toroweap, Lees Ferry, and Lake Mead up to Separation Canyon. In 1962 Dave ran the wild Colorado at the age of 14. He achieved multiple degrees in California, was a Vietnam era Air Force Navigator, worked for the BLM and then for the Washington State Legislature. He ran his own political consulting business until he retired. Dave has organized many Colorado River trips running replicated historic boats. He is on the boards of Grand Canyon Private Boaters Association and Grand Canyon Historical Society.

Naseem Rakha is a mom, a writer, a geologist, and an activist. She is the author of the novel *The Crying Tree,* a contributor to *The Guardian*, and was a journalist for public radio. Naseem lives with her son and husband and their animals in Oregon's Willamette Valley and spends as much time as she can reading, writing, knitting, hiking, and trying to save our public lands from the hands of destruction.

Scott Ramsey is a lifelong learner and has been exploring and running rivers since the early 90s. His quest for exploration and passion took him to Alaska, where he has been leading expeditions and teaching guides for over 20 years. He, his wonderful wife, Mandy, and his spirited little girl, Lily Jo, live off the grid in Haines, Alaska. He has a doctorate in Sustainability Education and is the owner and lead instructor of the Alaska Outdoor Science School (AOSS). AOSS celebrates nature's wisdom by providing multi-day environmental education and sustainability courses within Alaska's amazing classroom.

Jayson Ringel first became enthralled with river rafting in 1992 when he and his future wife, Barbara, were dating and saw the movie *The River Wild*. Twenty-five years later, Jayson and Barb are happily married with two children and a 16-foot cataraft. After a cancer diagnosis and a conversion to Buddhism, Jayson now views river trips differently. He approaches each river trip as a journey to enhance relationships, a means for personal growth, and as a prism through which to make sense of life's journey. Jayson lives with his wife and two children, Kieran and Aidan, at the confluence of the Icicle and Wenatchee rivers in north central Washington State.

Norma Sims Roche lives in Northampton, Massachusetts, and kayaks Class II–III whitewater, most often on the Deerfield River. In her day job, she's an editor of college textbooks in biology and geology. She writes mainly memoir, personal essays, poems, and fiction based on true events.

Shelby Rogala grew up in western Montana, raised by the rushing waters of the Salmon, Selway, and Bitterroot rivers. After spending a decade working in mountain towns across the world as a ski instructor, river guide, and grant writer, she has recently returned home to work as an outreach coordinator for the Darby School District—until the next adventure sweeps her away.

Duwain Whitis and his wife, Barbara Vinson, started boating with their children in 1985. They are the owners of RiverMaps, LLC, and started publishing map books for whitewater rivers in 2001. Duwain's day job for almost 30 years was as a consulting civil engineer, a career he still dabbles in on a part-time basis when he is not running rivers, playing flyball with dogs, or engaging in shooting sports.

Marty Wolf continues to be awed by nature and the planet, and is a lifelong supporter of its cleaner waters and air, with its birds and its flora (and humans and other fauna) in habitat transition under a changing climate. Settled in Colorado since 1974, he taught scientific honesty and environmental respect to 6th-9th graders in Colorado Springs for 30 years (in the face of local denial and resistance, with scattered support and appreciation). Having raised two amazing kids with his wife, he relishes living day to day, pursuing a handful of hobbies and passions.

Julie Yarnell is a Colorado native who makes her home in southwestern Colorado with her husband and two children. She enjoys traveling, doing CrossFit, writing, and gardening. She also loves exploring the beautiful outdoors with her family, mountain biking, hiking, and floating down rivers.